The Cook's Canon

Also by Raymond Sokolov

With the Grain

The Jewish-American Kitchen

Why We Eat What We Eat

How to Cook

Wayward Reporter

Fading Feast

Native Intelligence

The Saucier's Apprentice

Great Recipes from the New York Times

The Cook's Canon 101 Classic Recipes Everyone Should Know

RAYMOND SOKOLOV

HarperCollinsPublishers

HarperCollins books may be purchased for educational, business, or sales promotional use. For information, please write: Special Markets Department, HarperCollins Publishers Inc., 10 East 53rd Street, New York, NY 10022.

FIRST EDITION

Designed by Ph.d, www.phdla.com

Printed on acid-free paper

Library of Congress Cataloging-in-Publication Data

Sokolov, Raymond A.

  The cook's canon : 101 classic recipes everyone should know / Raymond Sokolov.—1st ed.
     p. cm.
  Includes bibliographical references and index.
  ISBN 0-06-008390-5
  1. Cookery, International. I. Title.

TX725.A1S566 2003

641.59—dc21   2003044966

03 04 05 06 07   ❖/RRD   10 9 8 7 6 5 4 3 2 1

To Johanna

This book, whatever its merits, could not have existed without the enthusiastic advice and editorial collaboration of Susan Friedland at HarperCollins. Kathy Robbins, my agent, was, as always, a wise counselor.

Contents

The Cook's Canon

Introduction

What Is a Canon and Why Do Cooks Need One?

In the academic world, the professors wrangle over which books everyone ought to read. They call this list of essential great books "the canon." The word itself is a classic: It derives from the ancient Greek word for measurement or standard of judgment. The Catholic Church governs itself through a legal system of "canon" law, by which judgments are made in ecclesiastical courts. When the Church selected the sacred books it would include in Holy Scripture, the selection process was described in the same language as the selection process for sainthood, which is called canonization. So it was that in 1545, the Council of Trent gathered in the Adriatic Italian city of Trento near Trieste and established a canon of officially anointed books to include in the Catholic Bible.

Today, college teachers have been unofficially conducting their own Council of Trent, arguing about what the literary canon of secular scripture should be. What authors should students absolutely have to read in order to consider themselves properly educated? Professor X has his favorites. Professor Y has his. And the authors on their lists can be as different as Shakespeare and the contemporary Guatemalan Mayan radical Rigoberta Menchú.

Whether you favor the traditional canon or the multicultural one, the distractions of modern life undermine it at every turn and lure potential readers away from Smollett and George Eliot.

A similar decline of literacy infects the kitchen. It started benignly enough as a rebellion against the calcified haute cuisine entombed in Escoffier's *Guide culinaire* and in the bloodless little *Répertoire de la cuisine* of Gringoire and Saulnier. With these two expressions of the canon of French food as it was after World War I (and continued to be during the paralyzing years of the Great Depression, the Second World War, and the postwar recovery), the flagship cuisine of the world seemed to have reached its apogee and then ground to an eternal halt.

Then the nouvelle cuisine got things moving again. Young chefs in the sixties and seventies threw out the stuffy garnishes and the gluey sauces of their teachers. New ingredients—kiwis, avocados—and new influences—Japanese decorative flair, aggressive new seasonings from the Americas and the Orient—all contributed to the breaking up of the gastronomic logjam I encountered in Paris as a foreign correspondent in the late sixties. By the seventies, the revolution had spread to restaurant kitchens around the world, inspiring local new cuisines: *nueva cocina, neue Küche, nova cozinha,* and American nouvelle cuisine.

In the United States, with its scattered and faltering regional traditions as well as its diluted or distorted presentations of classic European and Asian dishes, the nouvelle cuisine fever didn't have much of value or strength to rebel against. But it did produce two salubrious results right away. Sham foreign restaurants died off, victims of a crusade for culinary authenticity animated by a boom in tourism to Europe and by accurate cookbooks that documented what the major cuisines of the world actually were, or had been. More and more people in the know could spot inauthentic restaurants and shun them. Reservations declined and old standbys closed, pushed over the brink by the Nixon wage-and-price-controls recession.

Second, the American nouvelle cuisine was an engine for reviving the same American traditions that it had taken me considerable effort in the middle seventies to unearth in their native haunts as part of the research for my monthly column in *Natural History* magazine. Soon after my book *Fading Feast* appeared in 1979, hitherto obscure dishes or ingredients I'd written about as a sort of foodie folklorist began to appear on New York menus or in fancy food shops. A woodsman I'd interviewed in rural Michigan at the National Mushroom Championships became a supplier of morels to the Gourmet Garage. The foods of the Southwest were suddenly chic.

So far so good. But whereas in France, there was a stiff, archaic tradition for the Young Turk chefs to reform, in the United States, where most native chefs found everything exotic, from chocolate mousse to jambalaya, the nouvelle cuisine morphed into a novelty cuisine. What started as a respectfully creative attitude toward native and French ideas decayed into a rule-less creative anarchy, a riot of fusion cuisines in which nothing fused, a chef's finger-painting not disciplined by any sense of the past.

Of course this indictment does not extend to well-informed chefs basing their innovative menus on preexisting food ideas. I think of Douglas Rodriguez and his intelligent recalibration of Latin American tradition in various neo-Hispanic Manhattan restaurants or Annisa's Anita Lo and her recombinations of Asian and French ideas. In such places, there is the possibility, even, of learning about the historic dishes that inspired these clever inventions. But it will take more than this indirect kind of education to train the palates of a generation whose connection with traditional food has been short-circuited.

They can't roll back 30 years of change, but they can learn about where the food they like is coming from. Just as Professor X wants his students to read Shakespeare so that they can appreciate *Rosencrantz and Guildenstern Are Dead,* I want people to expose themselves to a canon of the world's great dishes. So here is my pantheon—101 classic recipes with historical and cultural and sometimes scientific information that tells in some depth where they came from, what they meant to the people who first ate them before they spread to other societies, and why they are important to us now.

By definition, you can't have a canon unless you decide what is canonical. From the thousands and thousands of worthwhile recipes human beings have developed over the millennia, how have I settled on 101? My criteria were simple:

1. Since this is aimed at American or English-speaking readers in other countries, it focuses mainly on foods from traditions that flowed into ours. This is, like a traditional survey course in the humanities, a book about the "Western" heritage. It is unabashedly Eurocentric and, more than that, it is Gallocentric, because French cuisine has shaped every other European and American cuisine. There are also plenty of dishes from other European cultures, sauerbraten from Germany, plum pudding from England. And there are crucial recipes from more distant places with great cuisines, from China, Morocco, India.
2. Every one of the 101 "divine" recipes in this pantheon justifies its presence by being delicious, obviously, but also by being famous and influential. These dishes often stand for entire national cuisines—paella for Spain, osso buco for Italy. Or they represent whole categories of food—cannelloni for pasta, blanquette de veau for stews.

Anyone can think of dozens of choices I might have made that would satisfy these criteria. One hundred and one is a very small number of dishes to pick from all of terrestrial gastronomy, but pantheons are inherently selective, books are finite, and judgment is, in the end, an arbitrary exercise of personal taste.

I hope that you will be moved to argue about these choices, because that will mean that you have thought passionately about the subject. I also hope that you will agree that this selection will contribute to a saner and better-informed culture of eating.

Perhaps it would be more accurate to say that the day of the apple has reached twilight after a long period of cloudless skies. The dazzling varieties of apples depicted in the color plates of *The Apples of New York* (1903), can now be found only in greenmarkets or hobbyists' orchards if they can be found at all.

Apple Pie

American folkways celebrate the apple as no other fruit. And there must be a reason for it. It can't be an accident that we don't talk about peach pie order, or say something is as American as pawpaw pie. Even though the pawpaw is a native fruit, and the apple evolved in early colonial times from the crossing of indigenous crab apples with European apple seed.

The apple is, in fact, the preeminent European fruit. Apples are recorded frequently in the annals of antiquity. By the time of the Romans, classical authors really are talking about true apples. In early Greek literature and myth, as in the Hebrew Bible, fruits called "apples" are very likely quince, because the words that later became reliable, specific tags for apples were originally applied to other globous, fleshy, small-seeded tree fruits. But in casting doubt on the identity of Eve's apple, the golden apples of the Hesperides, or the apple that distracted Hippolyta, I do not mean to discomfort you with non-apples. For centuries, apples have held sway over the succulent precincts of pomology (the science of fruit growing, which, significantly, has taken its name from a Latin word, *pomum,* that the Romans applied to any kind of fruit, including the one the French call *pomme*). But their preponderance in colonized North America has been their finest hour.

Perhaps it would be more accurate to say that the day of the apple has reached twilight after a long period of cloudless skies. The dazzling varieties of apples depicted in the color plates of *The Apples of New York* (1903), can now be found only in greenmarkets or hobbyists' orchards if they can be found at all. Now that we can store summer apples for a year in warehouses filled with nitrogen, farmers don't need to plant many varieties, some late-fruiting, some early, so as to have a continuous harvest from the end of summer until winter. Idiot consumers encourage the trend; they buy with their eyes and, surveys show, will always go for the reddest apple in the market.

As for apple pies, it has been a very long time indeed since they were cooked en masse and left out in the wintry chill, where they kept nicely and would make a solid meal for settlers like J. Hector St. John de Crèvecoeur (1735–1813), who describes this practice in *Letters from an American Farmer* (1782). He, like his Long Island neighbors and other colonists of English heritage, came to America with pies in their heads. Britain was pie central in early modern European cookery. You can see that today in any pub, where steak and kidney pie is only one of dozens on offer. Traditionally, they were double-crusted and contained many diverse ingredients, whence, perhaps, the name—pie coming from magpie, a bird that snaps up whatever goodies are around and fills its nest with them.

In North America, the full upper crust has given way for the most part to the open or latticed top, showing the apples, much like a French *tarte aux pommes*. So why isn't a pie a tart? The deep-dish shape of the crust and the straightforward, English-style filling mark our pies off from the shallow, prebaked French crust and *crème pâtissière* of a classic tart. But the line of demarcation isn't really all that clear. And yet, like the Supreme Court Justice trying to explain what he meant by obscenity, I may not be able to define a pie, but I know one when I see it.

1½ cups flour plus 1 tablespoon for the filling	2 cups peeled, cored, and sliced tart pie apples such as Greenings or Cortlands
½ teaspoon salt	
½ cup lard	½ cup sugar
1½ teaspoons cider vinegar	½ teaspoon vanilla extract
2½ tablespoons milk	⅓ cup heavy cream
1 egg	

1. In a mixing bowl, stir together 1½ cups flour and the salt. Cut in the lard a bit at a time with a pastry blender or two forks, until the dough has the crumbly texture of uncooked oatmeal.

2. In an electric mixer, beat together the vinegar, milk, and egg. Then fold into the dough gradually.

3. Divide the dough in half and refrigerate in Ziploc bags for an hour (or freeze until you are ready to use).

4. Stir together all the remaining ingredients (including the tablespoon of flour).

5. Preheat the oven to 450 degrees.

6. On a floured board or countertop, roll out one half of the dough into a circle large enough to come up and slightly over the sides of an ungreased 9-inch pie tin. Trim away the excess and crimp the edge of the crust with the tines of a fork. Pierce the bottom of the crust all over with the points of the fork.

7. Put the apple filling on the crust, spreading it evenly.

8. Roll out the second piece of dough. Moisten the edge of the bottom crust lightly with water. Roll the top crust around the rolling pin and then unroll it on top of the filling. Trim and then press it around the edges so that it sticks to the bottom crust. Slash through the

crust in several places or make a hole in the center to let the steam escape during baking. If you have a pie bird, stand it in the hole.

9. Bake in the center of the oven for 10 minutes. Then reduce the temperature to 350
   degrees and continue baking for another half hour. The pie is done when the crust has
   turned a golden brown and the apples offer no resistance to a trussing needle pushed
   through the top crust. Cook another 10 minutes if necessary. Cool on a rack.

Serves 6 to 8

Baked Alaska

Baked Alaska is a stunt that began as a joke. Actually, it could well have been one of the many jokes made at the expense of President Andrew Johnson's secretary of state, William H. Seward, after he bought Alaska from Russia for just over $7 million in 1867. Wags called the distant northern territory Seward's Folly and Seward's Icebox, so it was probably inevitable that someone would create a snowy dessert—consisting of ice cream covered with lightly browned meringue—and dub it baked Alaska. Although the name first made its way into print in the original (1896) edition of Fannie Farmer's *The Boston Cooking-School Cook Book,* the idea of baking ice cream inside an insulating sandwich of sponge cake and meringue had been around for much of the nineteenth century.

Thomas Jefferson dabbled with a "hot" ice cream pudding in 1802; the chef of the Chinese mission in Paris may have cooked ice cream in pastry in 1866, according to *Larousse Gastronomique* (1930).

But the underlying science, showing that the air in egg whites (and cake batter) acts as insulation, we owe to that genius of practical thermodynamics Benjamin Thompson, known as Count Rumford, who paved the way for baked Alaska with his work on the resistance of egg whites to heat in the early 1800s.

The French serve a similar dish, *omelette norvégienne,* thought to have originated around the same time as baked Alaska. Instead of resting on sponge cake, their ice cream sits on Grand Marnier–soaked genoise. After the meringue is browned, the dessert is often flamed with Grand Marnier at the table. Whichever dessert came first, the tipsy faux-Scandinavian French or the teetotaling, antiexpansionist American, either is a good trick that can (indeed has to) be thrown together at the very last minute—and guarantees a warm reception from the chilliest of guests.

2 pints ice cream, slightly softened

2 teaspoons butter, softened

½ cup cake flour

1 pinch salt

3 eggs, separated

1 cup sugar

½ teaspoon grated lemon zest

1 tablespoon lemon juice

4 additional egg whites, collected in a separate bowl

2 pinches cream of tartar

1. Line a 7-inch-diameter bowl with a 15-inch piece of plastic wrap, allowing the excess to hang over the rim of the bowl. Pack the ice cream into the bowl, smoothing out the top, and freeze until solid, at least 4 hours.

2. Preheat the oven to 325 degrees. Butter an 8-inch-diameter round cake pan with half the butter. Line the pan with an 8-inch disk of parchment paper, butter the paper with the remaining butter, and set aside.

3. Sift together the flour and salt into a small bowl and set aside.

4. Put the egg yolks into a mixing bowl and beat with an electric mixer on medium-high speed until pale yellow, about 1 minute. Gradually add ½ cup sugar while continuing to beat until fluffy, about 1 minute. Stir in the lemon zest and juice and set aside.

5. Put three egg whites into another mixing bowl and beat with clean beaters on medium-high speed until stiff but not dry peaks form, about 2 minutes.

6. Fold the whites into the yolk mixture with a rubber spatula. Fold the flour-salt mixture into the egg-sugar mixture in two batches, taking care not to deflate the batter.

7. Pour the batter into the prepared pan and bake until a toothpick inserted in the center comes out clean, 20 to 25 minutes. Set aside to cool completely, then invert onto a rack, peel off and discard the parchment, and set the cake aside.

8. Preheat the oven to 450 degrees.

9. Just before serving, put the remaining four egg whites and cream of tartar into a mixing bowl and beat with an electric mixer on medium speed until soft peaks form, about 1 minute. Increase the speed to high and gradually add the remaining ½ cup sugar, beating until thick, shiny, stiff but not dry peaks form, about 2 minutes.

10. Put the cake onto a parchment-lined baking sheet. Invert the ice cream onto the cake and peel off the plastic. Cover the ice cream and cake with the meringue. Bake until the meringue begins to brown, about 5 minutes. Carefully transfer to a cake plate and serve immediately.

Serves 8

Beet Borscht

If you think, and why shouldn't you, that borscht is a plain Russian beet soup, lightly soured with lemon juice and topped with a dollop of sour cream, you will be astonished to see how many variations there are on this homely theme in Russian cookbooks. Beets are the only common thread, which makes sense if you know that "borscht" descends from a word in the Russian language's predecessor, Old Church Slavonic. Now, in Russian, borscht refers only to the soup (or soups) with beets in them. (The modern Russian word for beet is etymologically unrelated to "borscht." It means cow parsnip, a member of the carrot family—*Heracleum maximum*—whose parsnip-like root was evidently the original ingredient of the soup.)

My friend Anne Volokh, now the publisher of *Movieline* in Los Angeles, was once a food writer for the Sunday edition of the Soviet newspaper *Izvestia*. After emigrating from the U.S.S.R., she published the definitive Russian cookbook in English, *The Art of Russian Cuisine* (1983), in which she recollects a culinary idyll she spent by herself as a teenager in a rented cottage in the Ukrainian countryside (she was born in Kiev) cooking the primordial borscht, the Ukrainian variety:

> *My peasant neighbors proved to be sympathetic and readily supplied me with beets, carrots, cabbage and new potatoes, cucumbers and tomatoes, parsley and dill from their vegetable gardens, and wonderful fresh pot cheese and sour cream from their kitchens.*

Ms. Volokh's Ukrainian borscht, recollected in prosperous exile in California, includes, among other extras: spareribs, ham, white beans, mushrooms, garlic, and tomato paste. She tells us of special borscht dumplings, too, and an even richer version of the soup that substitutes duck or goose for the humbler meats.

There are many more borschts (which should really be spelled borshch, as in Khrushchev, reflecting the Russian consonant, a single letter that the Russian aviatrix in George Bernard Shaw's *Misalliance* explains should be pronounced like fishchurch) in the Soviet-era *Ukrainian Cuisine,* published in Kiev in an English edition in 1975. Twenty-five to be exact. Among them: borscht with carp, with meatballs, with mushrooms and prunes, with eggplant, with buckwheat pastry "ears," and with beans. In other sources, you can find still others, the most distinctive including *rossl,* the fermented beet liquid, or *kvas,* a beer made from bread.

The prepared, bottled borscht sold in almost every U.S. supermarket is the streamlined preparation that Ms. Volokh calls cold beet soup (although hers has hard-boiled eggs). For me, this is the classic, the unembellished Platonic version, and also the one that has escaped from Russia and its pogroms and purges, brought by Jewish refugees to join the wide world as a universal dish.

Borscht is in this book to represent the vast and inventive world of Slavic cuisine, but it is also the poster child for the too-often overlooked beet in many other cuisines. Of all the root vegetables, beets are the most complex in taste, earthy and yet delicate, healthy in the extreme, and, of course, beautiful. One of the great chefs of the second half of the twentieth century, Michel Guérard, did not hesitate to put a profoundly red-blue beet puree into his repertoire. All Greeks celebrate the beet in a cold salad smothered in pureed garlic. Start your beet odyssey with borscht and never look back.

2 dozen medium beets with their greens	Salt
6 cups water	½ teaspoon sugar
1 tablespoon lemon juice	Sour cream
	Snipped dill leaves

1. Cut off the beet greens and wash thoroughly. Chop into 2-inch lengths. Peel and slice the beets.
2. Bring 6 cups water to a boil. Add the beets and greens. Stir in the lemon juice, salt, and sugar. Cook for 20 minutes or until the beets are tender but not mushy.
3. Remove the greens and reserve for use as a vegetable. Let the soup cool completely, then chill.
4. Serve well chilled. Pass the sour cream and dill separately.

Serves 10

Beurre Blanc
(White Butter Sauce)

White butter is the famous, some would say the notorious, sauce from Nantes, a traditional Breton center at the mouth of the Loire on France's Atlantic coast. *Beurre nantaise*, as it is also known, is the bugbear of busy chefs, because if kept too long, it melts down from an elegant creaminess into an oily mess. At home, it isn't such a problem. The very reduced and highly acid shallot-vinegar base easily emulsifies the cold chunks of butter plopped into it over very low heat.

This is a bland sauce and benefits from being made with salted butter. In the pantheon of fish sauces, *beurre blanc* is the chaste and gentle opposite of *beurre noir*, black butter, that dark brown product of high heat boldly flavored with vinegar and capers. *Beurre noir* has no clear regional association, whereas *beurre blanc* is the Loire's fairest offspring, the ideal accompaniment for its shad. Protestants and other proponents of freedom of religion should prepare it on April 13 or April 30, either of which may be the correct date of the Edict of Nantes,[*] in which Henri IV,[†] a Huguenot himself, who converted to Catholicism in order to become king of France,[‡] decreed that Huguenots[§] could worship freely as Protestants. Conversely, they can dine on *beurre noir* on October 22, the mournful anniversary of the revocation of the edict by Louis XIV in 1685, which sent the Huguenots fleeing from France to havens of tolerance in England, the Netherlands, the Rhenish Palatinate, New York, and the enlightened Brandenburg of Frederick the Great.

2 tablespoons finely chopped shallots	½ cup white-wine vinegar
¼ teaspoon white pepper	¾ to 1½ pounds (3 to 6 sticks or 24 to 48
½ teaspoon salt	tablespoons) salted butter, chilled

---

[*] I prefer April 13, because it is the day on which both my father and sister were born.

[†] He was a benevolent monarch and a gourmand, who promised that if he were made king, there would be a chicken in every peasant's pot every Sunday.

[‡] He converted with little conviction, saying, "Paris is worth a mass."

[§] I am writing this in a house in the Hudson Valley built by a Huguenot couple whose LeFevre ancestors came to America as a result of the revocation of the Edict of Nantes.

1. Combine 1 tablespoon of the shallots, white pepper, salt, and vinegar in a small saucepan. Reduce by three-quarters, to approximately 2 tablespoons. Do not underreduce. The final reduction must be as acid as possible without boiling away altogether.
2. Remove the reduction from the heat. While it is still hot, strain it into a clean, heavy, non-aluminum 4-cup saucepan.
3. Crush the remaining shallots lightly with the flat of a large knife and add them to the reduction. Set the saucepan over very low heat. Then add four pats of butter (about 2 tablespoons) and start whisking.
4. As soon as the first four pats of butter have almost melted, add four more. Continue in this manner until you have melted in all but one stick of butter.
5. Remove from the heat and whisk in the remaining butter. Correct the seasoning and serve immediately.

Three sticks of butter will give you an ample amount of sauce for six to eight people, about 1½ cups, but the reduction will absorb the full 1½ pounds if you are having a large dinner party and think you will need 3 cups of sauce to go with fish or lobster.

Billi Bi
(Mussel Soup)

Surfing the Internet will undoubtedly turn up plenty of useful niblets of information with little effort. But it is also an efficient way of reminding yourself how myths get established as facts if they are repeated often enough. Billi Bi is a case in point.

All the *sources* (none of them eyewitnesses or even secondhand) agree that this yolk-and-cream-thickened mussel soup was invented in France. The most widely attested version of the legend names Louis Barthe, the chef at Maxim's in Paris, as the inventor. Supposedly, he honored an enthusiastic consumer of the dish by calling it after him. The most plausible candidate for this distinction is an alleged American tin tycoon, William B. Leeds, aka Billy B., whence the exotically phonetic Billi Bi. Dates for this watershed moment in the history of dining range from the late nineteenth century to 1925, with 1925 getting the most votes on the Worldwide Web.

There is, however, a rival tale. It takes place shortly after the Allied invasion of Normandy at Ciro's in Deauville. Chef Barthe, the Zelig of the stove, pops up once again, waving his magic whisk and sanctifying another Yank named Billy B. This would be a GI formally known as William Brand. The soup was served at a farewell party for him and so, it is said in some quarters, Chef Barthe came up with the title Billy Bye, which yields Billi Bi when pronounced as if it were French. Although you might argue in support of this alternative version that Normandy is a logical place to be cooking mussels, it has never been a problem to find them in Paris either.

My own theory is a synthesis of the Maxim's and the Ciro's fables. I believe that they are both true and that Louis Barthe may even have invented Billi Bi at other moments when he crossed paths with an American William whose surname began with a B. Anyway, Billi Bi is a wonderful soup, easy to make in a hurry, cheap, and lends itself to embellishment with a pinch of saffron. As the recipe here indicates, it is also a twofer. Once you have cooked the mussels and strained their cooking liquid, you have a choice. Put the shucked mussels back in the soup or save them for a separate cold hors d'oeuvre. Either way, don't leave out the celery, which is the secret ingredient that sophisticates the broth.

3 pounds mussels, well rinsed and debearded	3 cups heavy cream
1 large onion, peeled and chopped	2 egg yolks
2 stalks celery, chopped	Salt
1½ cups dry white wine	White pepper
	Chopped chives

1. Put the mussels in a large pot with the onion, celery, and white wine.
2. Cover and bring to a boil. Simmer for a few minutes, until the mussels have opened.
3. Discard any mussels that have not opened. Remove the rest with a slotted spoon and remove from their shells. Reserve.
4. Strain the broth through a chinois or two layers of cheesecloth (bought in a kitchen supply shop; cheesecloth sold for other purposes such as washing cars may be impregnated with a nasty chemical).
5. In a saucepan, bring the strained liquid to a boil. Stir in the cream. Bring back to the boil, remove from the heat, wait 3 minutes, and then whisk in the egg yolks. Season with salt and white pepper. Add the reserved mussels (or mix them with mayonnaise and put them back in their shells—one per half shell—to serve as an hors d'oeuvre at another meal).
6. Sprinkle with chives and serve the soup hot or cold.

Serves 4 to 6

Blanquette de Veau
(White Veal Stew)

In this homely stew, an elegance of concept bordering on the philosophical shows the French spirit operating with perfect clarity and physical assurance. Blanquette de veau is the serene Apollonian yin to the dark Dionysiac winy tension of boeuf bourguignon. I've picked blanquette because it stands apart from most stews, those hearty, burly lads of which boeuf bourgignon is the *beau idéal*. Blanquette stands by itself, a white goddess in a swarthy rabble. Goddess? Maybe milkmaid would be better, someone pure *and* playful like Dorcas and Mopsa in *The Winter's Tale*.

Whiteness is all here. The veal breast, a lowly cut but the tastiest part of the milk-fed calf, is simmered in water until just tender. No harsh seizing against a dry pot bottom to give caramel color and jump-started flavor to the stew. What could be plainer?

Meanwhile, the cook gets the meat's white retinue together, the mushroom caps heated briefly in the oven, water gone, whiteness retained. Note that the stems (technically stipes) are not discarded; no waste in this household. And the pearl onions get treated like real white pearls: trimmed, deftly slashed so the butter bath they'll be stewed in can seep into the heart of them and melt it.

Then comes what Bogey in *Casablanca* calls a "wow finish." All the ingredients are brought together in the pot and enrobed in a stole of thick alabaster cream and egg.

The name of the dish is, for one, a clear guide to its essence. *Blanquette* literally means some little white thing, a "whitelet." There is a blanquette pear and a fizzy white wine of Provence, the Blanquette de Limoux.

Alan Davidson in *The Oxford Companion to Food* (1999) thinks blanquette is an etymological cousin of blanket, itself originally a white cloth. And he sees one metaphorical step beyond that, a giant metaphorical step, comparing the cloaking of the veal in a blanquette with white sauce to the batter coating that gives its name to the American pig in a blanket.

I've picked blanquette because it stands apart from most stews, those hearty, burly lads of which boeuf bourgignon is the *beau idéal*. Blanquette stands by itself, a white goddess in a swarthy rabble. Goddess? Maybe milkmaid would be better, someone pure *and* playful like Dorcas and Mopsa in *The Winter's Tale*.

2 pounds veal breast, cubed	12 white "pearl" onions
2 teaspoons salt	5 tablespoons butter
2 large carrots, scraped and finely diced	4 tablespoons water
1 medium onion, peeled and stuck with 1 clove	¼ cup flour
1 sprig thyme	1 pinch nutmeg
1 celery leaf	Pepper
1 bay leaf	2 egg yolks
8 mushrooms	⅓ cup crème fraîche
Olive oil for drizzling	1 teaspoon lemon juice
	1 tablespoon chopped parsley

1. Put the veal in a medium enamel saucepan. Cover with water, about 4 cups. Add 2 teaspoons of salt.

2. Bring to a boil very slowly over low-medium heat so that the meat will not seize up. By heating it gently you promote the throwing off of any scum. For about a half hour, skim this off with a slotted spoon, stirring with a wooden spoon and adding a bit of cold water from time to time to encourage the process.

3. Now add the carrots, onion, thyme, celery, and bay leaf. Return to the boil, cover partially, and simmer very slowly for an hour. The meat will be cooked but still firm.

4. Meanwhile, prepare the mushrooms. Cut off the tough ends of the stipes and discard. Then snap off the stipes and reserve. With a small pointed knife, cut away any of the stipe that remains in the caps. Reserve these scrapings with the stipes.

5. Preheat the oven to 350 degrees.

6. Place the caps, gill sides up, on a baking sheet. Drizzle with a small amount of olive oil. Put in the oven for about 8 minutes so that the mushrooms give up their water. Then, remove from the oven, invert the caps on the sheet, and set aside.

7. Place the white onions in a coarse strainer and immerse them in boiling water for a minute. This loosens the skins. Pull off the outer leaf and then the first white leaf. Trim both ends a tiny bit and then make a small crosslike incision in the root end with the point of the knife. In order that, as Madame Saint-Ange says, quoting Carême's poetic but firm subjunctive clause of purpose, "the heart of the onion should anoint itself [*prenne de l'onction*] and cook more quickly."

8. Put the trimmed white onions in a heavy saucepan with 2 tablespoons of butter and 4 tablespoons water. Cover and set over low heat. From time to time, shake the pan gently.

Cook until the liquid has reduced to about a tablespoon. The onions will be lightly glazed in their own juice and still white.

9.   When the veal is done, remove the meat to a large skillet (not cast iron), cover and keep warm. Strain the cooking liquid through a chinois or other very fine strainer. You should have about 3 cups. If there isn't that much, add hot water to bring up to 3 cups. If too much, reduce to 3 cups.

10. Make a roux with the flour and the remaining 3 tablespoons butter: In a 4-cup saucepan, melt the butter and then whisk in the flour. Lower the heat and continue whisking occasionally for about 12 minutes, long enough to cook the flour but not long enough to brown this white roux.

11. Whisk the veal liquid into the roux. Bring to a boil, add the mushroom peelings, nutmeg, and pepper. Reduce the heat and skim for 20 minutes. Remove from the heat.

12. In a bowl, whisk together the egg yolks, crème fraîche, and lemon juice. Then gradually whisk in ¼ cup of the roux-thickened veal liquid. Pour the egg-crème mixture into the main quantity of veal liquid and whisk vigorously while returning to the boil (the yolks will not scramble because of the flour in the roux). When the sauce boils, remove from the heat.

13. Put the mushrooms and onions with the veal in the sauté pan, taking care not to crush the onions. Pour the sauce from step 11 through a chinois over the meat, mushrooms, and onions. Sprinkle with the parsley and serve.

Serves 6

Brandade de Morue
(Salt Cod Puree)

Christianity brought many tests of faith to its adherents in Europe. Among them, one less bloody than the Crusades but with a more lasting effect on human life around the world was the commandment to eat fish on Fridays and many other days of meatless penance. Because cod, a member of the haddock family (Gadidae), spawned and flourished so greatly in the Atlantic, it fed the pious millions. And in a world without refrigeration, it was preserved in salt and later rehydrated.

Salt cod is quite a different fish from fresh cod. So the French have special names for each: *cabillaud* is fresh cod, *morue* for the salt. Italians call the salted kind *baccalà*, the Spanish *bacalao*. And because of the Spanish empire, recipes for this North Atlantic specialty abound in the warm, fish-blessed societies of the Caribbean. Perhaps Portugal (and now its prodigal child Brazil) do more with *bacalhau* than any other culture, but, for my money, the most interesting of all salt-cod preparations is this puree, emulsified with milk and oil.

This is a trademark dish of the South of France, and in particular of the city of Nîmes, where, by legend, in the eighteenth century, a band of Breton cod fishermen who caught their fish off Newfoundland (and were therefore known as les Terre-Neuvas) made a salt-buying trip to the salt marshes of nearby Aigues-Mortes. They left behind salt cod as payment and some local Nîmois hero, now lost to history, is supposed to have invented *brandade*.

The name derives from the Provençal verb *brandar,* to shake. This is a reminder of the laborious pounding the dish once required. The processor has changed all that, without any loss of quality in my view. But as with so many other peasant recipes, connoisseurs dispute almost everything else. Should the cod be salted with its skin on? Should mashed potato be included? And garlic? Yes, no, and maybe. Skinless *morue* had to be skinned, adding cost and the risk of delay in the factory, not to mention all that unnecessary manipulation by alienated fish salters.

Potato is to *morue* as Hamburger Helper is to hamburger. It is also untraditional in Nîmes, although permissible elsewhere. Garlic is in the palate of the inhaler. I'm including it, but you might want to leave it out for a brunch. Provençal usage varies. Either way, this is comfort food that allows you to feel righteous, unless you reflect that centuries of rabid fishing have finally put the cod at risk. Meatless Fridays are gone the way of the Latin mass, but the taste for salt cod persists. And for good reason.

2 pounds dried cod	Salt
1½ cups milk	White pepper
1½ cups olive oil	½ teaspoon ground nutmeg
1 clove garlic, peeled and smashed with the side of a knife	Juice of 1 lemon
	Thin slices of bread fried in olive oil

1. Soak the cod for 24 hours in a sink full of cold water. Change the water several times.
2. Skin and debone the cod. Cover with water in a saucepan. Bring to a boil, then drain immediately in a colander.
3. Pull the cod apart into small pieces. Place in a processor.
4. Pour in ½ cup of the milk, ½ cup of the olive oil, and the garlic. Process until well combined.
5. Pour in the rest of the milk and oil, a little at a time, through the tube in the top of the processor. After each addition, process until well combined. When you have added all the liquid, continue processing until you have a smooth, white puree.
6. Transfer to a saucepan. Season with salt, if necessary, and white pepper. Stir in the nutmeg and lemon juice. Heat gently for 5 minutes, stirring, until warm throughout. Serve with fried bread slices, as a main course at light meals, or as a fish course.

Serves 6

Bread

I enter this arena with fear and trembling. Home bread bakers are a fierce lot. They have greatly suffered for their devotion to the search for an honest crusty loaf they can produce in their own oven. I am not talking here about simple folk like me who were content, in the sixties, to knead all-purpose flour with activated dry active yeast, let it rise a couple of times, put it in a loaf pan from the supermarket, and pop it in the oven. We got nice light loaves that were much better than the Kleenex bread sold in stores. They were also tastier and less compressible than most commercial "French."

They were not, however, anywhere near as delicious and *croustillant* as the baguettes and other classic breads you could get in France. Why not? First, because we were not using professional baker's ovens with their steaming capacity; second, we weren't using bread flour with the right amount of gluten and degree of hardness; third, we did not let the yeast mature with a small amount of flour in a sponge, or *chef,* so as to yield the complicated and appealing flavor of a professional sour bread.

Before long, at least by the mid-eighties, a cult of neo-neo-home bread bakers (following the early lead of Julia Child in volume 2 of *Mastering the Art of French Cooking,* 1970) had mastered the art of domestic sourdough, with a bag of tricks that included bake stones and ceramic cloches, bricks, specialty flour, even their own, hand-built beehive ovens. Artisanal baking, as they called it—anglicizing an adjective they'd learned in France from foodies like themselves with romantic fantasies about a food world supplied by individual purveyors instead of rapacious agribusinessmen and factories—also took a lot of time. To keep your *chef* bubbling along at the right speed was almost a full-time career.

My wife informally retired from her day job for several weeks, until the very high and long preheating her recipe required burnt out our oven.

Most amateurs like her threw in the peel, especially if they lived in places where real professionals were producing first-rate "artisanal" bread to artisanophiles like themselves. Why bother to distort your life and kitchen to make bread that was almost as good as what you could buy in the neighborhood?

There is only one good answer to this question. It was always the reason for people in our post-pioneer era to bake bread at home. Bake your own bread because it is the only serious way to understand and appreciate the most basic of all civilized foods. If you don't learn how to make your own chocolate truffles or ice cream, your ability to enjoy commercial varieties will not be diminished. But bread is different. To experience for yourself the miracle of rising dough, and the equally miraculous capture of the CO_2 released during fermentation in tiny cells formed by the gluten in hexaploid wheat, cells that solidify when the bread is baked—to experience this extraordinary harnessing of natural forces by human ingenuity (hexaploid or 16-chromosome wheat, the only grain that has the right properties for making light white bread, did not occur in nature but arose over centuries of grain cultivation) is up there in majesty with the music of Beethoven—and anyone can play.

1 tablespoon dry active yeast	Vegetable oil for bowl and surface
1¾ cups warm water plus more if needed	of dough
4½ cups bread flour	Cornmeal for dusting
1½ teaspoons salt	1 cup water

1. If you are using dry active yeast, stir ½ teaspoon into ½ cup of warm water and let it stand for 15 minutes until it shows signs of life, foaming or bubbling.
2. In a mixing bowl, beat together 2½ cups flour with the activated dry active yeast mixture and up to another ½ cup of warm water to make a ball of moist but not sticky dough.
3. On a lightly floured board or counter, knead the dough for around 5 minutes.
4. In a lightly oiled bowl, place the kneaded dough, cover the bowl with plastic wrap, and let rise at room temperature until it doubles in bulk (a minimum of 2 hours).
5. Punch down the dough and return to the bowl. Cover and refrigerate overnight.
6. The next day, let the dough return to room temperature. You can speed this process by cutting the dough in several pieces, covering with a towel, and letting stand for an hour.
7. Combine the dough in a mixing bowl with the remaining 2 cups of flour, the remaining yeast, and the salt, as well as ¾ cup warm water or more, to make a sticky dough.
8. Knead for 5 minutes or so, repeatedly moistening hands.
9. Flour the counter. Transfer the dough with a spatula to the floured surface. Flour the top of the dough and your hands. Push the dough into an oblong shape. Let it sit for 3 minutes.
10. Flour your hands again and grasp the dough by both short sides. Don't try to lift the entire rectangle, just raise the ends and let the weight of the dough stretch it. Then fold over the stretched ends on each other, as if folding a letter.
11. Paint the surface with oil, dust with flour, cover, and let rest for a half hour. Then repeat the stretching and folding, oil and flour as before, cover, and let rise for 2 hours.

12. Cut the dough in half, into two rectangles. Watch that you don't deflate it in doing this. Sprinkle with flour on all sides. And with a spatula, set down on a floured dish towel. Pull up the towel to confine the two pieces of dough on their long sides. Then stretch and fold again. Oil and flour the tops of the loaves, cover, and let rise for an hour.

13. Put a bake stone in the oven on a rack positioned at the lowest level. Set another rack at the upper level and put a sheet pan on it. Preheat to 500 degrees. (If you don't have a bake stone, just put the empty sheet pan at the upper level and preheat the oven.)

14. Dust the bottom of another sheet pan with cornmeal. Bring a cup of water to a simmer. Fill a garden mister or squirt gun with warm water.

15. Gently set the loaves on the inverted pan. Stretch the loaves from the ends to make them around 10 inches long. Press down lightly on the middle to even out the height. Slide carefully onto the bake stone or just put the sheet pan in the oven at the bottom level. Put a towel over the open oven door. Then pour the hot water into the preheated sheet pan on the upper rack and close the oven. Wait a half minute; then squirt water at the back and side walls of the oven. Close the oven. Repeat twice at half-minute intervals.

16. Reduce the temperature to 450 degrees. Bake 15 to 20 minutes, until the loaves are golden brown.

17. Cool on a rack. Do not serve while hot. Expect that the crust will soften some during cooling.

2 loaves

Bread Pudding

This paragon of comfort food and brilliantly simple home cooking is not what the French call a *pouding au pain à l'anglaise,* an English-style bread pudding. It *is* what the English call bread-and-butter pudding. What distinguishes it from French "English" bread pudding (or, for that matter, from French French-style bread pudding) is both technical and spiritual. The English spread butter on whole slices of bread and steam them in a whole-egg custard in the oven. The French start with bread crumbs, which they soak in milk and sugar and then strain, before they add to them whole eggs, egg yolks, and stiffly beaten whites. The cooking method is the same, but the molds used are somewhat different. English pudding molds are really bowls with a raised ridge at the top. French bread puddings, says *Larousse Gastronomique* (1938), get steamed in a cylindrical metal mold with a *douille,* a central tube.

So much for the technical differences. But they embody a radical difference of spirit or attitude. The English pudding almost flaunts its lack of artifice, with plain slices of bread and unseparated, barely beaten eggs in a mold that's no more specialized than a mixing bowl and really isn't specifically necessary (as below). The French recipe is so ardently sophisticated, you might eat a *pouding au pain à la française* without knowing it had bread in it; the eggs are prepared in all three possible ways, whole, as lightly beaten yolks, and as whites whipped to stiff peaks; and the mold is not something most people would have around the kitchen. I like both kinds of bread puddings, but which came first?

This amounts to asking whether *pouding* is a franglais derivation from pudding or the reverse. And while we're at it, where does boudin fit into this cross-Channel intercourse? *Boudin noir* is, of course, a French sausage stuffed with congealed pig's blood and onion; in Britain, a black pudding has blood and cereal, usually oats.

My battered old *Larousse* dictionary says *pouding* is from the English "pudding." But it gives the etymology for *boudin,* which can hardly be unrelated to "pudding." Is this a second case of borrowing from England, or is it the original word, which spawned "pudding" and then traveled back to France as *pouding*?

By one theory,* *boudin* came first, starting in ancient Gaul, as a descendant of Latin *botellus,* the classical word for sausage, and even more closely derived from the colloquial or

---

* For another, see Plum Pudding, page 159.

Vulgar Latin *botellinus*. In 1066, the conquering Normans brought it to England. The leap from sausage to pudding (in our sense) is an easy one to imagine. Early puddings were steamed in bags, stuffed like sausages. Even now, the word "pudding" has both senses, although the dessert pudding first gets mentioned in written sources around 1670, after refined sugar was commonly available. And then the word (and the dish) crossed over to France, retaining most of its spelling and its basic meaning, which was a foreign concept in France (*boudin* never refers to a dessert).

Pouding may have been the first of a whole category of Gallicized English words that take on a French flavor over there (*faire un footing* = go for a jog; *un shampooing* = a shampoo). The most delicious of these traveling terms is *redingote*, French for morning coat, from English "riding coat."

While all this borrowing was afoot, in England pudding got transformed in the nursery, where it came to refer to almost any kind of sweet. Used by adults in this way, it has an intimate, self-consciously childish ring, like an allusion to Pooh.

½ loaf soft white bread, approximately	1 teaspoon vanilla extract
8 tablespoons (1 stick) butter, at room temperature	3 large eggs
1 cup milk	¾ cup sugar
2 cups heavy cream	¾ cup sultanas, soaked in hot water
¼ level teaspoon salt	¼ cup apricot preserves
	Confectioners' sugar

1. Slice the bread thinly and butter the slices lightly on one side. A 10-inch pie plate will fit nine or ten slices, approximately, depending on the size of the loaf and the thinness of the slices you cut.

2. Bring the milk, 1 cup heavy cream, the salt, and the vanilla to a boil. Remove from the heat immediately or it will foam over.

3. Beat the eggs and sugar together until smooth and lemon-colored. Then gradually whisk in the hot milk.

4. Preheat the oven to 350 degrees.

5. Butter a 10-inch pie plate that you intend to serve the pudding in. Arrange the buttered slices in the plate in layers. The third layer should rise just a bit higher than the edge of the plate.

6. Pour in the egg-milk mixture.

7. Set the pie plate in a bain-marie, a roasting pan, or other vessel that is ovenproof. Add water so that it comes about halfway up the side of the pie plate. Put the bain-marie with the pudding into the oven, at middle level. Bake for 40 minutes. The pudding will have set and the top layer of bread slices should be nicely toasted.

8. Drain the sultanas and scatter over the top of the pudding.

9. Heat the preserves, then push through a strainer and pour over the top of the pudding.

10. Dust with confectioners' sugar. Serve with the remaining cup of (unwhipped) heavy cream.

6 servings

Bstilla
(Moroccan Pigeon Pie)

Moroccan cuisine is one of the world's greatest, the apex of Berber and Tuareg civilizations as perfected in a royal court over many generations. Its perfumed and recondite spice mixtures, preserved lemons, and laborious concoctions never conceal the flavors of raw materials, and though often showy, never sacrifice taste for spectacle. *Bstilla* is the crowning glory of Moroccan cuisine, the legendary pigeon pie.

It is also a shining example of the impossibility of achieving authenticity far from the traditional culture that spawned a dish with highly local ingredients or techniques or both. But where the dish is built on a strong idea, it is still worth making in your kitchen.

Bstilla is a magnificent set piece even if you substitute chicken for squab. But if you find squab at a specialty butcher, I doubt you will ever make your own *warka* leaves for the pie's strudel-like pastry. Even in Rabat or Tangier, in the 1950s, no one made foolscap-thin but chewy *warka* leaves at home. They bought them from professionals.

Paula Wolfert devotes several pages and illustrations to explaining how to make *warka* in *Couscous and Other Good Food from Morocco* (1973). I have read those pages many times over 30 years, and I have never once tried to follow the directions. But I have seen someone make *warka*—in the Hopi Reservation in Arizona. Anyway, *piki,* the traditional, razor-thin corn "bread" of the Hopi, is made just like *warka.* The cook bounces a ball of dough against a greased iron surface, leaving a film of dough with each bounce. Working quickly, she (it is always a woman) makes a series of transparent dough circles, eventually connecting the disks to create a sheet.

Commercial *warka* is marginally available in the non-Arab world, but Shanghai-style egg roll wrappers aka spring roll wrappers are said by experts to be the closest widely available *warka* surrogate. They are far easier to work with than the ubiquitous phyllo.

Spring roll wrappers come in two sizes. You want the larger, 8-inch-square variety. They are sold frozen. When you want to use them, let them come to room temperature in the package. After opening the package, keep them moist under a damp dish towel. Spring roll wrappers are commonly available both in Chinese groceries and in Philippine markets, because the Filipino egg roll *lumpia* is made with the same Shanghai spring roll wrappers. A good mail-order source is: Chinese-American Trading Co., Inc., 91 Mulberry Street, New York, NY 10013 (212-267-5224).

½ pound butter, softened	1 cup water
3 squabs or one 3- to 4-pound chicken, cut into several pieces	1 cup slivered blanched almonds
1 teaspoon ground ginger	6 tablespoons sugar
2 cinnamon sticks	2 tablespoons ground cinnamon
1¼ cups grated onion	Juice of 1 lemon
¼ cup finely chopped flat-leaf parsley	8 eggs, lightly beaten
½ teaspoon turmeric	2 packages of twenty-five 8-inch Shanghai-style frozen spring roll wrappers
1½ teaspoons black pepper	1 egg yolk, lightly beaten
1½ teaspoons salt	Confectioners' sugar

1. Melt half the butter (1 stick) in a heavy skillet just large enough to hold the chicken. When the butter stops foaming, add the squabs or chicken, ginger, cinnamon sticks, grated onion, parsley, turmeric, pepper, and salt. Sauté the squabs or chicken slowly in this mixture for 10 minutes, shaking the pan or stirring so that the spices and turmeric completely permeate the flesh. Add a cup of water, bring to a boil, and simmer for 45 minutes or until the meat is tender and pulls easily away from the bones.

2. While the chicken is cooking, melt 2 tablespoons butter in a skillet and gently fry the almonds. Stir from time to time to avoid burning. Cook until honey-colored. With a slotted spoon, remove to a processor jar. Process coarsely, in brief spurts, with ¼ cup of the sugar and 1 tablespoon of the ground cinnamon.

3. When the squabs or chicken are done, remove with a slotted spoon, but do not discard the cooking liquid; leave it in the skillet. Pull off the skin and discard. Pull or cut the meat off the bones. Discard the bones. Shred or julienne the meat. Put in a bowl and toss with the remaining 2 tablespoons sugar.

4. Heat the squab or chicken cooking liquid in the original skillet with the lemon juice. Pour in the eggs and stir until scrambled on the dry side. Drain off the excess liquid and let cool.

5. Melt the remaining butter and use some of it to brush the inside of a 14-inch cake pan with sides at least 1½ inches high. Take six egg roll wrappers and set them around the outer edge of the pan. They will overlap and they should also drape over the edge of the pan about 2 inches all around. Brush them with some of the melted butter. Cover the center of the pan with another wrapper. Butter it.

6. Now make three sets of alternating layers of squabs or chicken, almonds, and eggs.

Proceed as follows: Spread a third of the squabs or chicken over the buttered wrappers in the pan. Take three wrappers and spread them around the edge of the pie, overlapping but spread apart enough so that they cover the perimeter of the pie but not the center. Butter the wrappers.

7. Follow the same method with a third of the almond mixture and then with a third of the egg mixture. Each time, cover the new layer with three wrappers, as above. Repeat this process until all the squab or chicken, almond, and egg are used up. Cover each new layer with three wrappers. For the final layer, cover the entire layer with buttered wrappers.

8. Fold the wrapper edges draped over the edge of the pan (see step 5) back over the pie. Put another wrapper over the center of the pie. Brush with the beaten egg yolk.

9. Turn on the oven to 425 degrees. Do not wait to preheat. Put the pie in right after you have turned on the oven. Bake for 15 minutes. This is enough to heat everything through and to bake the wrappers without drying them out.

10. Invert the pie onto a serving platter. Do not let cool. Sprinkle generously straightaway with confectioners' sugar. The sugar should completely cover the pie. Then sprinkle with the remaining tablespoon of cinnamon, making a pattern on the white field of sugar. Serve immediately.

Serves 8

Cannelloni
(Spinach-and-Ricotta-Stuffed Pasta Roll-ups)

An elegant neighbor lady invites us to dinner every other year and always serves cannelloni with a spinach-and-ricotta stuffing. Does she think we won't remember? If so, she is wrong twice over. She slights our memories and the high quality of her (only?) party dish. For me, cannelloni, literally big tubes, are among the finest of all pasta dishes. It would be folly to say that they are the best pasta dish Italy has to offer, but they epitomize this crucial category of Italian food at its highest level. And yet it would be wrong to see this casserole of oven-baked, rolled-up, filled squares of egg pasta as somehow typical.

Cannelloni do not come from the heartland of pasta, Emilia-Romagna, home of *spaghetti alla bolognese.* They are native in Piedmont and in Sicily (where a gratin of provolone replaces the more usual béchamel topping). They belong, not in the vast army of noodle pastas, but in that smaller, more laborious and calculated family of flat wide strips of pasta, along with lasagne and ravioli. Truly unique is the anomalous popularity of cannelloni in Spain.

Caneloni are on almost any menu in Catalonia, and they are a completely naturalized food from one end of the peninsula to another.

How did this happen? It is a happy remnant of Spanish hegemony over Italy in the sixteenth century, when cultural influences spread easily across the water from northern Italy to Barcelona. This is not to say that Spaniards don't realize, if they stop to think about it, that *canelones* have an Italian ancestry. The classic Catalan cookbook, Ignasi Domènech's *La Teca,* has three recipes for *canelons* (the Catalan cognate)—Rossini, a grand affair with several different meats in the stuffing, Florentina, with spinach and calf's brain, and the last, stuffed with a mixture of seafood for Christmas Eve vigil, a farinaceous reflection of the Italian custom of eating many kinds of fish to celebrate the Nativity.

Italian food has, much more recently, conquered the New World through immigration to the United States, Argentina, and Venezuela (among others). In these new areas, authenticity is gone with the wind. From Chef Boyardee to the fantasias improvised by adolescent American chef-prodigies, the spectrum of distortion is a dismal prospect. So roll out some egg dough with your hand pasta machine and take a stand for the way things ought to be (a thoroughly practical undertaking in this case). This recipe may look elaborate, but the machine makes it much easier than it may sound, and the result, misleadingly bland-looking, is an ideal comfort food, matching cheese and spinach and cream sauce in superb pasta.

It would be folly to say that they are the best pasta dish Italy has to offer, but they epitomize this crucial category of Italian food at its highest level. And yet it would be wrong to see this casserole of oven-baked, rolled-up, filled squares of egg pasta as somehow typical.

1 pound spinach, washed thoroughly and
   trimmed
1¾ to 2 cups ricotta cheese
7 eggs
Salt
Pepper

1 pound flour (about 3½ cups),
   approximately, for the dough plus 3
   tablespoons for the béchamel
Olive oil (if needed)
3 cups milk
3 tablespoons butter
Grated Parmesan cheese

1. Put the spinach in a saucepan over medium heat. Check frequently and stir. When the spinach wilts, drain and then squeeze gently to remove residual water.

2. Chop the spinach fine and mix well with the ricotta and 2 eggs. Season with salt and pepper. Set aside.

3. Pour the 1 pound of flour on a clean wood surface. Form it into a mound. Then scoop out a "well" in the center. Crack the remaining eggs into the well. Then, working with one hand, bring the flour from the sides over the eggs and mix until the flour and eggs have been amalgamated into a smooth moist ball of dough. To achieve this, push the dough away from you with the heel of your hand; then gather the dough into a ball and repeat. If the dough is too dry, add a little olive oil. If it sticks to your hand, add a little flour.

4. Let the dough rest for a half hour wrapped in a dish towel.

5. To roll out with a machine, follow the directions that come with the machine. For the Atlas hand roller, cut off a handful of dough and flatten it gently with your hand. Pass it through the rollers set at position 1. Sprinkle a little flour on one side of the dough, fold the dough over the flour and pass it through the machine again. Repeat in this way four times. Then reset the rollers to position 2 and repeat. Then to position 3 and so on until you have run it through at position 9. You should now have a long, fairly thin rectangle of dough 20 to 30 inches long and the width of your pasta machine, around 4 inches. Square off the ends. Continue in this way until the rest of the dough is rolled out. Keep moist under a damp towel. If you have a special cannelloni attachment, center a sheet of dough over the gap between the rollers, like a newspaper. Spread 1 tablespoon of the filling in the gap. Turn the handle slowly. A closed *cannellono* will appear underneath the roller. Repeat this operation until all the pasta and filling are used up. Place on a dish towel to dry. Separate individual cannelloni along the crimped lines between them. This should be possible by hand. If you do not have a special attachment, cut the rolled strips of dough into 3 by 4-inch rectangles.

6. If you are rolling out the dough completely by hand, take half the rested ball of dough from step 4 and begin rolling it with a rolling pin on a lightly floured surface. Keep rotating it as you roll until you get a circular sheet about ⅛ inch thick. Then roll up a quarter of it on the pin. Press your hands on the dough on the pin, stretching it sideways and rolling it up at the same time. Unroll, rotate slightly, and repeat the roll-up stretching several times until you can almost see through the dough. Cut it in 3 by 4-inch rectangles. Repeat with the other three-quarters of the rolled-out dough. Then repeat this step with the remaining half of the rested dough from step 4.

7. For either the machine-rolled and -filled cannelloni or the machine-rolled hand-cut unfilled rectangles or the completely handmade rectangles, bring 4 quarts of lightly salted water to a boil. Immerse five of the filled cannelloni or the rectangles at a time. Let the water return to a boil, wait a few seconds and remove with a slotted spoon to a dry towel. Pat dry and fill each rectangle with a tablespoon of the filling. Place the cannelloni, edge side down, in a single layer in a 9 by 14-inch lightly oiled baking dish.

8. Prepare a béchamel sauce: Heat the milk until it begins to foam; then remove from the heat. Melt the butter in another saucepan. Add the flour all at once to the melted butter and whisk it in. Stirring constantly, cook for 2 or 3 minutes. Then begin whisking in the hot milk, a little at a time. When it is all incorporated, continue cooking over low heat until it thickens a bit.

9. Preheat the oven to 400 degrees.

10. Cover with the béchamel, sprinkle generously with the grated cheese, and bake in the oven for 15 to 20 minues or until golden brown on top.

Serves 6

Ceviche de Lenguado
(Citrus-Cured Flounder)

Fish marinated in citrus juice or other acid liquids changes from raw to a gently "cooked" state. No heat is applied. The acid alone alters the protein, softens it and turns it opaque, but the freshness of the food or shellfish remains. This technique, so far as anyone knows, is native to several cultures. The most delicate form is found in the Philippines, where fishermen immerse freshly caught seafood in juice for a few seconds before eating it. Longer immersion, for an hour or so, produces what is known far and wide as ceviche, cebiche, or seviche.

Ceviche is popular in Mexico. But the most elaborate ceviche cuisine is Peruvian. The classic components include not only lime juice and chilies but sweet potato and the large-kerneled corn of the Andes known as *choclo*.

The late Felipe Rojas-Lombardi emigrated form Peru to New York and was a talented missionary for the foods of his heritage. This recipe is adapted from his *The Art of South American Cooking* (1991).

It would seem probable, given its omnipresence and high state of development there, that ceviche originated in Peru and spread to Mexico during the early days of Spanish colonization in the New World. In the present state of knowledge, it is impossible to say for sure. But the word itself may have emanated from the Old World and then been applied to this New World method. In an article in *Petits Propos Culinaires* (no. 20, 1985), Barbara Santich looked into its etymology in the three great Latin American dictionaries of local Spanish idioms, the dictionaries of Mejicanismos, Chilenismos, and Peruanismos. The Mexican lexicon referred her to the Chilean, which rather unpersuasively derived it from the English "shellfish." The dictionary of Peruvianisms sees it as a diminutive of *cebo,* a Spanish word for food, which itself derives from the Latin *cibus*.

Ms. Santich also entertains the notion that ceviche is a first cousin once removed of the well-known Mediterranean preparation of fried fish with vinegar (see page 70) called *escabeche*. Although the fish in *escabeche* is cooked in the normal sense before the acid medium is poured over it, the acidulation of fish in ceviche might well have reminded Spaniards of the *escabeche* they had grown up with at home. *Escabeche* itself comes from the Arabic *sikbaj* and crops up in the medieval Catalan cookbook *Sent Sovi*.

In Peru today, ceviche and escabeche exist side by side and nobody seems to worry about their possible common ancestry in Baghdad or Ispahan. In the food world of Lima, seviche is old news. The new news is *tiradito,* a hybrid of sashimi and ceviche invented by the large community of Japanese immigrants. The fish is cut in strips, marinated much more briefly than ceviche and tossed somewhat unceremoniously on the plate. The name means something like "tossed off" or "throwaway." It has emigrated northward to the elite New York restaurant Nobu, a temple of sushi run by a Japanese from Lima.

2½ pounds skinless flounder (or other
    flatfish—sole, turbot, halibut) fillet
2 cloves garlic, peeled
2 tablespoons coarse salt
¼ teaspoon ground white pepper
2 cups lime juice (12 to 14 limes)
2 or 3 fresh jalapeño or serrano peppers
1 small red onion, peeled and thinly sliced
¼ cup olive oil

GARNISH

6 to 8 Boston lettuce leaves, washed and
    dried
1 ear corn, cooked and cut into 6 to 8
    slices
1 cooked sweet potato, cut into 6 to 8
    slices
12 to 24 alfonso or kalamata olives
3 tablespoons chopped fresh cilantro leaves

1. Wipe the fish fillets with a damp cloth and cut on the diagonal into ¼ inch by 4-inch strips. Set aside in a glass bowl.
2. In a mortar with a pestle, pound the garlic, salt, and white pepper to a smooth paste. Add the paste to the lime juice and mix thoroughly. Pour over the strips of flounder. Let marinate for 1 hour, covered, in the refrigerator. Remove from the refrigerator, add the peppers, onion, and olive oil, and mix well. Let rest 5 to 10 minutes before serving.
3. To serve, place a lettuce leaf on 6 to 8 small plates. With a slotted spoon, scoop a helping of ceviche onto the leaf. Garnish each plate with 1 slice of corn, 1 slice of sweet potato, and 2 to 3 olives. Sprinkle with cilantro.

Serves 6 to 8

Chicken Adobo
(Filipino Chicken Stew)

When I visited the Philippines in 1990, most Filipino food experts believed that many foods from Spain and Mexico had been "adapted" by local cooks during the four centuries of Spanish colonial rule. They would point, for instance, to the rice dish *bringhe,* assertedly adapted from paella by the substitution of coconut milk for olive oil and saffron. And, of course, there is the most important case of all, adobo, the so-called national dish supposedly descended from Spanish and Mexican dishes of the same or similar names.

To an outsider, these "new" dishes did not look like adaptations. All the essential ingredients for *bringhe* were present in the Philippines before Magellan. The same is true for adobo. And for the Filipino tamale.

So I speculated that what really happened when Spain and the indigenous culture collided was not an adaptation of the two original cuisines to each other but a kind of lexical imperialism. Spanish colonists saw that certain native Filipino dishes were similar to dishes in Spain or Mexico. When Spaniards came upon them, it was natural for them to apply the name of something they knew to the Filipino dish. So they transferred the name *adobo,* which in Spain implied cooking in a wine marinade, to Filipino chicken or pork cooked in vinegar, soy sauce, and garlic. By the same process, Mexican dishes with chili-laden marinades had already been Hispanicized as adobo.

Similarly, I theorized, when the Spaniards alit from their galleons on the shores of Manila Bay, they saw leaf-wrapped, steamed rice cakes filled with meat strips and other oddments. These they called tamales, by analogy to what they knew from their experience in Mexico. And a big, festive dish in which rice was cooked with a spectrum of foods became paella, or if it kept its old name, *bringhe,* it was viewed as a local variation of the more authentic paellas seen in the big house of the Spanish plantation owner.

My whole theory was, in the small world of Filipino gastronomy, a radical notion. It called into question the most basic ideas on which the history of Filipino cuisine are based. After all, since adobo was the national dish, it was a wild claim I was making, but a claim that made sense, logically and emotionally, to Filipinos, who were eager to reclaim and sustain all forms of indigenous culture now that they were independent after centuries of subjugation to outsiders. But there was no documentation to support my idea.

I did find a willing ear, however, at a lunch in Manila with Doreen Fernandez, a remarkable person—scholar of English, restaurant critic, and a food historian of profound gifts. She went to her library and looked up adobo in a Jesuit dictionary from early colonial days. There it was plainly stated that "adobo" was a stew of *los naturales,* the natives. QED. I rest my case, but encourage you to try this extremely simple but original dish, worthy under any name to be a national emblem for 200 million people and a perfect example of their special gastronomic affinity for sourness.

One 3- to 4-pound chicken, cut in serving pieces

1½ cups soy sauce

¾ cup white wine or cider vinegar

3 cloves garlic, peeled and minced

1 bay leaf, crumbled

10 black peppercorns, crushed

1. Put all the ingredients in a pot. Bring to a boil and simmer, covered, for an hour, or until the chicken is tender.
2. Preheat the broiler.
3. Remove the chicken pieces and run under the broiler to brown. Meanwhile, reduce the sauce by half.
4. Put the chicken pieces on a serving platter. Pour the sauce over the chicken.

Serves 6

Chicken Soup

Many people think chicken soup is a cold medicine. And who am I to argue with the wisdom of the ages? But I will tell you that I am unwilling to wait until I or someone in my house falls ill before I make chicken soup. In fact, I prepare to make it every time I roast a chicken. I take the little package of giblets from the bird's cavity, put it in a plastic bag, and freeze it. Four or five chickens later, I put all the giblets in a pot with the disarticulated carcass from the most recent roast chicken, chop in an onion, pour in water to cover, and simmer for 45 minutes. After the solid ingredients are strained out (they have been drained of their flavor in the cooking process), I add salt and pepper and serve.

The recipe given here is based on a more elaborate chicken soup demonstrated to me 30 years ago by André Soltner, the chef of Lutèce in New York. I asked him to cook a few dishes he liked to make at home, away from his celebrated restaurant. If the very simple chicken soup I normally make will cure colds, this one should defeat pneumonia.

15 cups water	½ teaspoon dried thyme or 3 sprigs fresh
2 chicken gizzards, peeled	Pepper
Salt	¼ cup raw long-grain rice
8 chicken wings	1 large potato, peeled and diced
1 large carrot, scraped and finely chopped	1 slice bacon, diced, blanched in boiling
1 stalk celery, trimmed and finely chopped	water for 2 minutes, and drained
1 large onion, peeled and finely chopped	1 clove garlic, peeled and minced
6 sprigs parsley, reserve stems	1 teaspoon ground cardamom
1 bay leaf	

1. Bring 3 cups water to a boil, add the gizzards, lower the heat, and simmer, uncovered, for 30 minutes. Drain, dice, and reserve.

2. While the gizzards cook, bring 6 cups lightly salted water to a boil, add the chicken wings, and cook for 3 minutes. Drain. Pull out the bones. Chop into 2-inch-long pieces and reserve.

3. Combine the reserved gizzards and the wing pieces in a large pot with 6 cups of water along with the carrot, celery, onion, parsley stems, bay leaf, and thyme. Season with salt

and pepper to taste. Bring to a boil, reduce the heat, and simmer slowly for 1½ hours. Remove and discard the parsley stems, bay leaf, and fresh thyme, if any.

4. Add the rice and potato. Continue simmering for another half hour.
5. Meanwhile brown the bacon pieces, and chop the parsley leaves as finely as you can.
6. When the soup is ready to serve, add the bacon, parsley, garlic, and cardamom.

Serves 5 to 6 as a soup course or as a light lunch with bread and salad

Chiles Poblanos en Nogada
(Puebla Chilies Stuffed with Pork in Walnut Sauce)

After the Spanish conquest of Mexico, the pre-Columbian Aztec civilization persisted and mixed with the imported culture of viceregal Mexico. This *mestizaje,* or "mixing," affected every aspect of Mexican life. But the mélange is nowhere more noticeable, or more crucially defining, than in the kitchen and on the table.

The foremost Mexican gastronomic writer of the modern period, Salvador Novo, expounds this phenomenon almost ecstatically in his *Cocina Mexicana o Historia Gastronomica de la Ciudad de Mexico* (1967):

> *The encounter was a fortunate one, the marriages were happy, their offspring abundant. Atoles [a category of beverage] and cacao drinks benefit from sugar and milk; tortillas, after being fried or sprinkled with chorizo [a Spanish pork sausage], will transform them- selves into garnachas, chalupas, sopes, tostadas, tacos, enchiladas, chilaquiles, infladas, molotes, bocoles, pellizcadas. Tamales will be fluffier with lard . . . Refried beans will be more delicious than plain boiled beans; and beans as well as strips of chili fried with onion will accept the white, tasty caress of cheese and cream.*

It would be possible to go through dish after dish in this manner, sorting out the Aztec and Spanish contributions to each. But the most impressive part of the *mestizaje* in Mexican cuisine is how rapidly it took hold, both in agriculture and in the kitchen. Already in Cortés's lifetime, the process had permeated all sectors of Mexican life, and by the seventeenth century the invention of new, self-consciously Mexican dishes was pursued at the highest levels of the vicerealm.

In particular, well-born or well-connected women in convents created many hybrid recipes, notably a whole repertory of elaborate sweets. The greatest of Mexican sauces, the mole poblano, was according to legend invented by a religious, Sor Andrea de la Asunción, at the convent of Santa Rosa in Puebla. Whether the attribution is correct or not, the notion of Puebla as the origin of this savant sauce is convincing. A great colonial center, Puebla was a cosmopolitan place, open to new things. It was Puebla that welcomed a Chinese girl, the *China Poblana,* and made her into a folk symbol whose colorful dress is still recognizable to every Mexican—a charming relic of the seaborne trade with China.

Puebla in the seventeenth century was a hub of new things, just the sort of place where a refined nun would mix chocolate, chilies, and imported ingredients, such as cinnamon and coriander, for a sauce to go with the great Aztec bird, the turkey. If the final taste of the sauce seems Asian to us, perhaps our taste buds are hinting at a historical truth. Probably not, but the legend of mole poblano as an invented sauce concocted by a non-Aztec with Spanish and local pre-Columbian ingredients is itself worthy of note. Even if the account is only a fable, it is a fable that demonstrates how eagerly Mexicans embrace the idea of a *mestizo,* or "hybrid," origin for their national cuisine.

What seems clear, in any case, is that out of the extremely fertile period of Mexican sauce development in the eighteenth century, the mole (Nahuatl for sauce), which combines chocolate and chilies, emerged firmly identified with Puebla.

I emphasize this because the acme of refinement in classical Mexican cookery is another Poblano dish that, beyond any doubt, had to be invented at some point after the conquest because it combines chilies and milk. The chili is the big green chile poblano, the chili of Puebla. The dish is called *chile en nogada.* It is an elaborate member of a family of dishes that all involve stuffing chiles poblanos with one thing or another. *Chile en nogada* is stuffed with chopped pork and served in a sauce of ground nuts and cream. In some versions of this dish, peaches and pears, *acitrón* (the candied fruit of the bisnaga cactus), and other fruits are added to the stuffing. Perhaps this is a relic of a pre-Columbian, and therefore pre-pork, stuffed poblano dish in which the stuffing was all fruit.

Chile en nogada is still a seasonal dish of late August, but now the timing depends on another seasonal fruit, an Old World fruit, the walnut (called *nuez de Castilla* in Mexico to distinguish it from the native American pecan, which is simply *nuez*). Fresh walnuts and cream bathe the stuffed green chili, and ruby-red pomegranate seeds, also Old World in origin, provide the third color of the Mexican flag. Some people believe that the patriotic look of this "Old World" sauce for a New World chili stuffed with Old World pork is not happenstance. They say that *chile en nogada* was invented in Puebla for a banquet honoring Agustín de Iturbide, the self-styled emperor of newly independent Mexico, on August 28, 1821. Once again it doesn't matter if this tradition is true. The story still completes the symbolism of a great dish that is the epitome of a culture.

12 chilies poblanos

1½ pounds boneless pork shoulder, cubed

Salt

2 cloves garlic, peeled and chopped

1 onion, peeled and chopped

2 tablespoons corn oil

½ cup vinegar

1 cup water

2 tablespoons lard

1 pound tomatoes, blanched, peeled, seeded, and chopped

3 tablespoons raisins

10 blanched almonds, slivered

10 pitted green olives, chopped

Sugar

Pepper

1 crumbled bay leaf

50 walnuts, shelled (freshly harvested if possible, otherwise soaked in water overnight) and with inner skin removed

½ cup Mexican sour cream or crème fraîche

¼ cup sherry

2 pomegranates

1. Toast the chilies over a direct flame or under the broiler until blackened. Then leave in a paper bag for 20 minutes. They should now peel easily. After peeling, cut a lengthwise slit in each of them but leave the stem and tip end intact. Trim out the internal veins and remove the seeds. Set aside.

2. Cook the pork in lightly salted boiling water to cover, along with half the garlic and onion, for 45 minutes. Drain, reserving the cooking liquid, and chop the pork fine.

3. Heat the corn oil in a large saucepan and add the rest of the garlic and all but a tablespoon of the remaining onion. Add the chilies and toss until the onion is translucent. Then add the vinegar, a cup of water, and salt. Bring to a boil, reduce the heat, and simmer until the chilies are cooked through.

4. Meanwhile, finish cooking the stuffing (*el relleno*). Melt the lard in a skillet and add the remaining tablespoon onion. Sauté until translucent. Then add the pork, tomatoes, raisins, almonds, and olives. Stir together and add ½ cup of the reserved pork cooking liquid, sugar, salt, pepper, and bay leaf. Bring to a boil, reduce the heat, and simmer until the liquid has almost completely evaporated.

5. Make the walnut sauce (*la nogada*). Chop the nuts very fine and stir together with the sour cream. Then stir in the sherry. The sauce should be thick but pourable. Add more sherry if necessary to create this consistency.

6. Stuff the chilies with the pork mixture. Arrange them on a serving platter, cover with the sauce, and then sprinkle with pomegranate seeds.

Serves 6

Chocolate Fudge

This was called Vassar fudge by Maria Parloa, who published the recipe in a booklet distributed by Walter Baker & Co. in 1905. It was reprinted in the *American Heritage Cookbook* (1964). The headnote for the recipe said: "Fudge was popular in the late nineteenth century in women's colleges. Sometimes cooked over the gaslight, which hung from the center of the ceiling, it was used as an excuse for parties after 'lights-out.' "

The idyllic scene conjured in this passage will impress anyone who has made fudge herself even more than the reader who has only eaten it. Fudge is one of those apparently simple kitchen projects that is actually full of pitfalls, even when cooked on a stovetop, instead of on an overhead gaslight. That's because fudge requires precise attention to temperature and a knowledge of the chemistry of sugar.

The infallible Harold McGee, in *On Food and Cooking, the Science and Lore of the Kitchen* (1984), lays out the basics:

> As a liquid boils, it loses molecules from the liquid phase to the gaseous phase, while the solids stay behind. In a sugar syrup, this means that the sugar molecules account for a larger and larger proportion of all the molecules in the solution. In other words, the syrup gets more and more concentrated as the water boils off. . . . Generally, the more water the syrup contains, the softer the final product will be. At 235°F (113°C), or about 85% sugar, the cook can stop the concentration process and make fudge; at 270°F (132°C), or 90%, taffy; at 300°F (149°C), nearing 100%, brittles and hard candy.

Traditionally, these temperatures were not determined by thermometers, but by dropping a small amount of the syrup in cold water. At 235 to 240 degrees, the sugar forms a "soft ball" that can be molded easily and will be excellent for fudge. At 245 to 250 degrees, you get a "firm ball," ideal for caramels. At 250 to 265 degrees, the "hard-ball" stage is reached, just right for marshmallows or nougat. At 270 to 290 degrees, the sugar makes a cracking sound as it hits the water, the soft-crack stage, taffy time. The hard-crack stage is 300 to 310 degrees, perfect for butterscotch or brittle. Between 320 and 335 degrees, sugar browns or caramelizes. Wait any longer and the sugar burns, turning a stinky black.

The other issue for fudge makers is crystallization. This is a complex topic, but in the limited case of fudge, the following principles apply. Use a wooden spoon, a poor heat conductor that will not create local cooling areas. Do not agitate the hot proto-fudge. If you are using a thermometer, leave it alone as much as possible. Since crystals grow more quickly in hot syrups, the correct procedure is to cool the fudge dramatically before beginning to stir it. The stirring does indeed produce crystals, but tiny ones, just what you want for a creamy fudge. But you can't stop the stirring or the fudge turns grainy.

Do Vassar women still make fudge by night? Are they still as adept at judging temperature and strong enough to stir like mad? And what about the gaslights? No, no, and no more. Should we blame all this on the advent of coeducation?

2 cups sugar	1 cup light cream
2 ounces unsweetened chocolate	1 tablespoon butter

1. Heat the sugar, chocolate, and cream over medium heat, stirring until the sugar and chocolate have melted. When the sugar begins to boil, wash down any splashes that have stuck to the inside of the pan.
2. Then heat without stirring until the mixture reaches 238 degrees F on a candy thermometer (soft-ball stage).
3. Remove from the heat, add the butter without stirring, and cool to around 110 degrees. Then beat vigorously and without stopping until the fudge starts to stiffen. Pour into a lightly oiled pan.
4. When the fudge is cool but not completely hard, cut into squares with a sharp knife.

1 pound

What makes a great chocolate pudding? For one thing, it stands on its own, trembling with false modesty, secretly sure of itself, and unsupported by cornstarch. The cream and egg yolks are enough.

Chocolate Pudding

When David Page and Barbara Shinn opened Home Restaurant in a narrow space with thirty-four seats and a back garden in Greenwich Village, their aim was to serve American food without flourish but with plenty of skill and also modern sophistication about ingredients and techniques. Recently, they collected their favorite recipes in *Recipes from Home* (2001). Among them: evolved regional dishes like shrimp and andouille sausage gumbo or plum butter. And, of course, they included their trademark dessert, this mostly straightforward chocolate pudding. It is perennially the most popular thing they serve. For once, public taste is based on real taste, for this is a chocolate pudding superior to all other chocolate puddings.

I can make this claim because I have eaten it many times, not because, or only partly because David and Barbara moved into an apartment whose terrace overlooks our Village garden and replaced a tenant who threw noisy cocktail parties every summer afternoon. Before we met the new neighbors, we were grateful for the peace and quiet. They were never at home, but we soon learned why: they were always at Home.

Since we are very close to Home when we are at home, we go to their restaurant frequently to find out how the neighbors are doing, to ask them what's cooking, and to take pot luck with them. This is no gamble, particularly since chocolate pudding is always on the menu.

What makes a great chocolate pudding? For one thing, it stands on its own, trembling with false modesty, secretly sure of itself, and unsupported by cornstarch. The cream and egg yolks are enough.

Home's pudding straddles a fine line between liquid and solid. This is achieved not only by sensible treatment of basic ingredients but also through meticulous observation of the degree of doneness: See step 4 below. That quarter-size shimmy in the center is the dance of delight that keeps the customers coming back. It is what separates fine Home cooking from those stand-alone gravity puddings we used to invert over the table at school, knowing they wouldn't drop, or that pan of My-T-Fine I left out overnight at a campsite, where a raccoon ate everything else but spurned its congealed chemicals completely.

Not that you asked, but Home's chocolate pudding is a real American chocolate pudding, not a chocolate mousse misnamed. Chocolate mousse is, as its name implies, a foam aerated by raw beaten egg whites. Chocolate pudding is all yolk, steamed just right.

4 cups heavy cream

5 ounces bittersweet chocolate (see Note), finely chopped

6 large egg yolks

½ cup sugar

1 teaspoon vanilla extract

Pinch salt

Preheat the oven to 325°F.

1. Bring the heavy cream to a simmer in a large heavy saucepan, then remove the pan from the heat.

2. Place the chocolate in a large stainless-steel bowl, add 1 cup of the warm cream, and let stand until the chocolate is melted. Stir the chocolate mixture until it is smooth, then stir in the remaining cream.

3. In a separate large bowl, whisk together the egg yolks, sugar, vanilla, and salt. Gradually whisk in the chocolate mixture. Strain the pudding through a fine-mesh strainer and skim off the froth on the top.

4. Pour the pudding into eight 6-ounce ovenproof ramekins. Place them in a deep baking pan and put the pan in the oven. Add enough hot water to the pan to reach halfway up the sides of the ramekins, then cover the pan with aluminum foil. Bake the puddings for about 50 minutes. When gently shaken, they should look set around the edges but not quite set in a quarter-size area at the center.

5. Remove the ramekins from the water bath and let cool at room temperature. Refrigerate for several hours, or overnight. Serve chilled.

Serves 8

Note: *Bittersweet chocolate has sugar, vanilla, and lecithin added to the pure chocolate liquor and cocoa butter. Although semisweet usually has more sugar, the two are pretty much interchangeable in recipes.*

Choucroute
(Alsatian Sauerkraut and Pork Stew)

Like most overcelebrated regional specialties, choucroute is almost always inauthentic and unsuccessful. The word is some kind of French accommodation of a German word for cabbage, kraut, tacked onto the French word for cabbage, *chou.* This is the kind of mongrel word that mortally annoys French language purists, when they ought to be pleased with the creative absorption that takes place almost every time that some outlandish alien term gets swallowed up by the French language. I know this is an Anglo-Saxon attitude, but how can you not be charmed by the complete distortion of German kraut (literally an herb or leaf) into French *croûte* (literally crust of bread, and idiomatically, a metaphor for simple dining, *casser la croûte,* break bread).

Alsace sits at the frontier between two powerful cultures, but if the Germans from across the Rhine have often enjoyed the political power over the centuries, the French-leaning Alsatians have everything else. You have only to cross the big steel bridge over the border from bustling, elegant French Strasbourg to dreary German Kehl to believe unblinkingly in the superiority of French culture and civilization. But it is that emblematic German food, sauerkraut, which is the centerpiece of the emblematic Alsatian choucroute.

Still, if anyone ever needed proof that Alsace really belongs in France, choucroute provides it. All over the German-speaking world, pork and sauerkraut meet in a hundred guises, none of them unremarkable. In Alsace, the pig and the cabbage merge in a Rabelaisian profusion. On a bed of kraut, there sprawl bacon, ham, sausages, ears, tails, chops. And if you are living large, corned beef and goose. We are not holding back here. And the kraut tastes better with every new meat that's added to the pot. Try to remember, the kraut is the point.

So is porcine excess. But the connoisseur of choucroute will perk up and smell the cabbage, just as Serbs savor the chili-spiked sauerkraut under the turkey in *podvarak,* the truly national dish that is a well-kept secret in most of the non-Serb world.

It is tempting to see these dishes as little battlegrounds of culture, in which one culinary system overwhelms another. You could argue, as people will, that Serbian turkey and choucroute show what superior cuisines can do with flat-footed German food. Or you could opine that these wonderful dishes are the most successful and lasting vestiges of German hegemony at the margins of German expansion. Myself, I see a Hegelian synthesis here of German macho and French finesse yielding hybrid vigor and cruciferous concord.

3 pounds sauerkraut

½ pound fat (lard, goose fat, duck fat or other meat drippings)

10 juniper berries

2 cups white wine

½ pound bacon (and/or kielbasa, or cocktail franks)

1 pound salt pork (belly, hock, ear, or jowl), soaked for 2 hours in cold water

1½ pounds ham in a single piece

6 smoked pig's knuckles

1. Rinse the sauerkraut thoroughly to remove all traces of the brine in which it was cured. Soak for 15 minutes. Rinse several times in a colander, until the water comes out clear. Take the sauerkraut a handful at a time and squeeze out as much water as you can. Let the sauerkraut stand for a few minutes on a plate. Then leave to drain further in a strainer set over a bowl.

2. Preheat the oven to 350 degrees.

3. Put the sauerkraut in a heavy ovenproof pot and cover with cold water. Add the fat, the juniper berries tied up in a piece of cloth, and the white wine. Bring to a boil. Cover with a greased circle of wax paper. Put on the lid and set in the oven.

4. After 3 hours, add the bacon and other meats, mixing them into the sauerkraut and covering them with it. Continue braising for another 2 hours to completely cook the sauerkraut, which should completely absorb the cooking liquid by the end. Pay close attention to the two converging processes—the doneness of the cabbage and the imbibition of the liquid—toward the end of the 5 hours. If the absorption of the liquid occurs too soon, add more—half water, half wine—a glass at a time, as necessary.

5. To serve, separate the sauerkraut and the meats. Slice the meats as appropriate and put a selection of them with some sauerkraut on each plate.

Serves 6 to 8

Clam Chowder

French fishermen crossed the Atlantic long ago and took their favorite fish soup with them. Then, in the mouths of neighboring English speakers, the traditional French *chaudrée* turned into chowder. (It is also possible that the word chowder descends from *chaudière*, a French term for pot that is also applied to a Breton fish stew.) And in their hands, the former fish stew turned into a milk-based soup of hard-shelled clams brought together with bits of rendered salt pork and potato cubes.

This account of the origin of New England clam chowder leaves out a great deal. It does not explain why or when a quite original soup was created. As with most traditional recipes, no one knows how chowder got started. It is not hard to locate recipes for traditional French soups that mix cream and seafood. The Breton *cotriade* calls for a mixture of fish and a modest amount of *crème fraîche* added to the broth. Even closer is the Norman *soupe aux coques,* which brings together the little bivalve of the Norman shore known in English as cockle (*Cerastoderma edule*) with *crème fraîche.* But I have yet to find a really close analogue to our clam chowder in a French cookbook. And I doubt I will find one, because the plainness of our New England chowder is its hallmark and its genius.

Was the birthplace of chowder in Newfoundland where French and English colonists mixed? Nobody knows. And the exact moment of inspiration that mixed milk and bivalve, pork and potato, is lost in the mists of the early days of colonial North America. But the dish caught on and survived.

By the later eighteenth century, the word "chowder" had appeared in print. And by the mid-nineteenth century, it received its literary apotheosis in *Moby-Dick.* Melville devotes an entire chapter to Ishmael's chowder supper with Queequeg at the Try Pots in Nantucket. "Oh, sweet friends! hearken to me," he wrote. "It was made of small juicy clams, scarcely bigger than hazel nuts, mixed with pounded ship biscuit, and salted pork cut up into little flakes; the whole enriched with butter, and plentifully seasoned with pepper and salt."

This is rich stuff, but you could not use it as a recipe. It doesn't mention milk. It does not give a precise description of the salt pork, which should be chopped and crisply rendered. Purists will shudder at the presence of cracker crumbs (the pounded ship biscuit). And they will also shake their heads at the idea of tiny clams in a chowder. How could Melville have not known that you put big clams in chowder, after chopping them up? For true chowder-heads, this last requirement is no quibble. It is the heart of the matter. Even Queequeg must have known that chowder clams are known in New England as quahogs, pronounced *co-hogs*.

Don't let the name put you off. And try to forget about the sleazy-sounding scientific name of the delicious animal—*Mercenaria mercenaria*. By any of its more universal vernacular names (in ascending order of size and age) littlenecks, cherrystones, and quahogs, the quahog species has a hard shell and a short neck, or siphon, unlike the soft shell and elongated neck of the soft-shell, or steamer, clam (*Mya arenaria*). *M. mercenaria* goes by several names other than quahog. All three varieties of hard-shell clams can be and are used for chowder. But littlenecks and cherrystones are often served raw on the half shell. The larger, older, and tougher quahogs benefit from chopping and then light cooking. In my experience, these large hard-shells are sold outside New England as chowder clams. Any hard-shell will do fine. But you should avoid the lazy man's pitfall of steaming them open. Despite the extra work of opening them by hand, raw clams produce better chowder. You end up with tenderer clam bits and their "juice" is not adulterated with plain water from the steaming.

Actually, opening clams is not all that challenging if you remember to refrigerate the clams ahead of time. Cold relaxes their muscles. To open: Rinse off any mud with cold water. Then grasp the clam with one hand by the hinge. Insert a clam knife (or other strong, short, wide-bladed knife) into the crack between the shells opposite the hinge. Run the blade back and forth until the clam gives up and can be easily opened the rest of the way by hand. It is efficient to open chowder clams over a bowl so that the juice is automatically collected. Neophytes should wear a glove on the hand that holds the clam, to avoid unintended amputation.

2 dozen hard-shell clams, preferably quahogs* with shells more than 4 inches across, thoroughly chilled

1 piece salt pork, about 2 inches square and ¼ inch thick, finely diced

1 medium onion, peeled and chopped

1 stalk celery, trimmed and diced, optional

2 medium Idaho potatoes, peeled and chopped

1 quart milk

---

* Cherrystones are much easier to find outside New England than quahogs, and I will risk controversy by saying that they make a nice chowder. Put in a few more than 2 dozen if you want, to compensate for their slightly smaller size, but even just two dozen should be enough.

1. If the clams haven't been cleaned, brush them thoroughly under cold water. Then open them, reserving their juice. Strain the juice through a chinois or cheesecloth and reserve in a bowl. Mince the clams and add to the reserved juice.

2. In a pot you will ultimately use to serve the chowder, render the salt pork over medium heat until the pieces are well browned. Remove the solid pieces and reserve. Add the onion and optional celery. Sauté until the onions are translucent. Meanwhile, simmer the potatoes in the milk until almost tender, about 10 minutes.

3. Simmer the clams in their juice until just heated through. When ready to serve, combine all the ingredients and heat through, but do not boil after you have put in the clams and clam juice. If the milk boils, the chowder will curdle. No seasoning should be necessary.

Serves 4

Coq au Vin
(Burgundian Chicken Stewed in Wine)

There's no getting away from it: This is supposed to be a recipe for rooster in wine. I have never seen it that way; you have never seen it that way. It is always made with a regular, no-wattles chicken. My theory is that in some dark dawn of French life, farmers invented this dish as a vehicle for turning old roosters to account. These would have been tough old birds, literally, yeoman soldiers in the sexually lopsided economy of chicken husbandry.

If you have wondered why there are so many chickens and so few roosters, the answer is starkly simple. Males of the chicken species are not worth raising, except for the isolated rooster kept alive for mating. The females are the ones who lay the eggs and grow the tender flesh. So almost every male chick is destroyed, because it would be a total waste to feed him just to hear another cock-a-doodle-doo in the morning. In the modern chicken industry, highly trained chicken sexers flip newborn chicks upside down and scrutinize their nether parts to choose between the female chicks and the soon-dead yellow males.

The most perverse book I ever opened was an illustrated manual of instruction for chicken sexers. The diagrams were the poultry world's equivalent of pedophile literature. But if you like the low price we pay for chickens and eggs, you can't shrink from granting the sexers, most of them Japanese, credit for their creepy skill.

Without them, we'd be glad to eat rooster and tenderize it by long marination and cooking in wine. In the right hands, this would be a great delicacy, like a game-bird stew. And that is just what the great gastronomic researcher Austin de Croze discovered during his research for *Les plats régionaux de France* (1928), his compendium of French regional dishes as he found them just after World War I.

He came upon this "very old recipe" for *Le coq à la bourguignonne* on the menu at a restaurant called (luck favors the virtuous researcher) Le Coq au Vin. In almost every way it resembled the recipe below except that it begins: "Bleed a fine rooster, collecting the blood" for a marinade. So the mystery is solved. The justification for our modern coq au vin recipes is that they are really old-fashioned civets, stews containing the blood of game animals, stews intended to tame the animal without breaking its spirit.

So when we make the same dish, minus the blood, with a battery chicken, or even a glorious blue-footed, white-feathered *poularde de Bresse,* we are a big hop down the road from the original dish, but it is not really a step backward. Coq au vin has survived without rooster and rooster's blood, because it works well with the tender chickens those old Burgundian farmers would have valued too much to put in a stew.

Some day I may try it with a rooster, but meantime I am happy to honor the past with this most honored of all poultry dishes, using a chicken. And from time to time, I may also approximate the original civet by using a duck instead of a chicken. Under the whimsical name Le Bouribou, this was a specialty available in the sixties at a Paris restaurant near the Bourse named À l'Alliance, which had been a favorite haunt of Curnonsky,* who was a collaborator of de Croze in the revival of regional cuisine. I am sure that Le Bouribou was meant as a clever modern compromise in a world without roosters.

4 pounds chicken, in serving pieces	½ cup olive oil
1 bottle (3 cups) red wine	2 sprigs fresh thyme or ½ teaspoon ground
½ cup dry white wine	9 tablespoons butter
¾ cup cognac	2 dozen pearl onions, peeled and blanched
4 medium carrots, scraped and cut in rounds	5 tablespoons flour
2 medium yellow onions, peeled and quartered	Salt
	Pepper
4 to 6 cloves garlic, peeled	1 cup chicken stock
2 sprigs parsley	½ cup salt pork, diced and blanched
2 bay leaves	12 mushrooms, quartered

1. In a large bowl, combine the chicken pieces with 2 cups red wine, the white wine, ½ cup cognac, the carrots, yellow onions, garlic, parsley, bay leaves, and olive oil. Marinate overnight at room temperature. Remove the chicken from the marinade, drain and pat dry. Reserve the marinade.

2. Heat 4 tablespoons butter in a large heavy pot and sauté the pearl onions until lightly browned. Remove the onions with a slotted spoon and reserve.

3. Sauté the chicken pieces, a few at a time, in the same pot, until they just begin to color. Keep the pot covered.

* Curnonsky was the pen name of Maurice Edmond Sailland (1872–1956), a *bon viveur* and journalist known as "the elected prince of gastronomes [*le prince élu des gastronomes*]." "Curnonsky" is a Latin-Polish joke meaning "Whynotsky."

4. Put the browned chicken pieces back in the pot, in a single layer if possible. Sprinkle with 2 tablespoons flour and salt and pepper. Cook 10 minutes more, covered. Turn once.

5. Heat the remaining cognac in a small saucepan until it begins to vaporize. Pour over the chicken and ignite.

6. Strain the marinade and reserve the solid ingredients left in the strainer, discarding the garlic and bay leaves.

7. Pour the strained marinade over the chicken along with the chicken stock and all but 1 tablespoon of the remaining 1 cup red wine.

8. Sauté the remaining vegetables from the marinade in 1 tablespoon butter until the onions turn translucent. Add to the chicken. Add the pearl onions.

9. Cook the coq au vin slowly, covered, until tender, about 45 minutes. Remove the breasts if they are tender before the dark meat and reserve.

10. Remove the remaining chicken pieces to the pot you will serve them from.

11. Put the cooking liquid through a fine strainer into a clean saucepan. Reserve the pearl onions and discard other solid material. Skim off the fat from the strained liquid (if you are doing this a day ahead, refrigerate the liquid so that the fat solidifies and can be easily lifted away and discarded).

12. Beat together 3 tablespoons butter and the remaining 3 tablespoons flour to make a smooth paste, a beurre manié. Bring the defatted cooking liquid to a boil, lower the heat, and whisk in the beurre manié. Add the remaining tablespoon of red wine. Correct the seasoning.

13. Brown the salt pork and mushrooms in the remaining tablespoon of butter. Add to the sauce along with the chicken and the pearl onions. Cook briefly until heated through. Serve.

Serves 6

Coulibiac
(Russian Fish Pie)

After a multicourse banquet, two food-obsessed members of the New York chapter of the Confrèrie des Chevaliers du Tastevin, a society devoted to the appreciation of wines from Burgundy, took me out for a nightcap. And what did these *fines gueules* talk about at midnight on very full stomachs? Food, obviously.

With great urgency, the White Russian epicure I will call Igor expatiated on the absolute necessity of obtaining *vesiga* if you were even going to think about making (or in his case having your cook make) a *coulibiac de saumon*.

I was vaguely aware that coulibiac was the gaudiest jewel in the crown of prerevolutionary Russian cuisine: a fish pie containing layers of salmon and/or sturgeon with kasha (buckwheat groats) or the concentrated mushroom paste called duxelles. Igor assumed any fool had suffered through a glut of these concoctions, always lusting as he himself did for the essential but elusive ingredient, the spinal marrow of the sturgeon, called *vesiga* in Russian (I am unaware of a specific name for it in any other language). Among its other putative virtues, *vesiga* expands to five times its original volume when soaked in water. But in post-czarist New York, *vesiga* was as rare on the ground as *matzoh wasser*.* Igor, after strenuous searching, had located a mother lode at the Vita company, best known for its herring in sour cream but also a bulk processor of sturgeon.

"They throw it away," sneered Igor. "I got them to give me some, and now I can make the only authentic coulibiac anywhere west of the Caspian."

Igor did not fulfill his promise to invite me to the next coulibiac evening he staged. And I have never tasted *vesiga*. My sense is that it contributes a tapioca-like texture among the many layers of other foods inside the coulibiac crust. Even without it, though, a coulibiac is a dazzler. It is not hard to see why the great and peripatetic French chef Antonin Carême was impressed with it and brought it home to Paris after a visit to Russia in the early nineteenth century. Coulibiac became—and remains—the most celebrated of all haute cuisine Russian dishes.

---

* In Jewish folklore, *matzoh wasser,* or matzoh water, is a mythical sort of holy water of blessed virtue for making the unleavened dough for matzoh at Passover time. Because it is mythical, there isn't any. But if there were some, everyone would pay anything to get it. Whence the expression "It would sell like *matzoh wasser.*"

There is no classic recipe for this dish. The concept is clear: fish and a starch-enhanced fish paste baked in dough. But the details are up for grabs. What starch? Kasha predominates but I have seen a recipe that calls for Chinese cellophane noodles. What fish? Sturgeon or salmon or the European pike perch are only a few of those called for by reliable sources. And the dough? Brioche and puff pastry are both canonical. This recipe specifies a brioche dough. But with excellent frozen puff pastry sheets widely available, they seem like a convenient (!) alternative. Or you can bake the coulibiac in a Pâte Brisée (page 147).

1 package active dry yeast	¾ pound flounder or catfish fillet, cut in
¾ cup warm milk	smallish pieces
2½ cups flour	1 medium onion, peeled and finely chopped
10 tablespoons butter, softened	2 tablespoons chopped dill
2 egg yolks, lightly beaten	5 tablespoons (3½ ounces) coarse kasha
3 whole eggs, lightly beaten	groats
½ teaspoon salt	1¼ cups water
	1 pound salmon or sturgeon fillet

1. Stir the yeast into half the milk until dissolved and foaming. Beat in half the flour, form into a ball, and set to rise in a bowl covered with a damp dish towel.

2. When the dough has doubled in bulk (about an hour), knead in the rest of the milk and flour, 4 tablespoons of the butter, half the beaten egg yolks, two thirds of the beaten whole eggs, and ¼ teaspoon salt. Let rise a second time. Punch down, knead briefly, and let rise in the refrigerator overnight.

3. The next day, sauté the flounder or catfish in 2 tablespoons butter, along with the onion and the dill. As soon as the fish is cooked through and the onion is transparent, transfer to a processor and process with the steel blade until you have a smooth paste. Set aside.

4. Stir the remaining beaten egg yolk into the kasha in an ungreased skillet. Heat over low-medium flame until dry.

5. Bring 1¼ cups water to a boil with the remaining butter and salt. Add the kasha and simmer for 10 minutes, stirring. Then mix well with the fish paste from step 3.

6. Slice the salmon or sturgeon with the grain, as thin slices as you can manage.

7. Preheat the oven to 425 degrees.

8. Roll out the dough on a floured board into a long rectangle. Spread the center of the dough with a thin layer of fish paste. Then add a layer of salmon or sturgeon slices, then

a layer of fish paste, then a layer of salmon or sturgeon. Begin all over again with fish paste and continue until you have used up all the filling ingredients.

9. Pull up the long sides. Moisten the edges and press together to seal. Then pull up the ends, moisten and seal to the dough already pulled up from the sides. Let rise for a half hour on a cookie tray, covered with a damp cloth.

10. Brush with the remaining beaten whole egg and bake for 35 minutes or until a needle poked into the pie comes out clean. Serve immediately, before the dough dries out.

Serves 6

Couscous Chick Chick
(Moroccan Chicken Stew with Wheat Pellets)

In order to make a couscous, you need two things you might not have at home if you aren't a Berber. Go to a health food store and buy some couscous, a wheat product invented in North Africa. When you have a supply of those golden-yellow, highly absorbent tiny pellets, you'll want to steam them over a simmering stew in an ingenious cookpot called, unimaginatively, a *couscoussière*. Mine is aluminum and has a high, gracefully swelling lower vessel known in Morocco either as the *tanjra* or the *gdra*. The upper section is a shallow sievelike affair, the *kskas,* which nests in the *tanjra* or *gdra*. Both pieces have handles. Mine also has a lid, untraditional and completely unnecessary, since couscous is steamed uncovered, but it is helpful on those occasions when I use the *gdra* (I've made my choice, because *gdra* is shorter, though I can't pronounce either it or *tanjra,* or *kskas*) for boiling pasta and I want to expedite the coming-to-a-boil. The lid also proves the old adage, conventionally applied to young women in search of a husband, that there's a lid for every pot.

A *couscoussière* is not just another space-consuming object you could do without. Not if you are going to make couscous anyway, because the brilliant principle of a great cuisine's most versatile dish (its main rival for stardom in the Moroccan kitchen is bstilla (page 24) is that the couscous grains swell in the *kskas* and, at the same time, absorb the flavors of the stew below.

This couscous is only one of dozens and dozens of couscouses from North Africa and other places where it has traveled, from Sicily to Brazil. Paula Wolfert in the pioneering *Couscous and Other Good Food from Morocco* (1973), rattles off a long list of them, including couscous in the Berber style with chicken, turnips, and milk, couscous with fish, wild turnips, and fennel stalks as served on the coast at Essaouira, couscous with lamb's head, favas, and carrots—and on and on.

For the record, couscous is canonically the last course in a Moroccan meal, the coup de grace for overfed guests. And then there is dessert couscous, with dates, cinnamon, and sugar.

1½ cups dried chickpeas	6 tablespoons olive oil
3 chicken drumsticks	1 teaspoon saffron
3 chicken thighs	1 tablespoon finely chopped parsley
3 chicken breasts, with bone in	5½ cups water
3 tomatoes, sliced	1½ cups raisins
1 teaspoon salt	2 pounds couscous
1 large onion, peeled and chopped	1 tablespoon butter, melted
1 teaspoon pepper	

1. Soak the chickpeas overnight. Drain.
2. Add all ingredients except the water, raisins, couscous, and butter to the bottom of the *couscoussière*. Pour in 5 cups of the water. Bring to a boil, reduce the heat, and simmer for 30 minutes.
3. Add the raisins. Continue simmering for another 15 minutes. Remove from the heat until just before the meal.
4. Work the couscous together with ½ cup water in a mixing bowl. Tradition dictates using fingers, which are indeed the best tool for moistening all the grains and making sure they don't clump together.
5. Return the bottom of the *couscoussière* to the heat, bring to a boil, reduce the heat, and simmer. Put the couscous in the perforated upper portion of the *couscoussière* and set this on top of the simmering chicken stew. Do not cover.
6. Steam for 15 minutes. If steam leaks out of the join between the top and bottom of the *couscoussière*, cinch a dish towel around the join to seal it. Dump the couscous into a bowl. Stir in the butter. Then put the couscous back in the upper part of the *couscous-sière* and steam for another 20 minutes. Serve the stew and couscous separately.

Serves 6

Crayfish Bisque

In modern usage, bisque refers to a puree, usually a puree of shellfish, served as a soup. But in the nineteenth century, according to *Larousse Gastronomique* (1938), bisques were made from quail and pigeons. Moreover, a crayfish puree recipe from 1752 did not call it a bisque. It seems that at the time bisque referred to boiled fowl or game, unpureed. Shortly thereafter, bisque does appear in print as the name of a soup with quail topped with a puree of crayfish. So what began as a soup with meat in it garnished with a shellfish puree evolved into a soup entirely made from shellfish puree.

This was no accident, I wouldn't think. The superiority of the puree to the boiled fowl it was there to enhance must have been obvious and led to the creation of a new and delicious category of rich soup, a category held in high esteem at all times, for its flavor and out of respect for the labor it entailed.

An essentially untranslatable poem full of puns written by François Premier's chaplain, Mellin de Saint-Gelais, advises against consuming bisque when you are sick:

> *When you've fallen ill with a fever,*
> *Madame, you are really at risk,*
> *And for quite a long time,*
>
> *. . . . .*
>
> *Be sure never to eat a bisque:*
> *Such a powerful, tiresome risk*
> *Tsk, tsk, put it out of your mind.**

* Quand on est febricitant,
  Ma Dame, on se trouve en risque
  Et pour un assez long-temps,

  . . . .

  De ne point manger du bisque
  Si rude et si fâcheux risque
  Que je bisque en y songeant.

I can't say that I've ever tried a bisque when I wasn't feeling tip-top, but I once did decide not to order a lobster bisque at the Restaurant de la Côte d'Or in Saulieu when the great Alexandre Dumaine was chef, because I wanted to try his Coq au Vin (page 50) and the waiter advised me the bisque would be too heavy an introduction to a major Burgundian main course. You will not get this kind of advice in a three-star restaurant today, but then you would be hard put to find anything as relatively straightforward as Dumaine's dishes.

This recipe will accommodate most other shellfish: lobster, of course, crabs, shrimp. Real risk takers might even try it with pigeon.

¼ pound salt pork, diced	½ bay leaf
½ pound carrots, scraped and sliced in rounds	1 tablespoon cognac
2 medium onions, peeled and thinly sliced	½ cup white wine
18 crayfish, heads removed and discarded	1 quart chicken stock
Salt	3 ounces cooked rice
Pepper	5 tablespoons butter
2 sprigs parsley	⅔ cup heavy cream
1 sprig thyme	Cayenne

1. To make a mirepoix: Render the salt pork in a heavy cast-iron skillet. Remove the pork pieces as they brown. Then sauté the carrots and onions in the residual fat until the onions are transparent.

2. Add the crayfish with shells, the salt, pepper, parsley, thyme, and bay leaf. Sauté until the shells turn red. Then pour in the cognac, heat, and flambé. Add the white wine and reduce the liquid by two-thirds.

3. Pour in ⅔ cup chicken stock and the shellfish cooking liquid. Simmer for 10 minutes.

4. Remove from the heat and shell the shellfish. Reserve the flesh and shells. Discard inedible innards.

5. Break up or pound the shells into small pieces. Process into a puree with the rice and 1⅔ cups stock. Push through a regular strainer into a saucepan. Add the rest of the stock and bring to a boil for a few seconds. Then put it through a chinois or other fine strainer.

6. If you are using lobster instead of crayfish, slice the claw meat into several pieces per claw. In the case of crabs, pick through the meat and shred.

7. Just before serving, heat the puree with the butter, cut into small pieces, and the cream. Correct the seasoning and add a small amount of cayenne.

8. When heated through, serve immediately, garnished with the shellfish meat.

Serves 4 to 6

Crème Caramel
(Caramelized Pudding)

Caramelizing sugar—raising melted sugar to the precise point, a touch more than 300 degrees, where it turns a uniformly gold color but not beyond (when it will turn bitter and then burn)—is a tricky bit of kitchen chemistry possible in Europe only after refined white sugar became readily available, with the establishment of Caribbean plantations in the sixteenth century.

As a practical matter, caramelizing the interior of a pudding mold for crème caramel makes it possible to unmold the pudding without buttering the mold. And, obviously, the layer of caramel that remains on the outside of the pudding adds a beautiful, melting exterior and a seductively flavored "sauce" to an otherwise pristine dessert.

Eugénie Saint-Ange, author of the definitive French cookbook for the home, *La Cuisine de Madame Saint-Ange* (1925), is nowhere more impassioned and precise than in her discourse on caramelizing a mold:

> *The first rule to observe is to use a mold with a sufficiently thick and perfectly flat bottom, with no dents caused when somebody bumped or dropped it, or by some other mishap. A bumpy mold lets the sugar burn in the low spots and stick without melting on the high spots, which the heat does not reach with the same intensity. As a result, the caramel turns grainy and takes on a dull, uneven color.*

For a 4-cup (1-liter) charlotte mold, figure on ½ cup (100 grams) granulated sugar. Make sure the mold is completely clean. Add the sugar without water. Put the mold over low heat. Have a towel or heatproof pad handy so you can grasp the mold, as well as a large shallow container filled with a couple of inches of cold water for setting the mold in if necessary.

Do not leave the stove for an instant. Watch the sugar carefully as it melts. If the melting occurs on one side only, tilt the mold to even out the cooking. In this way, you will keep the sugar from caramelizing in a single spot. In any case, the color should not get deeper than a golden brown and the sugar should not be allowed to heat to the point where it gives off a bluish smoke, which would be a warning that it is about to burn and will have a decidedly unpleasant bitter taste. At the slightest sign of this, plunge the mold in the cold water to stop the cooking of the caramel.

When the sugar has reached the right degree of coloration, lift the mold from the heat

As a practical matter, caramelizing the interior of a pudding mold for crème caramel makes it possible to unmold the pudding without buttering the mold. And, obviously, the layer of caramel that remains on the outside of the pudding adds a beautiful, melting exterior and a seductively flavored "sauce" to an otherwise pristine dessert.

with both hands and tilt it back and forth so that the caramel flows from the bottom to the sides and coats them completely, right to the top. As a result, the whole interior of the mold will be covered with a glassy, transparent layer of caramel, like a piece of enameled silver. As the caramel cools, it will develop numerous small cracks (*craquelures*). These are inevitable and without importance.

The recipe here follows an old-fashioned method advocated by Madame Saint-Ange, in which the pudding is steamed inside a covered pot in the oven. It takes a few minutes longer, but gives reliable and splendid results.

1¼ cups sugar	5 yolks from large eggs
2⅓ cups milk	2 whole large eggs

1. Put ½ cup of the sugar in a 4-cup charlotte mold and heat very slowly to caramelize. Then, off heat, tilt and roll the caramel so that it covers the entire interior of the mold. Let cool completely. (For a detailed description of this process, see above.)

2. Heat the milk in a large saucepan until it begins to foam. Add the remaining ¾ cup of sugar to the milk. Stir once, remove from the heat, and cover. Let stand until the sugar melts completely, stirring from time to time.

3. Preheat the oven to 350 degrees.

4. Meanwhile, beat the yolks and whole eggs together until they are well mixed. Pour the milk-sugar mixture into the eggs a little at a time, whisking constantly, until you have a uniform mixture. Strain through a chinois or a regular strainer lined with a moistened dish towel, to remove any solid crumbs of yolk. Then pour the custard into the prepared mold.

5. Set the mold in a pot an inch larger in circumference than the mold itself. Pour enough boiling water into the space between the mold and the walls of the pot to come about a half inch up the sides of the mold.

6. Put in the oven. Cover the large pot and cook for 55 to 60 minutes. After 5 minutes, reduce the temperature to 325 degrees.

7. Before removing from the oven, test the pudding with your finger to be sure it is solid at a point an inch in from the side. The center should be not quite set. Let cool in the water for at least another 15 minutes. Then let cool completely on a rack at room temperature. Do not unmold until ready to serve.

8. Run a thin knife blade around the side of the pudding to separate it from the mold. Set a flat serving plate upside down over the top of the mold. With one hand on the plate and

the other on the bottom of the mold, invert the mold. Set the plate down and gently pull the mold away from the pudding. To extract any remaining caramel from the mold, add 2 tablespoons water and boil to melt the caramel. Pour over the unmolded pudding.

9. Decorate the pudding and the liquid caramel sauce around it with "petals" of orange peel cut with a vegetable peeler. This looks pretty and imparts a nuance of orange flavor to the syrup.

Serves 6

Crepes

In the movie *Groundhog Day,* Bill Murray plays a Pittsburgh TV weatherman who goes to Punxsutawney, Pennsylvania, on February 2, to see if the local pet *Marmota monax* will see his shadow. The weatherman has done this for many years, but this time a hitherto tedious assignment turns into a nightmare. A blizzard forces him to spend the night in Punxsutawney, and the next morning it is Groundhog Day again. And the next morning, and on and on, again and again, until love puts things right and the calendar resumes its normal advance.

Amusing as it is, this film has probably puzzled audiences outside the United States, since few people elsewhere are aware of Groundhog Day. On the other hand, Europeans do celebrate a holiday on the same date, the traditional Christian feast called Candlemas. Although it officially commemorates the presentation of the infant Jesus in the temple, as well as the purification of Mary after childbirth, Candlemas is, in name and in practice, a festival of light. It would seem that this is a survival from pagan days. As with Groundhog Day, light is the key to the observance, and the point of both celebrations must be, in my view, to pledge faith in the coming end of winter. Both the candle and the sun that tempts the groundhog out of his hole are early signs of spring.

Why do I think this? Because on Candlemas in France (the French call the holiday *Chandeleur*), it is *de rigueur* to eat crepes. For children, making these thin pancakes has a special folklore that disguises the underlying cosmological significance of the crepe. The successful crepe maker holds a coin (traditionally gold) in one hand and the skillet in the other. When the crepe is done on one side, the child flips the pancake in the air and catches it in the skillet after it turns over. Failing is bad luck. Napoleon, by legend, amused himself in the kitchen by making crepes just before his departure for Russia in 1812. He flipped four crepes successfully, but missed the fifth. The day that Moscow burned, he is supposed to have said to Marshal Ney: "It's the fifth crepe."

The real meaning of crepes, and of pancakes in general, is far more profound. Crepes are round, and they are fried in golden butter, symbolizing the orb of the sun and its golden rays (as does the gold coin French children hold in their hand).

Better known examples of the same pancake/light/sun/spring symbolic cluster occur on Shrove Tuesday, or Mardi Gras, when pancakes are traditional fare in England and Germany. The German *Pfannkuchen,* sometimes called *Ballen,* are spherical and even more heliomorphic.

Perhaps the most elaborate of these pre-Lenten pancake celebrations still occur in some places in Russia. For a whole week before Ash Wednesday, Russians have traditionally indulged in a gorging semifast called *maslennitsa* (Anne Volokh in *The Art of Russian Cuisine* [1983], translates it as "butterweek"). Everyone eats mountains of the medium-thin pancakes called blini doused in melted butter.

Blini (singular, *blin*) predate the arrival of Christianity in Russia. Indeed, the word itself derived from an earlier form, meaning milled. And every authority seems to agree that the pancakes, whether made from buckwheat or wheat or a mixture of the two, were associated with a pagan sun festival long before any Russian had heard of Easter.

Blini lie somewhere between the doughy true pancake and the much thinner crepe. The real difference lies in the batters, as a comparison of basic recipes will show. Harold McGee did such a comparison in his scientific analysis of the kitchen, *On Food and Cooking* (1984). He quantified common sense by determining that the main difference between regular pancakes and crepes was the relative dilution of the flour in their batters. Given equal amounts of flour, the ratio of water for pancakes and crepes was 15:23. In other words, crepes were 1.53 times more dilute than pancakes. This is why crepe batter spreads so easily across the bottom of a skillet. It also explains, says McGee, why crepes don't have baking soda added to them and pancakes do. The thicker pancake can hold the air bubbles, but during cooking, the thin crepe batter loses any air that a chemical raising agent might add to it at the batter stage.

Once you have a stack of crepes, however, the world is your oyster, so to speak. Whole restaurant menus have been concocted with crepes, sweet or savory, stuffed with scores of improbable ingredients. There are, of course, traditional crepe recipes of fabulous complexity, in particular some Hungarian crepe tortes. But the essential value of these delicate pancakes is their simplicity and delicacy, their connection with pagan days—a pledge of springtime sun on your plate.

1 cup flour

3 eggs

1 cup whole milk

2 tablespoons butter, at room temperature

½ teaspoon salt

½ cup raspberry preserves or caviar

½ pound (2 sticks) butter, melted

1. Whisk the flour into the eggs.
2. Bring the milk to a boil. As soon as it begins to foam, remove from the heat and add the 2 tablespoons of room-temperature butter and the salt. Whisk into the milk as it melts.
3. Pour the milk-butter mixture slowly into the egg-flour mixture. Continue whisking until you have a smooth batter.
4. Heat a 9-inch cast-iron skillet over medium heat.
5. Pour ⅓ cup batter into the skillet, turning the skillet back and forth to distribute the batter as thinly as possible.
6. As soon as the surface of the crepe begins to bubble, slip the point of a knife under it, pick it up with your hand and flip it over. After a few seconds the other side will have browned lightly. Slide the crepe onto a plate.
7. Continue as above until all the batter is used up. Pile each finished crepe onto the others. Keep warm until ready to serve. Then pass with the raspberry preserves or caviar (not both) and melted butter.

Approximately 12 pancakes or 4 servings

Croquetas
(Spanish Croquettes)

These are not your mother's croquettes. Yes, they are also breaded, deep-fried parcels of egg-bound solid ingredients, but the croquettes Mom made were a medium for re-serving leftovers. After you served the roast chicken on Tuesday, you could chop or slice what was left and stick the pieces together in a sticky medium of egg and flour. Roll that into Ping-Pong-ball-size spheres, bread them, and fry them until crisp. Not a bad thing. Indeed, such croquettes could hold their own proudly in the mini-cuisine of fried oddments that includes hush puppies, fritters, and doughnuts.

Please note, however, that those croquettes were all about their main ingredient—ham, shrimp, turkey. *Croquetas*, Spanish croquettes, are first and foremost about their batter, which is creamy and makes an elegant contrast with the crunchy exterior. And there is more of this dough, proportionate to the chopped solid ingredients mixed into them, than in the croquettes of American tradition.

This is a technical way of saying that *croquetas* are more interesting than croquettes. And that must be why in Spain you see *croquetas* at every tapas bar, why *croquetas* are more popular than ever with Spaniards, while croquettes, here and in France and Italy, have dropped out of sight. When you see a basket of freshly fried, sausage-shaped (they can also be oval, but cylindrical is the most common form) *croquetas* on a bar in Seville, you will be thinking about the unctuous centers and only secondarily about the solid-ingredient fragments that speckle them.

Did croquettes originate in Spain and spread north and east, to France and Italy, and from there to England and America? There Is no evidence for this, and since all the various words for croquette are clearly reflexes of the same basic word, this indicates a Latin archetype that evolved separately in all the Romance languages and then made the leap to England with the Normans in 1066. But there is no Latin word for croquette or even a related verb *crocare*, meaning crunch (with the teeth).

This much we know: that croquettes are little crunchies or crunchlets. We know it because French does have a verb *croquer,* to crunch, and a small list of colorful derived terms (the sandwich *croque-monsieur,* the crunchy cake, *croquembouche,* and the undertaker or corpse cruncher, *croque-mort*). So it could easily be that the verb *croquer* evolved in France out of medieval Latin or spontaneously, and that this new term provided a logical name for croquettes and that croquettes then spread across the continent, finding their apogee in Spain.

Other scenarios are, of course, possible. I am, nevertheless, certain about the value of *croquetas*, as a Spanish cultural icon and as, in their small way, the culmination of an idea that has spread throughout Western civilization.

1/3 cup olive oil plus olive oil for deep-frying

1 boneless chicken breast

1 small onion, peeled and chopped

3 tablespoons flour

3 1/2 cups whole milk

1/4 pound *jamón serrano* or prosciutto, finely chopped

1 egg, separated

Salt

1 pinch ground cinnamon

Bread crumbs for dipping plus 2 cups bread crumbs

1. Heat the olive oil in a small skillet and sauté the chicken until lightly browned and just cooked through. Set aside. Then sauté the onion in the same oil until translucent.
2. Whisk in the flour, blend well, and then whisk in the milk slowly to produce a smooth, lumpless béchamel.
3. Chop the chicken very fine. Whisk it and the chopped ham into the béchamel. Continue to whisk over low heat until the mixture thickens. Whisk in the egg yolk and add salt to taste. Scrape into a large bowl, sprinkle with cinnamon, and let cool completely.
4. Whisk the egg white until homogeneous and pour onto a plate. Put bread crumbs on another plate.
5. Form the croquette mixture into egg-size balls, one at a time. Dip first in egg white, then in bread crumbs. Shape into cylinders and let dry on wax paper for an hour.
6. Fill a 9-inch skillet halfway up with olive oil. Heat the oil until it just begins to give off a visible vapor. Then carefully slip four croquettes into the oil. Turn them gently after a minute or two and continue turning every 2 minutes until they are golden brown all over. Remove to a paper towel with a slotted spoon. Continue in this way until all the croquette mixture has been used up. Serve hot.

Serves 4 to 6

Daube de Boeuf à la Provençale
(Provençal Beef Stew)

I went with my parents and sister to several Michelin three-star restaurants in France in the summer of 1963. None was anything as lavish or intricately thought out in its food as the three-star restaurants of today. But they were temples of gastronomy nonetheless, and let you know it one way or another. Except, that is, for La Petite Auberge de Noves in a small town just outside of Avignon. It was a hot day in August. We ate outside in an atmosphere almost as simple as a picnic. When the distinguished, black-suited elderly owner came around to our table, my father said something about the heat. The old man decided to take this as a compliment. "*C'est la Provence,*" he beamed back with a twinkle. That's Provence.

La daube, c'est aussi la Provence. A daube is the essential one-pot meat dish of this region whose name descends from the name the Romans gave it before they were a world power: *Provincia.* It was also a Mediterranean region long before it was French, and the local language (language, yes, not dialect) is best referred to as Occitan, unless you want to offend people and assert, with much justice, that it is a very close relative of Catalan.

Not all Frenchmen are chauvinists, certainly not the learned and tireless editors of the twenty-volume series of region-by-region surveys of local French foods and recipes called *L'Inventaire du patrimoine culinaire de la France.* It is true that two of the team are American-born, but, all the same, in their volume on Provence-Alpes-Côtes d'Azur (1995), they include a recipe for fried breaded lambs' feet and come right out and say it comes from Barceloneta, a neighborhood in the port of Barcelona.

In her section of the book on traditional recipes, Céline Vence writes: "This daube is often put together at the end of spring or the beginning of summer, when the vegetables are young and tender; it is prepared with white wine. In general, people make twice as much as they can eat at one sitting, because they like to eat it hot, accompanied by pasta [*macaronade*] and to serve it as a cold dish, which is very pleasant."

At any rate, you will please note that this adaptation of Ms. Vence's recipe involves larding and other efforts to make the eventual liquid of this stew as gelatinous as possible. This begins with the marination in olive oil and wine and aromatics so typical of the region and ends with a chopped salad of daube, refrigerated in a mold until it has solidified and can be unmolded and served.

Please note the orange, an essential flavor. Without it, *ce n'est pas la Provence.*

4½ pounds chuck roast	2 stalks celery, trimmed and cut in thin
⅓ cup plus ¾ cup olive oil	rounds
1½ bottles dry white wine	¾ pound small white onions, blanched and
2 sprigs thyme	peeled
4 sprigs flat-leaf parsley, finely chopped	2 pounds tomatoes, blanched, peeled,
4 cloves garlic	seeded, and roughly chopped
1 tablespoon black peppercorns, crushed	½ pound black Mediterranean olives, pitted
½ pound bacon, preferably pancetta	1 orange
1 pound fresh pork rind	Salt
3¼ pounds carrots, scraped	Freshly ground pepper

1. Ideally, your Marseillais butcher will lard the roast for you, sewing it through two or three times with thin strips of pancetta or salt pork. But on the off chance that you do not have an agreeable Marseillais butcher, you can do it yourself if you acquire a larding needle. Larding is like sewing and will leave the beef veined with flavorful fatty pork. A larding needle looks like an instrument of torture. It has a wooden handle and a long, thin, channeled metal business end with a sharp point. You "thread" the needle by inserting the strip of pancetta or salt pork in the channeled slot that runs the length of the metal "needle." Push the point of the needle all the way through the roast, far enough so that the hinged flap at the end releases and permits the needle to be pulled back through the roast while leaving the strip of pork in place. This is simpler than it sounds. With or without lardoons, cut the beef in cubes (being careful to miss the larding, when you are slicing in the direction of the lardoons, if you have lardoons).

2. Put the meat in a large bowl and stir together with the ⅓ cup olive oil (reserving 2 tablespoons) and the wine. Crumble in the thyme, parsley, garlic, and crushed peppercorns. Stir again, cover, and refrigerate for 24 hours in the vegetable drawer.

3. Blanch the bacon in boiling water. Dice. Transfer to a Dutch oven and set over medium heat with the reserved 2 tablespoons of oil. Let the pancetta render its fat slowly.

4. Meanwhile, remove the meat cubes from their marinade with a slotted spoon. Reserve the marinade. Pat the meat cubes dry. Raise the heat under the Dutch oven and brown the cubes on all sides, a few at a time. Remove them, and the browned pancetta, to a bowl. Degrease the Dutch oven.

5. Preheat the oven to 325 degrees.

6. Cover the bottom of the Dutch oven with the pork rind, flesh side down. Place over low

heat. Add the carrots (whole if they are small, otherwise cut in 2-inch lengths), celery, onions, tomatoes, olives, and a strip of orange zest (only the outer orange part of the orange peel) about 6 inches long (a vegetable peeler is the tool of choice for this). Put the meat cubes on this bed of vegetables, along with whatever juice they have left in the bowl.

7. Strain the marinade through a chinois and pour over the stew. Add salt and ground pepper to taste. Cover and cook in the oven for 2 $\frac{1}{2}$ to 3 hours, until the meat is fork-tender.

8. Remove all the solid ingredients to a covered dish set in boiling water to keep the ingredients warm. Let the cooking liquid rest for a few minutes and then spoon away as much fat from the surface as you can.

9. Dice the pork rind. Put it back in the Dutch oven, along with all the other solid ingredients and the strained cooking liquid. Stir, cover, and set over very low heat for a few minutes before serving.

Serves 8

. . . when John F. Kennedy made his famous speech at the Berlin Wall. *"Ich bin ein Berliner,"* he said, declaring his solidarity with the people of Berlin. . . . By adding the indefinite article, *ein*, the President took himself out of geography and into the kitchen. To the German ear, he said, "I am a jelly doughnut."

Doughnuts

The word *doughnut* itself is apparently American, but the idea of deep-frying small pieces of dough belongs to many older cultures. In Italy, they call these yeast-dough fritters *zeppole,* in France *beignets,* in Spain *buñuelos.* They are all ways to use up leftover bread dough. But none of these "doughnuts" led to our toroidal snack. All evidence and all authorities agree that our doughnut came to us from Holland. The first occurrence of the word cited in the *Oxford English Dictionary* is in Washington Irving's *A History of New York* (1809). Peter G. Rose quotes the passage fully in her English-language edition of the preeminent Dutch cookbook of the seventeenth century, *De Verstandige Kock,* which influenced the kitchens of early Dutch colonists in New Netherland:

> Sometimes the table was graced with immense apple pies, or saucers full of preserved peaches and pears; but it was always sure to boast an enormous dish of balls of sweetened dough, fried in hog's fat, and called doughnuts, or olykoeks—a delicious kind of cake, at present, scarce known in this city, excepting in genuine Dutch families, but which retains its preeminent station at tea tables in Albany.

Olie-koecken, oly-koecks, olicooks, oliebollen—the spelling and names of these oil cakes or oil balls in American manuscripts cited by Rose grow more "American" over time—were all originally made from yeast-raised dough. And they were often enriched with raisins, citron, nutmeg, and even apple slices, following Dutch tradition as represented in *De Verstandige Kock*. But they had no holes.

The addition of the hole in the doughnut was a crucial step in the long march of simplification and blanding-out that led to the doughnuts we know today. Fortunately, Karen Hess has looked into this matter in the notes to her edition of Mary Randolph's *The Virginia House-Wife* of 1824 (1983). She was unable to find an actual early source for the first doughnuts with holes, since recipes in the period following Irving's book were "maddeningly uninformative as to shape." By 1883, however, there was a printed reference to a doughnut cutter in *Mrs. Lincoln's Boston Cookbook*. No doubt the practice began somewhat earlier, early enough to have inspired the manufacture of a metal cutter that required no explanation by Mrs. Lincoln.

Hess reasons that cutters facilitated cutting the centers of doughs raised with pearl ash instead of slower-acting yeast. Pearl ash is potassium carbonate, a form of potash leached out of wood ashes with lye. This substance would have been known to Indians, but it really came into its own with wheat flour, producing spectacular and very rapid aeration of dough, especially in the presence of sour milk or some other source of acidity. (Modern baking powders combine these formerly separate alkaline and acid components into one "double-acting" substance that goes into high [actually second] gear only in the presence of heat in the oven.)

As early as the end of the eighteenth century, Hess shows, American cooks were opting for the zip of pearl ash over pokier yeast. But this left them with doughs that were harder to handle, doughs that often produced doughnuts with soft, raw centers. The doughnut cutter solved both problems. It made the dough easier to maneuver and allowed for more dependably thorough frying.

This quick fix distorted both Indian and Dutch ideas, but yielded an original pastry that never lost its hold on American appetites. The dried fruits and apple slices and spices were lost along the way, sacrificed no doubt to the god of efficiency. But there is a fruit-flavored survival of olden doughnuts in every doughnut shop in the land, the holeless jelly doughnut. And where did the jelly doughnut come from? It seems reasonable to conjecture that Germans brought it to America. Modern German jelly doughnuts are deep-fried yeast pastries filled with apricot or plum jam and variously known as *Berliner Pfannkuchen, Silvesterkrapfen, Bismarcks, Fastnachts-kuchen, Faschingskrapfen,* or just plain *Berliners.* Sarah Kelly Iaia tells us all this in her definitive work, *Festive Baking: Holiday Classics in the Swiss, German, and Austrian Tradition* (1988). Although they originated as a specialty of Berlin, these jelly doughnuts are eaten all over Germany on Shrove Tuesday or New Year's Eve.

Berliners came to the world's attention some time ago when John F. Kennedy made his famous speech at the Berlin Wall. "*Ich bin ein Berliner,*" he said, declaring his solidarity with the people of Berlin. At least, he thought he was saying the equivalent in German of "I am a Berliner." But in idiomatic German that should have been, "*Ich bin Berliner.*" By adding the indefinite article, *ein,* the President took himself out of geography and into the kitchen. To the German ear, he said, "I am a jelly doughnut."

I am neither a Berliner nor a jelly doughnut lover. And since the classic "American" doughnut is the Netherlandish immigrant with the hole it acquired over here, I am pleased to offer this recipe as a practical modern version of the pioneer original.

1½ packages active dry yeast (¾ ounce)	¼ teaspoon ground mace
½ cup lukewarm water	1 tablespoon skim milk
3 tablespoons butter, at room temperature	3 eggs
⅓ cup sugar	1 cup water
½ teaspoon salt	5 cups flour

1. Dissolve the yeast in the lukewarm water. Let stand.

2. In a mixer or a processor with a dough hook, combine the butter, sugar, salt, mace, and skim milk. Mix at a low speed until well combined. Then mix in the eggs, one at a time. Then add 1 cup water and mix until absorbed. Or mix the same ingredients by hand in a bowl.

3. Add the flour and the yeast mixture from step 1. Mix thoroughly to make a smooth, moist, resilient dough.

4. Let the dough rest and ferment for an hour and a half at around 80 degrees, covered with a moist towel.

5. Roll out the dough on a floured surface to a thickness of ½ inch. Let it relax for 15 minutes.

6. Cut out doughnuts with a doughnut cutter (or the open end of a soup can). Cut as close together as possible. Take the scraps and roll out to a thickness of ½ inch. Let relax and cut more doughnuts.

7. Let the dough rest for 15 minutes before frying. Deep-fry at 375 degrees, two at a time. When the doughnuts are golden brown, drain on paper toweling.

2 dozen doughnuts

Duck à l'Orange
(Duckling with Orange Sauce)

Unless you hunt or know a hunter well, any duck you are likely to eat will be a domesticated fowl. And yet, despite their sedentary life and the generations of selective breeding that have favored lower and lower fat, modern ducks of commerce still have one leg in the wild. Traditional duck cookery has reflected this, often treating farm ducks like feathered game. As with other game, rareness was prized and the blood of the beast was at center stage.

How well I remember the gleaming silver duck press at La Tour d'Argent in Paris, standing ready to extract as much blood as possible from the carcass of Rouennais ducks, specially raised in semi-wild conditions and strangled to keep all their blood available to the waiter, who would first crunch the bird in full view of the diners and then prepare a sauce from it, adding the pan juices and flaming the mixture in cognac at tableside. A real *coup de théâtre*.

A lot less dramatic and easier to manage at home are roast ducks with sauces based on fruit (orange and lemon for an acid contrast to the fatty, bloody duck, cherries [*à la Montmorency*] for a sweet-sour counterpoint, and olives [yes, they are stone fruits, of the drupe category, like peaches], for a bitter balancing out.)

That, at any rate, is the unacknowledged theory of haute cuisine French duck. And duckling in orange sauce is the theory's big, global success. But somewhere along the line, the point of the exercise got lost and what started as a mildly astringent sauce made with sour bigarade marmalade oranges evolved into duck with marmalade itself or something very close in sweetness.

Bigarade oranges can be found in U.S. markets, but even the utterly formal chef's manual, Gringoire and Saulnier's *Le Répertoire de la cuisine,* recommends the ordinary orange juice and lemon juice mixture I'm suggesting here. It is, as they say, a viable alternative to bigarades and will save you a trip to a Hispanic *botanicas* store, where they are usually on offer along with ingredients for potions and other prescientific and pre-Christian activities.

Even modern ducks exude a considerable amount of fat while they roast. Do yourself a favor and save it, strained, in the freezer in smallish containers. Cold duck fat turns pure white and, if lightly salted, makes a delicious alternative to butter. Unsalted, it is a superb cooking medium.

Two 4-pound ducks	2 tablespoons boiling water
Salt and pepper	6 tablespoons red wine vinegar
3 marmalade or Seville oranges or 2	1½ cups beef stock
medium juice oranges and 1 lemon	1 tablespoon arrowroot or cornstarch
3 tablespoons sugar	dissolved in ½ cup beef stock

1. Preheat the oven to 450 degrees.
2. Pull away the excess fat from the inside of the ducks and reserve (see Headnote).
3. Prick the skin all over with a fork so that the fat can drain during roasting. Liberally rub birds with salt and pepper, inside and out. Place in a roasting pan on racks, breast up. Place in the middle level of the oven and roast for 45 minutes.
4. Turn the birds over, baste several times, and continue roasting for about 30 minutes. After about 15 minutes, baste with ice water.
5. While the birds are roasting, prepare the bigarade (Seville orange) sauce. With a vegetable peeler cut thin strips of the thin outer layer of the peel of the oranges and/or lemon. Stop when you have a quarter cup of the Seville orange peel or a tablespoon of lemon peel and 3 tablespoons of regular orange peel. Blanch in simmering water for 15 minutes, drain, cut in julienned strips, and reserve.
6. Juice two of the Seville oranges (or 1 ½ of the juice oranges and half the lemon if you are using it).
7. Caramelize the sugar by heating it in the boiling water in a small saucepan over medium-high heat. When the sugar turns light brown, immerse the pan in cold water to stop the cooking before the sugar burns. Add the juice(s) and 3 tablespoons vinegar to the sugar. Boil and reduce by half. Remove from the heat and add the julienned peel.
8. Remove the ducks to a serving platter and keep warm in the turned-off oven with the door open.
9. Remove as much fat as you can from the roasting pan and add to the reserved fat from step 2. Then deglaze the roasting pan over medium heat with the remaining 3 tablespoons of vinegar, scraping the bottom with a flat metal spatula. Off heat, pour through a fine strainer and add to the juice mixture. Whisk in the stock and the arrowroot or cornstarch mixture.

Serves 6 to 8

Escabeche of Vegetables
(Cold Braised Vegetables in Vinegar Sauce)

All around the Mediterranean, *escabeche* **is a prized method of preserving food,** mainly fish, in a two-part process that goes back at least to the medieval Arabs, who brought it to Europe from wherever they found it. Step one is frying in olive oil. Step two is immersing it in a vinegar sauce.

The word *escabeche* may be a linguistic ancestor to ceviche, that New World preparation of raw fish "cooked" heatlessly in acid citrus juice (see page 31). We know that *escabeche* itself goes back to an Arabic original, hispanicized—or catalanized—and written down in Spain in the fourteenth century. In her article on the subject in *Petits Propos Culinaires* (no. 20, 1985), Barbara Santich refers to a total of four medieval recipes from the Mediterranean region, all with typically medieval sweet-and-sour flavorings, such as almonds, currants, and dates to balance the vinegar. But escabeche is no antique relic. Venerable, yes, yet still a staple from Barcelona to Istanbul. Put a grave accent on the second *e* and the same dish is French.

In our day, the dish has evolved away from its origins, losing the sweetness, but keeping the vinegar.

Actually, *escabeche* is less an individual dish than a method, a method that can be applied to a whole range of foods other than fish. Here I offer a sumptuous vegetable escabeche, with a bit of nutmeg for a hint of its original medieval spicing. The next day—escabeches are meant to be eaten the next day or later on, and they will taste better for the wait—serve it cold, as a first course. *Escabeches* are ideal for warm weather, the climate they were invented for long ago, when the role of vinegar was much larger than it is now.

2 quarts cold water	8 cloves garlic, peeled
1 lemon	2 medium onions, peeled and sliced into
8 small artichokes	¼-inch rings
3 tablespoons kosher salt	3 large carrots, scraped and cut into
4 quarts water	rounds
1 head broccoli, blanched	2 pickled (canned or bottled) jalapeño
1 cauliflower, blanched	peppers, seeded and cut into
2 cups olive oil	matchstick strips

In her article on the subject in *Petits Propos Culinaires* (no. 20, 1985), Barbara Santich refers to a total of four medieval recipes from the Mediterranean region, all with typically medieval sweet-and-sour flavorings, such as almonds, currants, and dates to balance the vinegar.

1 bay leaf

12 black peppercorns

12 sprigs oregano or 1 teaspoon dried

¼ teaspoon ground or (preferably) grated whole nutmeg

1 cup red wine vinegar

1 bottle white wine

1. Fill a bowl with 2 quarts of cold water. Squeeze half the lemon into it.
2. Trim the artichokes: Snap off the stems. Cut away the outer skin of the stems and drop in the water. With a knife, level the bottoms of the artichokes. Rub the bottoms with the squeezed lemon half. Cut off the first inch of the tops of the leaves. Pull off the small leaves at the bottom. With a scissors, cut off the points on the remaining whole leaves. As you make these cuts, rub with the lemon.
3. Slice the artichokes in half, lengthwise. Remove the fuzzy chokes and put the cleaned halves into the lemon water with the stems.
4. Bring 4 quarts of water to a boil. Add 1 tablespoon of the salt and the juice of the remaining half lemon. Add the squeezed lemon halves and the artichoke halves and cook for 15 minutes or until they are just tender. Remove from the water with a slotted spoon and let drain, cut sides down, on a rack.
5. Cut the broccoli and cauliflower into flowerets.
6. In a large flameproof earthenware casserole or other heavy large pot, heat the olive oil. Add the garlic and sauté over medium heat for a second or two. Then add the onions, carrots, jalapeño pepper strips, bay leaf, peppercorns, chopped (or dried) oregano, nutmeg, and remaining 2 tablespoons salt. Stir-fry for 2 minutes.
7. Add the artichokes, broccoli, and cauliflower. Stir-fry for 1 minute. Then pour in the vinegar and white wine. Mix well, bring to a boil, reduce the heat and simmer for 5 minutes. Remove from the heat and let cool to room temperature. Remove bay leaf before serving. Serve. Or refrigerate in a tightly covered vessel for as long as a week, before serving at room temperature.

12 servings

Fresh Ham with Star Anise
(Tipan)

This Chinese wedding dish shows its Szechwan origins in the dried chilies and brown peppercorns that flavor its cooking liquid. But it is not one of those fiery Szechwan dishes that neophytes remember primarily for their heat. Indeed, it showcases the very distinctive flavor of the star anise and the richness of the ham itself. In China, this is a dish of celebration.

3 pounds fresh ham	2 teaspoons Szechwan peppercorns
3 scallions, trimmed and cut into green and white sections	⅔ cup soy sauce
	⅓ cup Chinese rice wine
One 3-inch piece fresh ginger	2 tablespoons sugar
½ cup dried mushrooms, unsoaked	1 tablespoon sesame oil
2 star anise	1 teaspoon salt
3 dried red chilies	10 ounces well-washed spinach

1. In a pot just large enough to fit the ham, combine the ham, scallions, ginger, mushrooms, star anise, chilies, peppercorns, and enough water to cover the ham. Bring to a boil, skim, cover, and cook for about an hour at a fast simmer. After a half hour, turn the ham. Continue cooking, until the liquid has reduced to half its original depth. Keep turning the ham every 15 minutes.

2. Add the soy sauce, rice wine, and sugar. Reduce the heat and simmer, covered, for another hour.

3. Add the sesame oil and 1 teaspoon salt. Then raise the heat and boil, uncovered, until the liquid has reduced to one-quarter its original depth. Serve straightaway with steamed spinach (see next step) or refrigerate for as much as 4 days before reheating.

4. Just before you are ready to serve the ham, put the spinach in a saucepan. Cover and cook over low-medium heat. After a couple minutes, check the spinach. It is done as soon as it wilts, but before It loses its brilliant green color. Drain thoroughly and array on a serving platter with the ham. Pour the ham cooking liquid over the ham.

Serves 6 as a main course in a Western-style meal with appetizer and substantial dessert

Fried Rice

Fried rice is a universal idea, as widespread a dish as there is. But no one can tell you which is the fundamental fried rice. Is it the classic Cantonese favorite, in which the rice itself is a foil for mildly sweet Chinese sausage or a panorama of other possible ingredients? Or is it the Indonesian national dish, *nasi goreng,* resplendent with a rainbow of vegetables and red-hot with chilies?

None of the above qualifies as the ur-fried rice, the Platonic ideal on which these national or regional embellishments have been hung. Fried rice is a concept so humble and inevitable that it belongs to no culture in particular and to all cultures that cook rice as a staple.

In such cultures, leftover rice is a fact of life—cold rice, not delicious by itself but too precious to waste. So it is resuscitated in hot oil, which it readily absorbs, along with other ingredients and seasonings. The fried rice I offer here is a stripped-down Chinese fried rice, unadorned but not at all to be sneered at. Anyway it makes my point, and if you cook it, you will see with clarity the strength of the idea. And then you can add whatever you like, whatever is around the kitchen and quickly stir-fried.

Fried rice, among other things, is fast food. The fastest version I know is a typical Filipino breakfast concoction called garlic rice. The name says it all, last night's rice made pungent with plenty of garlic and little else except the oil for the frying.

This is not the way restaurants and cookbooks with their best ethnic feet forward deal with fried rice. A Cantonese restaurant makes steamed rice especially for fried rice. Sri Owen, the Sumatran-English author of the *Classic Asian Cookbook* (1998) advises you to cook the rice and then wait 3 hours for it to cool, before getting down to business for *nasi goreng.* And I am certainly not trying to say that the deliberate preparation of rice to be fried later on is somehow inauthentic or soulless. Indeed, I think that people from many rice-eating cultures might find fried rice reduced to its bare essentials, as in garlic rice or the fried rice below, unfestive or dull, so I am offering some optional additions.*

---

* In China's regional Chiu Chow cuisine there is a famous theatrical "fried rice." It is not fried at all, just steamed and mixed at the table while still hot with an array of just-cooked garnishes, a sauce, and poached eggs. To the Chiu Chow, this is a fried rice because, like fried rice, it tosses together rice and other ingredients, instead of serving them separately.

2 scallions

2 tablespoons peanut oil

1 egg, lightly beaten

2 cups leftover rice

1 cup leftover chicken, skinned, boned,
and julienned, or flaked salmon or
sliced okra

Soy sauce

1. Trim the scallions and slice in rounds, keeping the green and white separate.

2. Heat the oil in a skillet until it begins to smoke. Toss in the white scallion rounds and stir a few times. Pour in the egg and continue stirring until it begins to set. Then, without hesitation, stir in the rice, leftover chicken, salmon, or okra, and keep stirring until any clumps have been broken up, all ingredients are well mixed together, and the rice is heated through.

3. Remove from the heat, stir in soy sauce to taste, and transfer to a serving bowl. Sprinkle green scallion pieces on top.

2 to 3 servings

Gaeng Pet Gai
(Thai Red-Curry Chicken)

Thai food in New York in the early seventies consisted of a small restaurant on Baxter Street near the courts and a tiny grocery store on upper Broadway that sold Thai fish sauce, *galanga, kaffir* lime leaves, holy basil, and lemongrass, all those other exotic condiments that make Thai and Lao food unlike other cuisines. The obvious interest of this food, and the industry of Thai immigrants put Thai food on the map overnight, or almost. Today, we can buy domestic lemongrass in rural supermarkets that also carry whole lines of canned and bottled products for non-Thai consumers.

This red-"curry"* chicken combines most of the characteristic flavors of the cuisine. Once you have the ingredients, the dish is a piece of cake to make. It is highly spiced—no surprise—and the coconut cream gives it body and mouth feel. I buy my Thai ingredients from a Thai grocer on tiny, steep Mosco Street at the edge of Chinatown in lower Manhattan. Bangkok Center Grocery, 104 Mosco Street near Mott Street (212 732-8196). But if this isn't convenient for you, there is a first-rate Thai food Web site at www.templeofthai.com.

Red-curry chicken won't look red, because the name comes from the red chilies. Thai green curry contains green chilies.

¼ cup vegetable oil	¼ cup Thai fish sauce
2 cloves garlic, peeled and chopped fine	2 teaspoons sugar
2 tablespoons Gaeng Pet (Red Curry Sauce) (see opposite)	¾ pound boneless chicken cutlet, julienned
1 cup coconut cream, at room temperature	4 kaffir lime leaves, chopped fine
	30 holy basil leaves

* As latecomers to the ethnic food scene in the English-speaking world, Thais did not hesitate to market their food with terms borrowed from other, more familiar Asian cuisines. Their food was hot, like Indian curries, which also took their flavor from spice mixtures, but not at all so exclusively from pounded pastes as the Thais do. But they called those pastes curries anyway, a shrewd piece of harmless misinformation. In the same spirit, Thai restaurateurs abroad served their food with chopsticks, even though in Bangkok chopsticks are as foreign as they are in Little Rock.

None of this seems to bother Thais, a confident people who were never colonized by anybody. They have definitely learned many things from their more powerful neighbors in India and China (Buddhism comes to mind), but the originality of their food shines through the usual crosscultural smokescreen of mutual misunderstanding.

1. In a wok or skillet, heat the oil. Stir-fry the garlic until lightly browned. Stir in the red-curry sauce, then the coconut cream. Heat until it melts and thickens. Stir in the fish sauce and sugar.

2. Add the chicken strips and stir-fry until the meat is no longer pink. Stir in water if the sauce seems too thick and let cook briefly. Add the remaining ingredients, cook for 2 minutes, and serve.

Serves 2 (or more as part of a multicourse meal)

Gaeng Pet (Red-Curry Sauce)

12 to 30 dried red chilies, with stems and seeds removed

3 pieces *galanga*

3 pieces kaffir lime peel, julienned

Bottom 6 inches of 2 lemongrass stalks, cut on the bias in one-inch segments

3 tablespoons finely chopped garlic

1 small onion, peeled and chopped fine

2 teaspoons shrimp paste

⅓ cup finely chopped coriander root, if available

1. Soak the chilies, *galanga,* kaffir lime, and lemongrass in warm water for 30 minutes. Drain and discard the water. Julienne the *galanga.*

2. Chop the soaked ingredients finely and pound to a paste with the remaining ingredients using a mortar and pestle or a food processor.

About 1 cup

Gazpacho, White and Red
(Two Cold Spanish Soups)

The gazpacho everybody knows is a cold liquefied salad with a tomato base. It has a Spanish origin but everything else about it is obscure. Actually, the historic record offers descriptions of many soups called gazpacho, but there are two main ones—the tomato and the non-tomato known as *ajo blanco* or white garlic soup. Since no soup with tomato was possible in Europe or in the Moorish Middle East before the Columbus voyages, *ajo blanco* is probably the original gazpacho, and its use of almonds helps link it to other medieval Iberian recipes.

Both *ajo blanco* and tomato gazpacho have important common bonds. They are prepared and eaten cold. They contain bread and vinegar. If we look for an original source or condition where a cold dish with bread and vinegar might have arisen, the most likely vector of transmission into Spain would have been the Roman army. Who more than soldiers on the move would favor a cold dish with yesterday's bread and vinegar, which wouldn't spoil outdoors. The word gazpacho itself has no definite etymology but may derive from the pre-Roman *caspa,* fragment or leftovers.

We know that the ancients in the Mediterranean world refreshed themselves with vinegar. You will recall what Boaz says to Ruth when he comes upon her gleaning among the sheaves in his fields: "At mealtime come thou hither, and eat of the bread and dip thy morsel in the vinegar." When Jesus on the cross asked for something to quench his thirst, Roman soldiers passed up a sponge soaked in vinegar for him to drink, or so it says in the Gospel According to John. This was not, as is sometimes supposed, a gesture of contempt. People really did happily drink vinegar. *Ajo blanco* adds grapes and a paste of almonds and garlic to the basic broth, giving body to a humble refreshment.

The first testimonial for gazpacho comes from an important epicure. Sancho Panza (paunch) liked gazpacho. He resigns in fury from the governorship of the isle of Barataria (Cheapery) because a harpyesque Dr. Recio (harsh) keeps snatching food from under his nose. "Make way, My Lords," he says, "and let me return to my former liberty . . . I would rather stuff myself with gazpachos than be subject to the misery of an impertinent physician who kills me with hunger."

Did he mean white or red gazpacho? Either was possible by the end of the sixteenth century when Cervantes was writing *Don Quixote.* Or Sancho might have meant the scraps from which the soup was made. I vote for the *ajo blanco,* as being more Sancho's sturdy style.

Ajo Blanco con Uvas (White Garlic Soup with Grapes)

¼ pound bread, with crusts removed

1½ cups blanched almonds

2 cloves garlic, peeled

⅔ cup olive oil

1 tablespoon sherry vinegar

Salt

4 cups cold water

1 pound seedless green grapes, peeled* as you would an orange, but gently, with a small knife

1. Moisten the bread.
2. Grind together the bread, almonds, and garlic in a mortar, adding the olive oil gradually until you have a smooth paste. Work in the vinegar and salt; then whisk into the cold water. Refrigerate until ready to serve.
3. Pour the soup into a serving bowl. Add the grapes and serve.

4 servings

Tomato Gazpacho

½ pound stale bread, with crusts removed

2 pounds tomatoes, peeled

2 green bell peppers, seeds and white pith removed, chopped

2 cloves garlic, peeled

¼ cup white wine vinegar

⅔ cup olive oil

2 teaspoons salt

1 small onion, peeled and chopped

½ medium cucumber, peeled, seeded, and chopped, about ⅔ cup

1 hard-boiled egg, chopped

1. Soak half the bread in water, then squeeze gently to remove excess liquid.
2. Process the bread, all but one tomato, 1 green pepper, the garlic, vinegar, oil, and salt until smooth. Chill.
3. Mix the remaining ingredients in individual bowls. Pour the gazpacho over them. If the soup is too thick, dilute with cold water before pouring into the bowls.

4 to 6 servings

* I can hear you saying, "Sure, peel me a grape, Beulah." But this is not as much trouble as you think, and the result, sublime, is worth it once a summer.

Something very like genoise is also the stuff of madeleines, the little molded, shell-shaped cookies, which, on a fateful day for literature, Marcel Proust remembered eating as a child. One memory led to another and filled the seven volumes of Proust's novel *A la recherche du temps perdu* (*In Search of Lost Time*).

Genoise à l'Orange

Gênes is the French name for Genoa and a *génois* is a Genoese. So this pinnacle of French cakes is nominally Italian.

Don't believe it. The classic French repertoire is full of cosmopolitan geography, Maltese sauce and Norwegian omelet, almost all of it whimsical or poetic (the omelet is like a Baked Alaska (page 4), therefore cold, therefore like Arctic Norway). As for genoise, I can think of nothing Genoese or even Italian in a cake made of universally available ingredients: eggs, sugar, butter, flour. The technique is what makes it special.

To make a genoise is a difficult thing. When I was the food editor of the *New York Times* in the early seventies, I printed a recipe for genoise—once. The angry phone calls from cooks who had failed convinced me I should lay off genoise.

Why did they fail? Because few of them had the true grit or persistence to beat whole eggs and sugar until they had taken in enough air to "make the ribbon." The test of this is to let some of the mixture drip off a spoon into the rest. If it leaves a ribbonlike trace behind it, you are there.

The classic method was laborious indeed. You warmed the mixing bowl, put in the eggs and sugar, set the bowl in a pan of hot water itself set over a moderate flame, and just whisked away, lifting the mixture with the whisk to aerate it, and continued until you had the ribbon. Oh yes, then you kept on whisking until the mixture had cooled. Then it was time to whisk in the flour, immediately, or the mixture would lose its loft, and you should be careful to see to it that that the flour falls like snow.

On the other hand, an electric mixer helps a lot (see below). Once you get good at making it, genoise is versatile. If you bake it in a shallow, rectangular pan, a *moule à génoise*, you can then easily cut it in squares and turn them into all manner of petits fours. Something very like genoise is also the stuff of madeleines, the little molded, shell-shaped cookies, which, on a fateful day for literature, Marcel Proust remembered eating as a child. One memory led to another and filled the seven volumes of Proust's novel *A la recherche du temps perdu* (*In Search of Lost Time*).

The orange flavor in this recipe is a nifty extra. I tasted such a confection at L'Auberge du Père Bise on the shore of idyllic Lake Annecy in eastern France near Geneva.

3 cups water

½ cup (approximately 3) eggs, at room temperature

⅓ cup sugar

1 ½ tablespoons butter

½ cup plus 1 tablespoon flour

2 teaspoons grated orange peel

1 tablespoon Grand Marnier

GLAZE

1 tablespoon Grand Marnier

3 tablespoons apricot preserves, melted and strained

6 tablespoons confectioners' sugar

1. Preheat the oven to 350 degrees.
2. Boil 3 cups water in a 6-cup saucepan. Before you start this, make sure the bowl of your electric mixer will sit comfortably on the saucepan's upper rim or nest partway into the saucepan. Reduce the heat to low-medium. Then put the eggs and the sugar in the mixer bowl, set it on the saucepan but do not allow the bowl to touch the water, and whisk the eggs and sugar vigorously with a wire whisk for 1 minute.
3. Remove the bowl from the heat and attach it to the electric mixer. Beat at high speed for approximately 5 minutes. The beating is done when the mixture is pale and straw-colored, and drips off a wooden spoon in a ribbon. Do not beat longer than necessary.
4. While the mixer is at work, clarify the butter: melt it and spoon away as much of the white milk solids as possible. Pour through a fine strainer and reserve. Butter and flour an 8-inch cake pan.
5. With a rubber spatula, fold the flour, grated orange peel, and 1 tablespoon of Grand Marnier very gently into the egg mixture. Fold in the butter, which should be warm but not much above blood heat.
6. Pour the batter into the prepared cake pan and bake for 30 minutes. The top will brown.
7. Cool on a rack for 10 minutes. Then unmold onto the rack.
8. The completely cooled cake should be moved to a serving dish (there is no need to invert it again; just slide it off the rack, leaving the original bottom side facing up). It can be served as is (my preference) or it can be glazed: Whisk together 1 tablespoon of Grand Marnier with the apricot preserves and confectioners' sugar. Keep at this for several minutes. Then spread over the top and sides of the cake. An unglazed genoise will keep for a week in the refrigerator in plastic wrap (wait until you are ready to serve before glazing, to avoid physical damage to the glaze and possible decomposition in the refrigerator).

Serves 8

Gravlax

Gravlax means cured salmon in Swedish. In practice, that means the salmon is cured in salt and sugar. The cure is a dry cure, not a wet cure. Gravlax is not smoked, so it is closer to the raw state than smoked salmon and not as salty as salmon that has been cured in brine. This does not mean that gravlax is better than brined and smoked salmon. But it does have a romantic edge on its more completely processed and artificially flavored cousins.

Does it matter if you start out with farm-raised salmon instead of wild fish? Since the price difference is huge, and you might be concerned about the overfishing of wild salmon for a global luxury market competing for an elite food that travels well, stores for long periods, and can be eaten right out of the cryopack, you might want to give farmed salmon a chance when you decide to make gravlax. You will hear that wild salmon are superior because they have led a vigorous life in stream and ocean (salmon in nature are anadromous, living in salt and fresh water at different stages in their lives). Since I have yet to see or hear about a blind tasting of wild and farmed salmon judged by impartial people, I am not ready to pronounce on this matter. My instinct is that the wild fish are better, but my hope is that they aren't, at least not for this preparation, which does not require the fish to stand up to the direct, high heat of standard cooking. My last gravlax was, in fact, made with farmed salmon. It was so delicious that I can't imagine ever curing a wild salmon again. I will save them for the poacher.

3 pounds thick salmon fillet, skin on	3 tablespoons white peppercorns, crushed
¾ cup kosher salt	with a mortar and pestle
¾ cup sugar	3 bunches fresh dill
	Dill-Mustard Sauce (see page 92)

1. Even though the salmon fillet is farmed, check it for pinbones that penetrate deeply into the flesh. With a needle-nose pliers, pull them out, being careful not to damage the salmon.
2. Stir together salt, sugar, and peppercorns in a bowl. Rub this mixture into both sides of the salmon.
3. Put the salmon into a large plastic Ziploc freezer bag. Pour in the rest of the salt/sugar/peppercorn mixture, on the flesh side. On top of that, place the dill. Set the

bag, salmon skin down, on the counter, and let sit for 3 hours. Then refrigerate for 2 to 3 days.* There is no need to cure the salmon any longer, because you are not attempting to preserve it, only to make it deliciously tender and beautifully flavored.

4. Before serving, remove from the bag, discard the dill, and brush off the curing mixture. Then, using a very sharp, long thin knife, slice the salmon crosswise and on the bias (so that the knife is tilted at about a 45-degree angle to the fish).

Serves 10 as an appetizer

Dill-Mustard Sauce

3 tablespoons mild brown mustard

1 tablespoon sugar

2 tablespoons white wine vinegar

½ cup peanut or corn oil

5 to 6 tablespoons chopped fresh dill

Salt

Pepper

1. Beat together the mustard, sugar, and vinegar.
2. Beat the oil into the mixture from step 1.
3. Stir in the remaining ingredients.

About 1¼ cups

* Scandinavians have traditionally weighted gravlax while it cures. A Swedish wannabe I know in Greenwich Village puts canned goods in a skillet and then sets it on the salmon in the refrigerator. This promotes the flow of juices from the salmon, juices which are then basted over the fish on the three occasions per day when pseudo-Gunilla also turns the fish. I have had spectacular results without weights, basting, or fish-flipping. All of this fuss makes sense if you are a subsistence fishwife in Malmö hoping to preserve the salmon catch through the winter. For the urban twenty-first-century cook intent on serving the whole shebang within the week, weighting gravlax is only make-work that squashes good fish.

Hollandaise Sauce
(Dutch Sauce)

In the year 1948 BCE (Before the Child Era), hollandaise was, for American home cooks, the only classic sauce they made from scratch themselves. At least I cannot recall my mother or anyone else preparing mayonnaise or béarnaise or any brown sauce more complex than a gravy thickened with beurre manié. But hollandaise was the exception: it bathed—and still bathes—those poached eggs over broiled ham on toasted English muffins named after E. C. Benedict (1834–1920), the Connecticut yachtsman who supposedly invented the dish, and even unsophisticated cooks sent it out with poached salmon or as a dress-up for vegetables like asparagus or broccoli.

How did hollandaise attain this solitary eminence? Considering its difficulty—much the same as the difficulties one faces with the other emulsified sauces—you wouldn't think that housewives caught up in the Eisenhower-era mania for labor-saving devices would have unhesitatingly taken on the last-minute tensions of a highfalutin sauce. But they did, just as they also whipped up other tricky items, hard sauce (page 160), or Yorkshire Pudding (page 198).

In this bag of tricks, made fashionable in the cooking schools and women's magazines of pre–World War II America, most of the stunts were right out of ye olde England, and I think further research will show that hollandaise itself came to us from the assimilating Victorian machine operated by Mrs. Beeton.

I am certain, moreover, that no one has ever been under the misapprehension that hollandaise was Dutch, in origin or inspiration. *Larousse Gastronomique* (1938) tells us that in the French kitchen of long ago, hollandaise was a code word for fish served with melted butter. It's easy to see how that might have evolved into our hollandaise, but it is impossible to believe that no one in France served melted butter with fish until some traveler happened to import the idea from a visit to Rotterdam or Maastricht.

Today, you could attend a lifetime of dinners and lunches, not to mention restaurant meals, without laying your eyes on a silken smooth and butter-yellow hollandaise. In the nouvelle cuisine, it vanished from the foreground and survived only as a means of thickening sauces without using flour. In the home, it was suppressed because of its cholesterol and calories and possibly because it was too *vieux jeu*. In hollandaise's favor are elegance, a svelte acidity, and a moonlight splash of yellow that brightens up green vegetables and plain white fish.

½ pound (2 sticks) butter	¼ teaspoon white pepper
½ cup white wine vinegar	4 egg yolks
½ teaspoon salt, approximately	1 teaspoon lemon juice

1. Melt the butter and allow it to cool partially. It should be warm when used in step 3.
2. In a heavy, nonaluminum 1-quart saucepan, stir together the vinegar, salt, and white pepper. Reduce by half, to about ¼ cup, and remove from the heat. Let cool to room temperature.
3. Whisk the egg yolks into the vinegar reduction. Place the saucepan over very low heat and whisk constantly, until the yolks have turned white and thickened visibly. Remove from the heat and immediately begin whisking in the warm butter a drop at a time. As you progress, after the sauce has clearly "taken," you can gradually increase the amount of butter you add. Incorporate all of the butter.
4. Strain the sauce through a warm chinois or other very fine strainer into a warm, clean saucepan.
5. The sauce is now ready to serve. Lighten it, if necessary, with a few drops of cold water. Whisk in the lemon juice. Taste the hollandaise and add more salt or lemon juice if necessary. Serve in a hot, dry sauceboat.

About ½ cup

Homard à l'Américaine
(American Lobster)

The authors of the Brittany volume in that august survey of French food region by region, *L'Inventaire du patrimoine culinaire de la France* (1994), call this *Homard à l'armoricaine*, Armorica being an old name for Brittany. But even these scholarly devotés of French cuisine concede that there is no evidence one way or the other for choosing between it and the equally traditional *américaine*. The dish could be of American origin; or it could be Armorican. This is charmingly unchauvinistic, not to mention true to the facts, or rather to the lack of them. But I think that it falls into the trap of supposing that because a dish in the classic French repertoire is called American or Javanese, it actually started out in America or Java as part of a primordial food patrimony.

Usually, the geographic designation is pure fantasy. In this case, I believe it is obvious that America v. Armorica is a false problem, arising from a purely orthographic confusion. Call it whatever you like, Armenian or Arabian, this is a French dish. Armorican makes sense as a name, because Brittany is a major lobster fishery. But the great lobsters of the world are from the other side of the North Atlantic; so the chef who named this wonderful dish may have wanted to borrow some of the glory of *Homarus americanus* and apply it to its less fabulous cousin *H. gammarus L.*

But why am I so sure this is a French recipe? First, because it requires killing the lobster with a knife instead of boiling it to death, unseen, in a pot. Americans are too squeamish to have thought up a recipe that involved stabbing. But a French chef used to bleeding hares and serving up larks with their heads still on, wouldn't have hesitated, especially because he would have reasoned, correctly, that if he didn't stab the lobster, he couldn't very easily cut it up and cook it raw as if it were a chop or a chicken breast.

In other words, *Homard à l'armoricaine* is, in its essence, a culinary treatment of lobster, something impossible if you started out with a lobster that was already cooked and that couldn't profitably be cooked again.

This passion to really "cook" something is traditionally French. Americans, by nature, have taken the quick way with a lobster: throw the thing in a pot and it will taste very good anyway, without the knifework and the flaming, la-de-da. Americans have a limited point. French chefs offer the slightly more ambitious and bold cook a path to the sublime.

One 2-pound lobster	2½ tablespoons cognac
4 tablespoons oil	1⅓ cups dry white wine
10 tablespoons butter	3 canned Italian tomatoes, drained, seeded,
2 large shallots, peeled and chopped	and chopped
1 small clove garlic, peeled and crushed	A pinch cayenne

1. Preheat the oven to 350 degrees F.
2. Punch the point of a large chopping knife into the lobster just behind its eyes and then slice the thorax (the main body section) in half lengthwise. The lobster is now dead, even if it continues to twitch or writhe for a few moments. Remove the sac near the head and discard. Remove the claws, legs, and tail from the body of the lobster. Crack the claws partially with a nutcracker. Slice the tail crosswise into sections at each joint. Remove the coral and reserve in a bowl.
3. Heat the oil and 3 tablespoons of the butter in a large heavy ovenproof skillet for which you have a cover. When the oil and butter are very hot but not smoking, put in the lobster pieces and sauté them until the flesh turns opaque and the shells are bright red. Turn the pieces so that they cook evenly on all sides.
4. When the lobster pieces are done, put the lid on the skillet and pour off as much of the oil and butter as you can. Then sprinkle the lobster with the shallots and garlic. Pour in the cognac and heat it until it vaporizes. Ignite.
5. Let the cognac flame off heat. When the flames have died away, add the white wine, tomatoes, and cayenne.
6. Set the skillet over high heat and bring the liquid to a boil. Cover the skillet and cook in the oven for 20 minutes.
7. Remove the lobster pieces with a skimmer or a slotted spoon, letting as much liquid as possible drain back into the skillet. Remove the flesh from the claws and tail sections. Reserve, along with the other pieces, on two dinner plates in a warming oven.
8. Reduce the lobster cooking liquid to about ¾ cup. While it boils down, pound the coral and 2 tablespoons of butter into a smooth paste. Add this lobster butter to the reduced liquid in the skillet. Blend the sauce with a whisk and strain through a chinois or other very fine strainer. Hold the sauce in a bain-marie until ready to serve.
9. Finish the sauce off heat by whisking in the remaining butter, cut in small pieces. Pour over the lobster pieces.

Serves 2

Hong Kong Salt Shrimp

Once you have the Szechwan peppercorns and five-spice powder, which are available at any Chinese grocery and will last for as long as other spices, this is the simplest possible example of the stir-fry method. It is obviously very quick, especially if you can drop your prejudice against shrimp veins. Taking them out is boring fussy work, and there is no point to it. They are harmless and once you've cooked the shrimp and sauced them, no one will realize the veins are still there.

Yes, you say, but what about the shrimp shells? Leave them be. They soak up flavor, and once you get over your belief that they shouldn't be eaten, you will join hundreds of millions of Asians who like their crunch. Guests who don't want them can easily remove them with a fork and knife or chopsticks. If they raise their eyebrows when they notice you scarfing those shells, just say eating them is authentic.

1½ teaspoons Szechwan peppercorns	1 pound medium shrimp, shells on, heads
4 tablespoons salt	and legs removed
1½ teaspoons five-spice powder	Vegetable oil for deep-frying
1½ teaspoons black pepper	

1. Spread the Szechwan peppercorns on a hot skillet and toast them briefly, until they darken and begin to give off an aroma. Remove to a mortar and grind to a rough powder.

2. In the same skillet, heat 3 tablespoons salt and stir for 3 minutes over medium heat, or until the salt turns gray. Scrape into a bowl with the Szechwan peppercorns. Mix together with the five-spice powder and the black pepper.

3. If you are squeamish about shrimp veins, remove them. Otherwise don't bother. No one noticed them, and I haven't lost anyone from shrimp vein poisoning yet.

4. Heat the oil to 350 degrees in a deep-fryer or a wok (filled about halfway with oil). Slip in the shrimp and fry until they turn red, less than a minute. Remove with a slotted spoon.

5. Heat a skillet. Put in the remaining tablespoon of the salt along with the shrimp. Toss the shrimp in the reserved salt mixture until they are well coated. Transfer to a serving dish. Pass the rest of the mixture in a bowl.

Serves 4 to 6 as a first course

Hummus bi Tahini
(Lebanese Chickpea Puree with Sesame Cream)

Anissa Helou, like any Lebanese, has a special attachment to chickpeas. They are an indigenous veg-etable all over the Mediterranean. We know this because early Greek poetry refers to them, and they are the essential ingredient in the most fundamental food of the Levant, the tahini-flavored puree known throughout the world as hummus.

Chickpeas start out looking a bit like garden-variety peas. As Helou writes in *Lebanese Cuisine* (1998): "There is a short moment in early summer when chick peas are available fresh. Green bunches laden with the peas still in the pod are sold by street hawkers, usually to children who spend hours squeezing each pod open to extract and eat the green chick peas. A very healthy snack."

Chickpea flour is a traditional staple in Nice and elsewhere, all the way to India. But the world recipe is hummus. It is everywhere now, in degraded industrial, flavored hummus products that give no inkling of the "smooth ivory" texture Helou talks about. And almost as important as the basic preparation of the puree is the ingenious traditional method of serv-ing (see steps 5 and 6 below) in which hummus spread out on a shallow plate is mounded slightly at the edges and the center, creating a natural receptacle for olive oil and a platform for displaying a few whole chickpeas.

This arrangement was clearly designed for a circle of people all scooping up hummus and moistening it in oil with a little pouch of pita bread held in the right hand. It also looks beau-tiful, and it inspires thoughts of Arab hospitality going back centuries.

Tahini is the other crucial ingredient, a thick "cream" made from pressed, roasted sesame seeds. Quality varies greatly between brands, Helou favors imported tahini from the eastern Mediterranean. You can easily test this proposition by staging a blind tahini tasting. Serve rosewater-tinged martinis and make hummus to go with them from the tahini brand you pick.

2 cups dried chickpeas	½ teaspoon cayenne, optional
3 cloves garlic, peeled and minced	1½ teaspoons cumin
Juice of 2 large or 3 small lemons, about ⅓ cup	2 to 3 tablespoons olive oil
1 cup tahini	Cumin or paprika to sprinkle on hummus
Salt	Pita wedges

1. Soak the chickpeas overnight.

2. Boil the chickpeas in plenty of water for at least an hour, until they can be mashed with a fork.

3. Save ½ cup of the cooking water. Drain away the rest and put the chickpeas and the ½ cup water in the jar of a blender (reserving 6 for a garnish) with the garlic and half the lemon juice. Blend until smooth. Scrape into a mixing bowl.

4. Work in the tahini and beat until completely mixed. The color will lighten. Add salt to taste. Add more lemon juice if you want a sourer spread. Add ½ teaspoon of cayenne if you want a bit of heat.

5. When you are ready to serve the hummus, spread it over a shallow plate. Run the back of a serving spoon in a circle through the hummus so as to leave a trough between the center and the edge. Put the reserved chickpeas on the mound at the center.

6. Heat 1½ teaspoons cumin briefly in the olive oil. Then drizzle it around the trough in the hummus. Sprinkle additional cumin or paprika around the raised outer rim of the hummus.

Serves 6 to 8 as an hors d'oeuvre with pita

"There is a short moment in early summer when chick peas are available fresh. Green bunches laden with the peas still in the pod are sold by street hawkers, usually to children who spend hours squeezing each pod open to extract and eat the green chick peas. A very healthy snack."

—Anissa Helou

Jambon Persillé
(Parsleyed Ham)

Before you can make a Burgundian parsleyed ham, you need a ham. In the Burgundian farmhouses where this most delicious of all "cold cut" preparations was first practiced, they cured their own hams, to preserve the abundant meat without refrigeration, which traditional, premodern farms didn't have. Old-time farms did have a superabundance of pork after a pig was slaughtered (usually in cold months). Very little of the fresh pork could be eaten before it spoiled; so farmers took the hams, the thick part of the hind leg, and preserved them in salt, so they would keep through the rest of the year. During that time, boredom with the delicious meat would set in. Jambon persillé was a brilliant and festive solution to this problem. Charcuterie in a bowl, no casings necessary.

Should you want to cure your own ham, here's how:

First, make sure you have a curing area with a constant temperature between 38 and 40 degrees Fahrenheit (the temperature at which a refrigerator should run). Then buy 10 pounds of fresh pork picnic shoulder with the bone in. Cut away the rind, scrape as much fat off it as you can, and set aside. Bone the meat (the bones can be used in soup), cutting it into large slabs.

In a bowl, mix 1½ cups sea salt, ¼ cup sugar, 1 teaspoon saltpeter (available at pharmacies, especially those near boys' boarding schools), 1½ teaspoons crushed juniper berries, ¾ teaspoon white pepper, ¼ teaspoon allspice, ½ teaspoon ground thyme, and 1 crumbled bay leaf.

Rub half the mixture thoroughly over the surface of the meat and rind. Pack the meat, with the rind on top, into an enamel bowl, cover with plastic wrap, weight down with a brick, and refrigerate for 5 days. (If you have a uniformly cool cellar, you can follow farmhouse tradition and dispense with refrigeration, but for most of us the refrigerator provides an indispensable save of reliable cold.) The rub in the rest of the salt mixture, cover and weight again, and refrigerate for another 10 days or for as long as 6 weeks. Turn the meat every few days and do not discard the brine.

This is the way French farm wives have been curing every known cut of pork—from jowls to hams—for centuries. Smoking would add its special taste, but it is not necessary. Even the renowned hams of Bayonne in the southwest of France and the prosciuttos of Parma are merely salt-cured and then, usually, sliced and served raw.

How does a salt cure work? Macroscopically speaking, the salt incites the juices to flow out of the meat, while the salt itself penetrates into the meat. In time, the process reverses itself, but the flavor of the salt and spices remains. The sugar prevents the salt from overly hardening the meat. And the saltpeter produces an attractive red-pink color. Microscopically, the salt acts as a bacterial filter, killing microorganisms we don't want but permitting a desirable pickling of the meat by others.

4 to 6 pounds salt-cured pork with rind if any, soaked in cold water overnight to leach out excess salt

1½ cups chicken stock

1 bottle (750 milliliters) dry white wine

3 cloves garlic, peeled

1 bay leaf

5 sprigs parsley for the cooking liquid

3 sprigs fresh thyme or 1 teaspoon ground dried

1 package (1 tablespoon) gelatin, optional

1 cup finely chopped parsley

White wine vinegar

1. Set the pork and the rind in a large pot with the chicken stock, wine, garlic, bay leaf, parsley sprigs, and thyme. Add enough cold water so that the meat is covered by an inch of liquid. Bring to a boil, reduce the heat, and simmer partially covered for 2½ hours, or until the meat falls apart easily when pressed with a fork.

2. Remove the meat, discard the rind, drain, cool, and pull apart into pieces roughly 1 by 2 inches.

3. Strain 2½ cups of the cooking liquid and refrigerate. A layer of fat will congeal at the top. (You can treat all of the cooking liquid in this manner and reserve the excess for aspic.)

4. Dribble a small amount of the chilled liquid from step 3 into a saucer. Set in the refrigerator for 15 minutes. If it solidifies, go on to the next step. Otherwise, dissolve a small amount of gelatin into the 2½ cups of chilled liquid, no more than a teaspoon, and repeat the refrigerator test. Continue adding gelatin by half teaspoonfuls until your test sample gels.

5. Meanwhile, put the chopped parsley in a bowl and pour on enough vinegar so that the parsley just begins to float. Let stand approximately 30 minutes.

6. Pour off the vinegar. Then press the parsley lightly to get rid of any remaining vinegar that will drip away under gentle pressure.

7. Combine the parsley and the chilled liquid. Pour a thin layer over the bottom of a glass bowl large enough to hold all the pork with a bit of room to spare.

8. Arrange the pieces of pork in a layer on top of the layer of parsley mixture in the bowl. Try to pack in the pieces of meat so that they dovetail fairly well, as in a mosaic. Continue alternating the parsley mixture and meat until the meat is entirely used up. Finish by pouring on enough parsley mixture to cover the last meat layer completely. Refrigerate overnight, or until the dish has completely solidified. Serve cold, unmolded, or directly from the bowl, in pie-like slices.

16 to 24 servings

Kibbeh Nayeh
(Lebanese Raw Lamb with Bulghur)

Lurking within the pan-Islamic cuisine spread around the Middle East by the Ottomans are a handful of local dishes that withstood Turkish gastronomic imperialism and continue to express the individual histories of their regions. In Egypt, for example, *mouloukhia,* the soup made from an indigenous green, dates back to the time of the hieroglyphs. Couscous is the emblematic food of North Africa, as preserved lemons are the characteristic flavor. In the Levant, kibbeh takes us back to the dawn of civilization in the Fertile Crescent, where the cultivation of grain in the Old World began.

The Lebanese have spread kibbeh around the world, wherever they have migrated. I have seen it in the Dominican Republic, hispanified as *quipe.* The recipe here is based on one published in *Lebanese Cuisine* (1998) by my friend Anissa Helou, who lives in London. The processor makes quick work of what once was a labor-intensive job, because of the chopping of the raw lamb.

For the outsider, coming to this dish in a restaurant for the first time, the smooth, svelte raw meat dominates the experience. But the intermixed bulghur wheat is the backbone of this inspired feat of earthy elegance.

According to the scholar Michael Abdalla, the oldest reference to bulghur is on an Assyrian cuneiform tablet of the ninth century B.C., in a discussion of a feast at the court of Ashurnasipal II. Abdalla's description, in a paper submitted to the Oxford Food Symposium in 1989, of how Assyrian villagers in Iraq process bulghur even now (or at least before their lives were disrupted by the Mother of Battles) is a Rousseauean idyll in Mesopotamian garb:

Each family prepares 100–200 kg. of recently harvested wheat for this purpose. First the grain is carefully cleaned: it is sieved manually, sorted on large round trays (every odd grain is removed), rinsed in water several times and dried in the sun. . . . In addition to family members, neighbors also take part in these activities. The activities last a few weeks and are done in leisure time, usually in the afternoons of long summer days.

Next the grain is boiled until it is softened to the point of edibility, called danoke *or* shleeqa. *The* shleeqa *is then spread thinly on rooftops or other outdoor surfaces and dried for one to three days. The grain darkens and contracts and looks like wrinkled peas.*

The second stage of bulgur preparation is shelling. The dried grains are sprinkled with water to make them flexible. Then they are struck with wooden hammers in a stone hole called a gurno, in effect a large mortar. During the work, Abdalla says, "men often want to show off in front of their wives and strike the grain with all their might. The hosts' daughters prepare meals for their hard-working parents and at leisure time encourage their fathers. This stage of bulgur preparation is very colorful and truly folkloristic. It is often accompanied by folk songs sung by the children."

One such song was recorded in Syria in 1972:

Himma u haye, himma u ha, Come girls, come ha . . . The girls have run and have come! They gathered around bulgur in silence. They rolled up their sleeves and stood ready. They looked more beautiful to the eyes of the boys. Himmu u haye, strike ha.

After the grain is pounded, it is sun-dried again, to facilitate shelling and to enhance its nutty taste. Eventually, the grain is winnowed: cupfuls are poured on the ground and the wind blows away the bran. Finally, the grain is cracked in a quern, a sort of primitive mill consisting of a stationary stone and a movable stone. The cracked grain is sieved so as to separate it into three grades of fineness.

You can buy it at the supermarket. *Himme u ha.*

1 pound lamb from the thick part of the leg, with skin, fat, and tendons removed	$^2/_3$ cup fine bulghur
1 small onion, peeled	1 quart lightly salted water
1 handful fresh basil or mint leaves	Olive oil
2 teaspoons ground cinnamon	Pine nuts
2 teaspoons ground allspice	Scallions, trimmed
½ teaspoon finely ground black pepper	Sprigs mint
Salt	

1. Process the lamb to the consistency of hamburger. Set aside.
2. Process the onion and basil or mint leaves until they make a smooth paste. Add the lamb, cinnamon, allspice, pepper, and salt. Process until smooth but no more. Overprocessing will eliminate the pink color.
3. Put the meat in a mixing bowl.

4. Put the bulghur in another bowl. Pour in some of the salted water, enough to cover the grain. Drain and repeat twice more. Drain well and add to the meat.

5. Mix together with your hands and then knead for a few minutes, until smooth. Periodically moisten your hands and the kibbeh with the salted water.

6. Taste and adjust the seasoning. Then pull a serrated knife through the kibbeh to remove any remaining gristle. Continue until no more gristle appears on the knife.

7. Transfer the kibbeh to a serving plate. Shape it into a flat, shallow circular cake.

8. Run a finger along the center of the meat to make a shallow trough. Make two other troughs on either side of the first one. Pour a little olive oil into each trough. Scatter the surface of the kibbeh with pine nuts. Decorate the platter with scallions and mint sprigs. And serve immediately.

4 servings

Lamb Biryani
(Indian Lamb and Rice Ragout)

Like most of the standard Indian main dishes, *biryani* is a method of cooking; you might even call it a concept. Some meat or vegetable is parcooked with spices. A substantial amount of rice is also parcooked. Next the meat or vegetable is spread in a layer at the bottom of a casserole, the rice put over it, and finally saffron and milk go on top. This is a rich festive dish brought to India by the Persian Mogul conquerors. Its distinctive features include the two-track preparation, the final cooking of rice and meat together, and the saffron-milk braising liquid added at the end.

Other familiar Indian dishes rarely explained on menus are also distinctive approaches to food rather than specific recipes named for their principal ingredients (e.g., veal birds or duck in orange sauce).

Here is a brief analytic lexicon of common Indian "concept" dishes:

BHOONA (OR BHUNA). Stir-frying. It begins with the frying of spices mixed with a bit of water, replenished as necessary to keep the spices from burning. Meat or vegetables are then added, and the heat is lowered. At the end, high heat boils off any liquid. Bhoonas have no sauce.

DOPIAZA. A Muslim method from Bengal, the word means double onion, because onions are added to it twice, in the initial sauce and then later.

JALFREZI. Leftover meat reheated with hot spices.

KHEEMA. Ground meat.

KORMA. Braising. Meat is browned, then cooked with a small amount of liquid in a sealed pot. A Mogul dish, therefore often rich and creamy with almonds or cashews.

VINDALOO. Meat cooked with vinegar and garlic. Highly spiced. A legacy of the Portuguese presence in Goa.

These are some of the basic categories. But they are not rigid concepts, and in practice they are combined. *Bhoona*-cooked food is often embellished further. And I recently learned about a *kheema biryani,* made with ground mutton. I made this discovery on the leading Pakistani Web site, Pakwatan.com, which has an interesting food page. It was a useful reminder that we too often speak glibly of Indian food as if it were a monolithic system confined within the political borders of India, when actually the foods that most diaspora "Indian" restaurants prepare with the methods discussed above are native to three countries, India, Pakistan, and Bangladesh, countries with large Muslim populations descended from the Moguls and still eating their food.

1 cup basmati rice	½ teaspoon ground nutmeg
1 pound lamb, cut in 1½-inch cubes	½ teaspoon ground cardamom
1 tablespoon minced fresh ginger	½ teaspoon caraway seeds
1 tablespoon minced garlic	One 1-inch stick cinnamon
Salt	1 teaspoon finely chopped mint leaves
1 onion, peeled and sliced	2 fresh green chilies, finely chopped
1 tablespoon raisins, plumped in hot water	1 tablespoon lemon juice
3 tablespoons ghee (or clarified butter)	¼ cup yogurt
4 cups water	1 pinch saffron
	¼ cup milk

1. Soak the rice while you prepare the other ingredients.
2. Rub the lamb cubes all over with a paste made by pureeing the minced ginger and garlic with the salt in a mortar or a mini-processor. Cover and let marinate for an hour.
3. Sauté the onion slices and the raisins in a tablespoon of the ghee in a heavy, six-cup saucepan, so as to produce nicely browned rings. Set aside. Then brown the meat cubes and leave them in the saucepan.
4. Bring 4 cups of water to a boil. Drain the rice and cook it in the water, at a full boil until just softened but not fully cooked, 5 to 10 minutes. Drain and reserve.
5. Combine the meat with the nutmeg, cardamom, caraway seeds, cinnamon, mint leaves, and the chilies, half the onion, the lemon juice, and the yogurt in a layer that covers the bottom of the saucepan. Cover with the rice. Sprinkle with the saffron, the rest of the onion, and the raisins. Drizzle with the remaining ghee. Then pour on the milk.
6. Cover, set over medium-high heat, and cook until the ghee sizzles audibly. Continue cooking for 3 to 5 minutes, until the rice is soft. Stir together and serve.

Serves 2 to 4, depending on the other dishes served

Lasagne al Forno
(Bolognese Baked Wide Flat Noodles)

Lasagne, as everyone knows, is a dish of wide flat noodles, sometimes green from spinach (*lasagne verdi*), sometimes with ruffled edges (*lasagne ricce*). The classic, austere verson from Bologna alternates layers of lasagne with meat sauce (*ragù*) and béchamel. I am giving a more exuberant example below. There are many others, including the *lasagne di vigilia,* Christmas Eve lasagne, involving very wide noodles that remind the faithful of the baby Jesus's swaddling clothes.

Lasagne (Lasagna is the singular but it is almost never used. Ditto for other pasta types: who would ever lapse into speaking of a single spaghetto, except in humor) is first and foremost a noodle, not a specific dish. It may be the primordial Italian pasta noodle, or at least the oldest known word in the modern pasta vocabulary. In one way or another, lasagne seems to derive from the classical Latin *laganum.* But what was *laganum?* Something made of flour and oil, a cake. The word itself derived from a Greek word for chamber pot, which was humorously applied to cooking pots. And like many other, better-known cases of synecdochical food names,* the container came to stand for the thing it contained. And eventually, by a process no one knows with any certainty, *laganum* emerged as a word for a flat noodle in very early modern, southern Italy.

If you are persuaded by all the evidence collected by Clifford A. Wright (cliffordawright.com/history/macaroni.html), you will be ready to believe that in Sicily, an Arab noodle cuisine collided with the Italian kitchen vocabulary and co-opted *laganum* and its variant *lasanon* to describe the new "cakes" coming in from North Africa.

Would you be happier about this theory if you had evidence of a survival of an "oriental" Arab pasta in Sicily? Mary Taylor Simeti provides one in *Pomp and Sustenance, Twenty-Five Centuries of Sicilian Food* (1989). *Sciabbò*, a Christmas noodle dish eaten in Enna in central Sicily combines ruffled lasagne (*sciabbò* [indat French for a ruffled shirtfront]) with cinnamon and sugar, typical Near Eastern spices then and now.

* Terrine, tagine, timbale, Jell-O mold.

½ pound ground beef	4 cups tomato puree
¼ cup milk	6 ounces tomato paste
2 tablespoons chopped flat-leaf parsley	6 quarts water
Salt	1 pound lasagne
Pepper	¾ pound mozzarella cheese, sliced thin and
2 tablespoons olive oil	then cut in ¼-inch strips
1 large onion, peeled and finely chopped	1¼ pounds ricotta cheese
2 cloves garlic, peeled and finely chopped	1¼ cups grated Parmesean cheese

1. In a mixing bowl, stir together the beef, milk, parsley, salt, and pepper. Form into balls the size of olives.

2. Heat 2 tablespoons of olive oil in a skillet and brown the meatballs a few at a time. Drain and reserve.

3. In the same skillet, add the onion and garlic and sauté until the onion is lightly browned. Then stir in the tomatoes and tomato paste. Simmer for 15 minutes.

4. Bring 6 quarts of water to a boil in a large pot.

5. Add the meatballs to the tomato mixture from step 3 and continue cooking for another 30 minutes.

6. Meanwhile, liberally salt the boiling water and add the lasagne. Cook until al dente, about 10 minutes. Drain in a colander.

7. Preheat the oven to 350 degrees.

8. In a shallow ovenproof pan, roughly 12 by 9 by 2 inches, spread a thin layer of the sauce (no meatballs) from step 5. Then spread a layer of overlapping lasagne one strip thick (don't let the strips run up the side of the dish). Cover that with mozzarella slices and then 5 tablespoons ricotta. Sprinkle with the Parmesan and then spread on a quarter of the sauce *and* meatballs. Begin again with a layer of lasagne and continue as above until all the ingredients are used up, ending with the Parmesan cheese.

9. Bake for 20 minutes. If the cheese on top hasn't melted, run under the broiler briefly. Then let the dish rest at room temperature for a few minutes.

Serves 6

Macaroni and Cheese

An entire book could be written about this deceptively simple all-American dish. The first chapter would trace the origin of macaroni to a Sicilian dialect term from the Middle Ages, showing its probable connection with medieval Arab cookery and taking another swipe at the myth of Marco Polo as the Johnny Appleseed of pasta. Chapter 2 would look at Italian antecedents of our mac and cheese, since it must have begun as a transplant of some recipe for *maccheroni al forno,* baked elbow macaroni.

It is not hard to find such a recipe in modern Italian cookbooks. For example, in *L'Antiartusi* (1978), in Anna Maria Dell'Osso's recipe from the restaurant Bernalda in Matera, a town in the poor, isolated Basilicata region at the instep of Italy's boot, you will find tubular macaroni (*pasta bucata*) and a quarter pound of grated cheese (Parmesan). There is also a *soffrito* of tomato, oil, garlic, and spices. No white sauce and certainly none of the "inventive" ingredients that celebrity chefs in North America add to the dish today, when they want to pretend they have the common touch but can't quite get down.

The Italian original (or some modest variation of it) found its way into the hearts and minds of American cooks at some point in the later nineteenth century. The new "tradition" split into two great streams, both flowing thickly with American cheese, often of the processed variety. In one stream, the cooked macaroni are topped with a cheese-béchamel sauce and baked with bread crumbs on top. In his *Simple Cookery* (1989), John Thorne dismisses this as "macaroni with cheese sauce" and blusters that "every cookbook in which it appears should be thrown out the window."*

The other style mixes the macaroni with an egg-cheese custard.

Mr. Thorne dazzled his readers with a third way, a custard macaroni and cheese that is stirred several times while it bakes. It is a fine, if fussy, method, which Mr. Thorne came upon in *The Home Comfort Cook Book,* published in 1937 by the Wrought Iron Range Company as a handout to purchasers of the Home Comfort wood-burning kitchen stove. His mother "adapted" it for the Thorne dinner table (he doesn't say how) and then Thorne himself

---

* Fortunately, the testy Mr. Thorne wrote those words from his eremitical refuge in Vermont, where a defenestrated book carries less menace to innocent bystanders than it would if tossed from a Manhattan penthouse (see page 121).

"adapted" it (he doesn't say how) for his readers. The final stage of this saga occurred in the meticulous, not to say pedantic, test kitchen of *Cook's Illustrated* magazine. *CI*'s editors preferred the Home Comfort/Thorne method but corrected its main flaws: It took 20 minutes in the oven and came out tepid. At *CI*, they discovered you could collapse all that stirring and oven-door banging into 5 minutes of stove-top "baking."Here is a recipe that combines the best of the best, a creamy white sauce with plenty of cheese custard, all of it stirred together and briefly finished in the oven. Call it consensus mac and cheese. And if you want a Proustian jolt of school cafeteria *déjà gouté,* be sure to hunt up some Velveeta.

3 quarts water	3 tablespoons flour
Salt	1 cup half and half
½ pound elbow macaroni	2 eggs
1 cup bread crumbs	Pepper
8 tablespoons butter	Cayenne
2¾ cups grated American processed cheese or mild Cheddar	

1. Bring 3 quarts of lightly salted water to a boil. Pour in the macaroni and cook, uncovered, for about 10 minutes or until al dente. Meanwhile sauté the bread crumbs in 2 tablespoons of the butter until lightly browned. Let cool. Then stir in ¼ cup of the grated cheese.

2. Make a white sauce: Melt 2 tablespoons butter in a small skillet. When the foam subsides, whisk in the flour until blended. Whisk in the half and half and continue whisking until thick and sleek. Whisk in the eggs, salt, pepper, and cayenne to taste, and the remaining 2½ cups cheese.

3. When the macaroni is cooked, drain and return to the pot over low-medium heat. Toss with the remaining 4 tablespoons butter until the butter melts and coats the macaroni. Pour the egg mixture over the noodles and stir until the cheese melts. Stir for a few minutes until the mixture is creamy.

4. Pour into a 9 by 9-inch baking dish. Spread the bread crumbs over the top and broil briefly, 6 inches from the broiler, just long enough to brown the top.

5. Remove from the oven and give it a few minutes to solidify. Serve while still hot.

Serves 6

Macaroons

I bite into a macaroon. It clings deliciously to my teeth, the perfect end to any meal. That meal could be an interminable Passover seder. Or it could be a brisk lunch in the Stanford White dining room of a mid-Manhattan club whose name I am forbidden to mention in print.

Macaroons fit any situation. But where and how did they start? From the name, we are led straight to Italy, even though modern Italian dictionaries don't mention them. That's because the word goes back to an archaic verb *maccare,* meaning to grind or pound. This makes sense, since the standard macaroon until the twentieth century was based on almonds pounded in a mortar. Chocolate and a whole rainbow of other flavors are now common in professionally baked macaroons. But the best and the first recipe, authoritatively traced to Renaissance Venice by Antonio Piccinardi in his *Dizionario di Gastronomia* (1993), is a confection of ground almonds, egg whites, and sugar. Venice, with its links to Constantinople, may have acquired the recipe from the Middle East.

In modern Italy, bakers from Sardinia to Liguria add bitter almonds (the almond-like seeds found inside apricot pits) to this mixture, to produce amaretti (from *amaro* or bitter). Italy also has regional macaroon varieties, ranging from the tiny, almond-shaped treats of Salsomaggiore near Parma to the pine-nutted *pinoccate* served at Christmas and Epiphany in Perugia. Jews, no doubt those living in the original ghetto in Venice, embraced the macaroon for Passover because it is flourless and satisfies the holiday's prohibition against leavened bread and other foodstuffs that might be confused with it and are spontaneously leavened by airborne yeasts. In England, macaroons with bitter almonds have been called ratafias, and crumbled macaroons are ingredients for traditional English trifles and syllabubs.

The ideal macaroon, whatever its flavoring, should be thinly crusted on top with shallow little fissures everywhere, but sublimely chewy inside. I like mine to have the same diameter as a fifty-cent piece (remember them!), but size mustn't matter with macaroons, texture rules.

1½ cups blanched almonds	Salt
1 cup sugar	Confectioners' sugar for dusting
1 jumbo egg white or 2 large egg whites	

1. Preheat the oven to 300 degrees. Butter a cookie sheet.

2. Grind the almonds fine in an electric coffee grinder (a carefully cleaned electric coffee grinder), turning it rapidly off and on to prevent turning the almonds into a paste. Or, if you have one, use a hand nut grinder.

3. In a mixing bowl, beat together the ground almonds and the sugar. Then beat in the egg white and a pinch of salt.

4. Divide the mixture into twenty-four equal pieces and roll them into balls. Space them on the cookie sheet and then tap them with the back of a spoon to flatten them a bit. Dust with confectioners' sugar.

5. Bake the macaroons in the middle level of the oven for 12 minutes or until they have just begun to brown. Cool on a rack and store, unrefrigerated, in a cookie tin.

Around 24 macaroons

Maiale in Latte
(Italian Pork Roast in Milk)

This brilliant Italian dish begins with pork half-submerged in milk. In the course of long cooking, the milk breaks down into a dark and delicious sauce, whose main character comes from the browned milk solids that remain after most of the water in the milk has boiled away. The roast picks up a delicious crust along the way and remains moist inside.

In Sumatra, there is a similar dish, *rendang,* which stews water buffalo in coconut milk. After a time, the white coconut milk breaks down into a clear oil and the meat cooks and browns very much as pork roast does in cow's milk. In the interest of practicality, I am not giving a recipe for *rendang,* but perhaps there is a basis here for future research into cultural similarities between Bologna and Palembang.

1 tablespoon butter	4 coriander seeds
1½ pounds boned pork shoulder, tightly tied	2 tablespoons finely chopped ham
Salt	1 onion, peeled and very finely chopped
Pepper	3 to 3½ cups milk
1 clove garlic, peeled	

1. Melt the butter in a heavy saucepan slightly larger than the pork. Rub the pork all over with salt and pepper. Push the garlic clove into the center of the rolled meat, along with the coriander seeds.

2. Brown the pork on all sides in the butter. Add the ham and onion and lightly brown.

3. Bring the milk to the boiling point, but stop there, before it foams up and erupts. Pour over the pork and cook for about an hour and a half, uncovered. The milk should bubble noticeably. Turn the meat and baste from time to time. After about an hour, stir the skin on the surface of the milk back into the milk once or twice, scraping it from the sides of the pot. After another half hour, the milk will have reduced markedly and converted into a nice brown sauce with toasted milk solids in it. Cut off the string from the pork and discard.

4. Place the roast on a serving platter. Slice and serve with its sauce.

6 to 8 servings

Marmalade

This is an adaptation of Alan Davidson's recipe. In addition to being the world's leading expert on sea fish, an aficionado of screwball comedy in the movies, and a founding chairman of the Oxford Symposium on Food and Cookery, he makes 75 pounds of marmalade a year in London. As he points out in his authoritative *Oxford Companion to Food* (1999), marmalade went through a cosmopolitan and labyrinthine evolution before it took its current, essentially British, form.

The word and the conserve began in Portugal, where a sweet, solid quince paste was called *marmelada*. By 1500, it had reached England, where it was called quiddony (in France, it was and is *cotignac*). From then until the eighteenth century, Davidson (following the research of C. Anne Wilson, the Boswell of marmalade) explains, various other fruits, including those of the citrus family, were made into similar, nonviscous preserves, all called marmalade, and all intended to be cut into eatable pieces and consumed as finger food.

The earliest spreadable marmalades—jellies with bits of citrus peel or other fruit in them—began to appear in the eighteenth century but did not take over the market from the solid pastes until the price of sugar plummeted in the late nineteenth century. Soon it acquired a special English stamp, reconquering the British Empire and taking over the world market. Many fruits are still marmeladized but orange is the standard. All sorts of oranges are used, even in England, but the acid Seville orange is the traditional variety.

5 pounds Seville oranges (bitter or bigarade oranges, sold in U.S. Hispanic markets and *botanicas* as *naranjas agrias*)	1 lemon Sugar (for amount, see below)

1. Wash the oranges and the lemon. Remove the little rosettes at the stem end and clean out any foreign matter. Chop the fruits (unpeeled) by hand or machine, but not too finely.
2. Put the chopped fruit (including the peel) in a large pan with water to cover and to spare (see Note). Bring to a boil and cook, uncovered, for 20 to 30 minutes or until reduced by a third.
3. Measure the result and return to the heat. For every 575 milliliters (if your measuring cup isn't graduated metrically—most glass ones are today—then figure that 2.43 [a little less

than 2½] U.S. cups is the closest practical equivalent), add 1 pound sugar, gradually, stirring until dissolved. Return to a boil and continue cooking until a small amount of the mixture sets readily in a room-temperature saucer or until a candy thermometer reads 222 degrees. Remove from the heat immediately and let stand for 5 to 10 minutes.

4.   Stir, then ladle into clean jars. Fill them very nearly full. Ensure that the top surface is level—no chunks of peel sticking up. Float a little alcohol, such as brandy, over the top if you wish, as a preservative measure.

5.   Seal by whatever means you prefer. Davidson uses screw-top jars and screws the tops on tight once the marmalade has cooled to just warm.

Note: *As Davidson points out, the precise quantity of water is not crucial, since the final boiling of the marmalade will reduce the mixture to the correct balance of water and sugar, the sign of this being either a temperature reading of 222 degrees or the capacity of the mixture to set.*

Mashed Potatoes

By a chain of circumstances too trivial to bother rehearsing now, I found myself in the dining room of the Auberge de l'Ill in Alsace with my two-year-old son Michael in the spring of 1967, on the very day that the restaurant received its third Michelin star. I hadn't intended to bring Michael along, but when Chef Haeberlin heard that he'd been left with his mother in the hotel, he insisted that I go get them.

But what did he intend to serve Michael? This was a place renowned for its *foie gras en brioche* and stag St. Hubert, not foods for a toddler. The chef, a parent himself, knew that well. First he sent out poached eggs, twin suns nestled in cumulus clouds. Michael looked at them with obvious delight and said: "Apricots."

It was an impressive observation, visually accurate and a sign of a large vocabulary in one so young. The next course taxed my own vocabulary. Haeberlin had announced he would make a mousseline. A muslin?

From a kitchen feverish with excitement over the sudden attention of the world came silken mashed potatoes worthy of their elegant French name, *pommes de terre mousseline*. I try to think of that moment whenever I hear adults clucking about their children's unadventuresome palates. A great chef knew that epicures are not born but bred, slowly. I also like to think of that day as a reminder of how fusion cuisine began long before someone made chipotle mayonnaise in a mall south of L.A.

On its native ground, high up in the Andes, the potato was not traditionally mashed. Descendants of the indigenous peoples dehydrated their tubers in the mountain air, so they would keep forever and didn't weigh much. Rehydrated, *papas secas* go in soup or get chopped and fried. You do not find mashed potatoes in Cuzco next to your *cuy chactado*.*

But when the first round of globalization, d/b/a the Spanish Empire, brought potatoes to Europe, it didn't take long before cooks were boiling them until soft and then crushing them into a puree. The same civilization that had crushed a hemisphere took easily to turning hard tubers and other fleshy vegetables into malleable pastes smoothed out and improved in taste with fat.

You can tell that I am not one of those who admire lumpy mashed potatoes. I hold with

* Split grilled guinea pig, head still attached.

This was a place renowned for its *foie gras en brioche* and stag St. Hubert, not foods for a toddler. The chef, a parent himself, knew that well. First he sent out poached eggs, twin suns nestled in cumulus clouds. Michael looked at them with obvious delight and said: "Apricots."

Roy Finamore and Georges Blanc, godfathers of this recipe, in wanting to manipulate the potato so that it will remind us as little as possible of its solid, starchy, gluey nature. "Cook over matter" is my motto.

2 pounds Yukon gold or russet potatoes, peeled and cut in quarters (or eighths if the potatoes are very large) Salt	10 tablespoons butter, at room temperature 1 cup heavy cream, approximately White pepper Duck or goose fat, optional

1. In a large, nonaluminum pot, cover the potatoes generously with cold water. Toss in as much salt as you can grab with the fingers of one hand. Bring to a boil and reduce the heat so as to produce a gentle bubbling.

2. When a fork slides easily into the largest potato chunk (start testing after 15 minutes of boiling), drain in a colander and then return to the pot. Stir the potatoes over medium heat to steam out excess moisture. The mashing comes later: You are interested here only in a relatively brief exposure to mild heat. Remove from the heat when you notice a thin layer of potatoes collecting on the bottom of the pan.

3. Dump the potatoes into a mixing bowl. Then put them through a ricer (hand mashers and food mills do not do the job as easily or as well; food processors tend to produce library paste) held over a clean saucepan.

4. Put the riced potatoes over low heat and beat in the butter, cut in small pieces, with a wooden spoon. When the butter has all melted and merged with the potato, start beating in the cream, a quarter cup or so at a time. Continue adding the cream until you have the consistency you want. More cream makes for silkier, lighter, looser, richer mashed potatoes.

5. You can stop here, after seasoning with salt and white pepper (black pepper will leave black specks in your pure white puree) and serve while still warm (this dish is not improved by holding, even in a double boiler, for long periods). But if you want to get the smoothest possible result, push the puree through a drum sieve (tamis) and, for an extra dollop of richness, melt in a couple of tablespoons or so of duck or goose fat.

Serves 6

Mayonnaise

Of all the emulsified sauces, mayonnaise is the easiest to make, has the most applications, and is the most universally known. Unfortunately, its popularity is based on the completely inauthentic bottled by-blow sold as mayonnaise in supermarkets. You can tell it is not real mayonnaise because it is white and keeps almost forever if refrigerated. It also doesn't taste or handle like real mayonnaise, which is a short-lived, yellow, trembling suspension of oil in egg yolk.

The farouche English food writer Elizabeth David once wrote an essay attacking bottled mayonnaise and the chef who invented it. I have no such quarrel with Hellman's or its congeners. On a BLT, why not? Of course, you can do much better by making an exalted version of the classic sandwich with real bread, garden tomatoes, and lettuce—and your own mayonnaise.

Some people won't eat real mayonnaise anymore because they fear that the raw egg yolks in it may be contaminated by salmonella. For me, the tiny risk of death by mayo is no more frightening than the prospect that someday I may walk out of the house and be hit by a set of barbells falling from a window overhead.*

Mayonnaise, if grossly mishandled, can curdle or break. This happens when someone in a rush tries to beat a very large amount of oil abruptly into the yolks. Slow and steady wins the game here, especially as the first of the oil is added. Ignoring this easy requirement puts too much pressure on the surface tension of the yolk and, *voilà,* you have to try to recover your sauce by whisking a bit of hot water into a small amount of the spoiled sauce and then carefully whisking back in the rest.

Two *trucs:* Use fresh eggs, whose yolks are better at absorbing oil. And don't hesitate to

---

* This actually happened to my parents' friend Alvin M. Rodecker, who, on a visit from Detroit to New York in the summer of 1960, was strolling up (or perhaps down) Park Avenue when weights accidentally pushed out of the window of Arlene Francis's apartment, allegedly by a cleaning lady, killed him. It made the papers because Miss Francis was a panelist on the popular TV quiz show *What's My Line?* Whether the weights belonged to her or her husband, the actor Martin Gabel (whose surname means "fork" in German and therefore justifies the inclusion of this anecdote in a cookbook), was not reported. I prefer to think that both of these celebrities liked to work out with those barbells and were quarreling over whose turn it was when their struggle turned physical and ended up widowing Catherine Rodecker.

put a little mustard in at the start. It improves the chemical underpinnings of the operation, and contributes a nice spiky taste to boot.

Are you wondering where the name *mayonnaise* came from? You are in good company. Antonin Carême, the Newton of haute cuisine, rejected the various etymologies current in his day (the early nineteenth century). The leading candidates then were all geographic designations. Carême reasoned thus: Since a great many other sauces had spurious geography in their names, mayonnaise probably ought to have a similar pseudo-regional appellation. The trouble was there is no Mayon or Mayonne. So, before Carême considered the problem, other gastropundits had flailed about and come up with Bayonne (bayonnaise>mayonnaise), the ham-producing town in southwest France and Port Mahon (mahonnaise>mayonnaise) in Minorca.

Backers of the Mahon option went on to credit the duc de Richelieu, grandnephew of the nemesis of the Four Musketeers, with the invention of Mayonnaise, because he had conquered the Mediterranean island of Minorca, after crushing its capital, Port Mahón, in 1756. By legend, Richelieu invented mayonnaise under battle conditions when a cold condiment was all that was feasible (this fable resembles the possibly true tale that Napoleon's cook Dunand invented chicken Marengo on the battlefield after the French victory over the Austrians on June 14, 1800, at the village of Marengo in the Piedmont region of northern Italy).[*]

Carême, showing his ability to think outside the box, decided mayonnaise must have started out not as a phony geographic provenance but as *magnonaise,* from the verb *manier,* to handle or manipulate, on the theory that mayonnaise did get manipulated. But as Prosper Montagné pointed out in *Larousse Gastronomique* (1938), you could say the same thing about almost all sauces. For his part, Montagné reached back to the early days of the French language and found an obsolete word for egg yolk, *moyeu,* which, he speculated, gave its name to a sauce originally called *moyeunnaise.*

[*] As was his custom, Napoleon took no food at Marengo until after the battle was decided. The supply wagons were too far away to be used for the quick dinner he demanded; so Dunand had to forage. He located three eggs, four tomatoes, six crayfish, a small chicken, some garlic, a little oil, and a pot. With these ingredients he improvised chicken Marengo: a chicken sautéed in oil with garlic and tomato, garnished with fried eggs and the crayfish. It was really a turn on chicken à la provençale, with eggs and crayfish added. Napoleon, the legend goes, loved it and ordered Dunand to make it after all future battles. Somewhat later on, when a better-supplied Dunand added wine and substituted mushrooms for the crayfish, Napoleon exploded. "You have suppressed the crayfish," he said. "It will bring me bad luck. I don't want any."

So the crayfish became traditional in Marengo dishes, at least those following the real tradition, not the majority of chicken Marengos, which are served without egg and are crayfishless.

In all this dithering, why has no one come up with the obvious origin for the name? It simply must be Mayenne. Mayenne? Yes, La Mayenne, the French *département* south of Normandy, which is named, like most *départements,* after the river that runs through it,[*] the Mayenne. There is also a town called Mayenne, in La Mayenne, on the banks of the Mayenne. So I propose Mayenne>mayennaise>mayonnaise.

1 egg yolk	1 teaspoon Dijon mustard
1 teaspoon vinegar or lemon juice	1 cup oil, approximately
Salt	1 tablespoon hot water
Pepper	

1. Whisk together the egg yolk, vinegar or lemon juice, salt, pepper, and mustard.
2. Whisk in the oil a drop at a time. After a time, the mayonnaise will "take," gaining body and coalescing into a recognizable mayonnaise. Then, you can begin whisking in the oil at a faster pace, whisking all the while. Continue until all the oil has been used up. To stabilize the mayonnaise for storage, whisk in a tablespoon of hot water. Even then, avoid storing the mayonnaise for more than a couple days, covered, in the rerigerator. To reuse, whisk briefly and let return to room temperature.

About 1 cup

[*] Sixty-eight of ninety-five, plus one river source (Vaucluse, from the Fontaine de Vaucluse, source of the Sorgue), one gulf (Morbihan), and one (English) channel (Manche). Most of the others are named after mountains.

Meat Loaf

I hadn't expected to find an entry on meat loaf in Alan Davidson's magisterial *Oxford Companion to Food* (1999). Indeed, I only looked it up there so I could say that meat loaf was a great and ubiquitous dish that everyone snubbed. Meat loaf, I intended to say, is a kind of joke. In fact, I can think of two funny things about meat loaf right off the top of my head. One is an off-color parting wish you have already remembered. The other is a rock star, the Texan known as Meat Loaf, who once was referred to in an important newspaper as Mr. Loaf.

Alan Davidson let me down. He had plenty to say about meat loaf, the food. Viz.: ". . . a dish whose visibility is considerably higher in real life, especially in N. America and Britain, than in cookery books. This situation might be changed if it had a French name (*pâté chaud de viande hachée, préalablement marinée dans du vin de pays et des aromatiques*), but it does not. In the United States the term was only recorded in print from 1899, in Britain not until 1939 (although liver loaf and ham loaf occurred earlier). The use of 'loaf' is particularly appropriate as most recipes include bread, usually in the form of soft breadcrumbs. Also, it is shaped like a loaf and may indeed be baked in a loaf tin or something similar. A worthy dish, which can embody the sort of rusticity which the word 'peasant' evokes, but can also exhibit the kind of refinement associated with bourgeois cookery. Its range, however, does not extend into the realm of haute cuisine.

"The editors of the *OED* assert that meat loaf is usually eaten cold in slices."

As much as I love the thought of the editors of the *Oxford English Dictionary* sitting down in their palatial offices and tucking into some sliced cold meat loaf, I think they should take a break from their lucubrations and try hot meat loaf with gravy in a Greek diner on Route 17 in New Jersey, or maybe a meat loaf sandwich. As for my friend Davidson, I'm not sure why he doesn't give the French a break here. *Larousse Gastronomique* (1938), in its lengthy and earnest two pages on *hachis,* a category that includes everything chopped from hamburger to lobster hash (the operative cognate), gives many fine examples of chopped meat concoctions served in various kinds of molded forms, primarily the truncated cone called timbale, from the drum it resembles, but not neglecting various earthenware containers. They have a way to go over there in the meat loaf department, but you can't fault them for trying.

I owe this recipe to the most ardent meat loafer I know, Susan Ruth Friedland, a native

New Yorker and my editor, for her sins, on this book. Susan is the Escoffier of meat loaf and the Lucullus of publishing. Blame her if you don't like this meat loaf.

2 pounds ground beef

Meat from 3 hot Italian sausages (squeezed from casings)

½ pound ground veal

1 to 2 teaspoons salt

½ cup freshly grated Parmesan cheese

1 cup bread crumbs

3 garlic cloves, minced

1 cup minced onion

½ cup minced parsley

1 teaspoon crushed rosemary or ground marjoram

1 teaspoon freshly ground black pepper

3 to 4 eggs, lightly beaten

Peel of 1 lemon, grated

1. Preheat the oven to 425 degrees.
2. Combine all the ingredients with your scrupulously clean hands. Arrange in a standard 9¼ by 5¼ by 2¾-inch loaf pan lined with oiled aluminum foil and bake for 30 minutes.
3. Reduce the oven temperature to 350 degrees and continue to bake 30 minutes longer, basting with water as necessary. The meat loaf is done when an attractive brown crust has formed on top and the juices run clear.
4. Let the meat loaf stand for 10 minutes. Then grasp the top of the aluminum foil at both ends of the loaf and pull it out of the pan and onto a serving platter. Raise the loaf off the foil with a spatula and slip out the foil.
5. Serve with ketchup and/or the hot sauce or chutney of your choice. Like all meat loaves, this one is excellent eaten at room temperature.

Serves 6 to 8

Moules Marinière
(Mussels Steamed in Wine)

Mussels (*Mytilus spp.*) are a perfect food—cheap, good for you, tasty, versatile, and easy to cook. Why they are not part of the core foodways of the Anglophone tradition is open to speculation. My guess is that they did not compete well with oysters and clams when our culture was defining its tastes. Why? First, because they aren't appealing raw. Second, they had to be cleaned because of their "beards" and other attached debris. Third, in the past, even the not-so-distant past, oysters and clams were dirt cheap.

That doesn't explain why Belgians and Greeks and Turks have doted on them for centuries. The mussel "parks" where most of Europe's mussels are now cultivated (on elevated artificial perches or *bouchots* that allow cleaner and more efficient mussels to thrive above the mud their forebears inhabited) are descendants of medieval mytilicultural operations dating from the thirteenth century.

The modern mussel is sold precleaned. Since he is almost always served cooked, most of the risk you face in eating raw shellfish is eliminated, unless you are allergic to shellfish or an unscrupulous shipper has ignored reports of some marine plague infecting local mussel beds—a risk fortunately rarer than that of getting stabbed in the dark at the movies. Dead mussels are easy to spot—they don't open.

The most basic mussel recipe isn't even a recipe: just toss a few dozen on a grill and serve them with long tongs after they open and take on a smoky hue. Next in simplicity (perhaps first, on reflection, because you don't need to buy a barbecue or build a charcoal fire) is the North Sea specialty offered here. *Moules* are mussels in French. A *marinier* is a bargeman (*marin* is a sailor or seaman), which suggests a colorful origin for the dish (full name, *moules à la marinière*, literally mussels bargee-style), as a Belgian boatman's dinner.*

---

* Belgium brings out the worst in the French. If you think Frenchmen are anti-American, you should hear them sneer at their francophone neighbors. Baudelaire raised Belge-baiting to a high literary level. But non-poets love to substitute *Belge* for *bête*, when they want to say something is dumb *(c'est Belge)*. You can always get a laugh imitating a Belgian by saying the archaic *septante* or *nonante* instead of the standard French, nondecimal (and therefore pointlessly illogical) words for seventy and ninety (*huitante* for eighty survives only in Switzerland, where *septante* and *nonante* are also in use). And then there are the Belgian jokes.

Q. Why are there so many frites on the ground in Brussels?

A. Whenever one Belgian asks another the time . . . (the speaker now consults his watch, inevitably rotating his wrist and spilling an imaginary paper cone of French fries).

In Belgium, mussels with French fries (*moules frites*), washed down with one of the remarkable Belgian beers, is the unofficial national dish. Of course, there are dozens of variations on the basic dish. And if you tire of steamed mussels, there are soups (see Billi Bi, page 10) and a cookbook's worth of other recipes, from Levantine mussels cooked and stuffed back onto a half shell to mussel pie to Turkish mussels fried in a yeast batter.

But these culinary mussel exploits are for the day when you are bored with *moules marinière*. Meanwhile, don't leave out the celery, the secret ingredient that gives character to the broth.

2 quarts mussels	4 tablespoons butter
1 small onion, peeled and finely chopped	Pepper
2 large stalks celery, trimmed and cut in rounds	1½ cups white wine

1. If necessary, brush the mussels with a wire brush and pull at the hairy "beards" protruding from inside the shells until they come out. Rapidly wash in several changes of cold water. All of this is unnecessary with bagged, pretreated mussels. But either way, discard any mussels that are open or noticeably heavy with sand.

2. Put all the ingredients except the mussels in a large pot, bring to the boil, cover, reduce the heat, and simmer for 3 to 5 minutes, until the celery is softened.

3. Add the mussels, bring the liquid to the boil, cover, reduce the heat, and simmer for a few minutes, stirring every couple of minutes with a large spoon, until the mussels have opened.

4. Serve directly from the pot into large soup bowls. Sprinkle with parsley.

Serves 4

Moussaka
(Eggplant Baked with Ground Lamb)

Even the most chauvinist of Greek authors concede that this casserole of eggplant (*Solanum melongena* L.) and ground meat came to them (as did so much else) with the Ottoman occupation. Evidence on the ground supports this: Moussaka without the white-sauce topping prevalent in Greece is eaten throughout the Middle East, and called moussaka. And it is hard to see how such a dish would have spread from Greece to the rest of the Turkish empire, and then become simplified. In any case, moussaka is not a Greek word. The Turks brought "moussaka" to Athens from Egypt, where it is colloquial for "chilled." Perhaps it was originally eaten cold.

There is no fixed recipe. The full-dress Greek version can be respectably produced with lamb or beef or even veal, but lamb would seem to be the inevitable choice for a Middle Eastern dish. When did Greeks add tomatoes? Almost certainly after they had learned to make moussaka. Purists can simply eliminate the tomato, just as they can opt (as I have) for a yogurt-based white sauce. Then there is the matter of how to parcook the eggplant slices: fry or grill? Claudia Roden says grilled slices are lighter, but are they more delicious? She says yes; I disagree, but the huge amount of oil that eggplant absorbs in frying makes me line up with Ms. Roden.

The most fundamental question—where did moussaka start?—is easier to resolve. Eggplant itself originated in India. So it must have reached the Middle East through contact between Islamic and Indic cultures. The obvious mechanism for the eggplant diaspora was the Mogul (Persian) conquest of India in 1526. The ensuing migration of eggplant westward can be tracked linguistically, beginning with Hindi *brinjal,* evolving naturally into Arabic *al-berenjena,* which produced *aubergine* (French and then British English), *berengena* (Spanish), and *melanzana* (Italian).

That moussaka, so deeply rooted in the Islamic Middle East, should be known as Greek in the Christian West, is a small sign of the way Greece and the Balkans have served as a point of entry for a multifarious family of cuisines that merged during the Ottoman centuries but which are fundamentally either Turkish or were fused with Turkish food. This is the culinary side of an ironic fairy tale in which the culturally unoriginal post-Byzantine Greeks enjoy an unearned prestige in Europe, because of an ancient Greek civilization whose language they can no longer read and a cuisine they picked up from their Turkish masters.

2 pounds eggplants, unpeeled, but trimmed
       and cut in rounds about ½ inch thick

Salt

3 tablespoons oil

1 large onion, peeled and chopped

1½ pounds ground lamb

½ cup tomato puree

2 teaspoons ground cinnamon

2 teaspoons sugar

Pepper

3 tablespoons flat-leaf parsley, finely
       chopped

2 cups plain, whole milk yogurt

3 eggs, lightly beaten

¾ cup grated cheese (Gruyère, Cheddar, or
       kefalotyri)

Grated nutmeg

1. Put the eggplant slices in a large colander. Toss them in salt and let stand to drain for at least a half hour.

2. Heat 3 tablespoons oil in a large skillet. Brown the onion with the lamb. Stir in the tomato puree, cinnamon, sugar, and pepper to taste. Lower the heat and continue cooking until all the liquid evaporates. Stir in the parsley and let cool.

3. Rinse the eggplant slices; pat dry with a paper towel.

4. Grill or broil the eggplant slices until they are lightly browned.

5. Preheat the oven to 375 degrees.

6. In a bowl, whisk together all the remaining ingredients and season with salt and pepper.

7. Lightly oil the inside of a 10 by 14-inch ovenproof dish. Cover the bottom with a layer of half the eggplant slices. Then spread on it a layer of all the lamb mixture. Finally add the rest of the eggplant in an even layer. Pour the yogurt mixture over the top and bake in the oven for about 45 minutes until golden brown on top.

Serves 6 to 8

Navarin de Mouton Printanier
(Lamb Stew with Spring Vegetables)

Here is another example of the insidious Greek talent for getting credit they don't deserve. During the Greek war of independence, the combined armada of Britain, France, and Russia decimated the fleets of Turkey and Egypt at Navarino in 1827. In honor of this great victory, according to legend, a traditional French ragout of lamb and vegetables was named *navarin*.*

This is plain wrong. The *navarin* as such predates the battle. It was originally a ragout of lamb and turnips (*navets*), a real tradition that persists in non-lamb stews with turnips, which chefs also call *navarins*. When the lamb *navarin* includes spring vegetables as well as turnips, it is a *navarin printanier,* from the French *printemps,* spring.

Chalk one up for the lowly turnip. It gets no respect in France. Not only did the resident turcophobes try to steal its culinary thunder, but a whole nation of turnip-scorners diss the vegetable every time they sneer at a bad play or film. In the idiom of the French theater, a *navet* is a turkey.† And a weakling has turnip blood (*sang de navet*) in his veins.

Turnips deserve better. They particularly deserve better cooking that does not kill their subtle, peppery flavor. Turnips do not have to be dull. And in *navarin,* they attain their unpretentious apogee.

---

* This bogus piece of eurocentrism deserves a jihad. Thanks to Byron and a continent full of romantics with classical educations, freeing the Greeks from the Ottoman "yoke" became a fashionable cause in London and Paris. Moscow wanted to join the club, defending the original Orthodox Christian nation. And so they crushed the Ottoman navies in the Bay of Navarino. And where is Navarino? On the southwestern shore of the Peloponnese. The *Columbia Encyclopedia* identifies it succinctly: "Navarino (now Pylos)."

   Now Pylos!!! Please, you sleepy encyclopedists, try to remember your Homer. Pylos (now actually Pilos), invariably referred to in the *Iliad* as "sandy Pylos," was the home of Nestor, wisest of the Greeks at Troy. Navarino is its Italian name; so one effect of the battle was throwing off Italian imperialism.

† The American expression mocks the bird, not the country. A turkey was originally a pompous, strutting person, but came to be applied exclusively to ham acting, then to all stage embarrassments, and coming full circle, to people who are losers.

2 tablespoons oil

3 pounds stewing lamb (shoulder, breast, or neck), cut in 1½-inch cubes

Salt

Pepper

Sugar

2 tablespoons flour

4 cups water

2 sprigs parsley

1 bay leaf

1 clove garlic, peeled and smashed

2 tablespoons butter

15 pearl onions, peeled

20 cubes of potato, about the size of walnuts

20 inch-long chunks of carrot

20 pieces of white turnip cut to the size of the carrot pieces

½ pound peas

1. Heat the oil and brown the lamb pieces in it a few at a time. Season with salt, pepper, and a small amount of sugar. Reserve in a bowl.
2. Preheat the oven to 325 degrees.
3. Return all the lamb to the pot, sprinkle with the flour, toss over medium heat for a few minutes, then add 4 cups of water as well as the parsley, bay leaf, and garlic. Bring to a boil, cover, and cook in the oven for 45 minutes to an hour, until the meat is very tender.
4. Meanwhile, heat the butter in a small skillet and brown the onions in it.
5. Pour off the cooking liquid from the lamb and degrease.
6. Put the lamb and all the remaining ingredients in a clean large pot. Return to oven, cover, and cook until the potatoes and turnips are softened. Baste frequently. This dish, like most stews, improves overnight. The flavors balance and intensify; so you would ideally prepare a *navarin* a day in advance. It will keep several days in the refrigerator.

Serves 8

Omelet

Like many physical feats, making an omelet is all in the wrists. Or almost. In addition to the snap that makes the omelet slide, it helps to have a nonstick pan. Rubbing that pan with olive oil allows you to bring the surface to a higher heat than with butter alone.

Omelets are like ice cream in that they provide a basic texture that can merge with a very wide spectrum of flavors. The New York omelet restaurant Mme. Romaine de Lyon offered more than five hundred varieties. There is no single classic omelet, but the trinity of cheese, fines herbes, and mushrooms are the all-time favorites, and for good reason.

Salt

Pepper

3 large eggs, lightly beaten until the whites and yolks have blended

Olive oil

1 tablespoon unsalted butter, at room temperature, plus a little for rubbing on the finished omelet

FOR THE FILLING

4 teaspoons finely chopped parsley, tarragon, or chervil or 2 tablespoons grated Parmesan cheese or ½ cup roughly chopped mushrooms, sautéed in butter

1. Whisk a pinch of salt and a pinch of pepper into the beaten eggs.
2. Coat the bottom and sides of a 7-inch nonstick omelet pan with olive oil. Wipe off with paper towel.
3. Melt 1 tablespoon of butter in the omelet pan over high heat. When the foam subsides, but just before the butter browns, pour in the egg mixture so that it covers the bottom of the pan and set over high heat. Count to three.
4. Tilt the pan slightly and give it a sharp jerk. Do this once a second, three or four times, until the eggs have begun to thicken. Pour the filling over the middle of the omelet.
5. Tilt the pan up to a 45-degree angle, so that the omelet rolls over on itself at the far edge of the pan. Hold it there for a second to brown the bottom. Turn the omelet out onto a plate (tilting the plate and the omelet pan toward each other) so that the browned side of the omelet is on top. Rub with butter and serve.

Serves 1

Onion Soup

Onion soup is Holy Writ. Just ask anyone old enough to have made the midnight pilgrimage to Les Halles, the central market of Paris, to have a bowl of cheese-topped *soupe à l'oignon* under the giant iron and glass pavilions filled with produce being pushed around by burly fellows (*les forts des Halles*) who took time off from their work to mock tourists or couple with the *putes* hanging out nearby on the boulevard de Sébastopol.

Long since torn down, the market has moved out to suburban Rungis where no one has ever gone for fun, to be replaced by the Pompidou Center's forced post-industrial gaiety. Because of the cheese melted over it, the Halles-style onion soup is familiarly called a *gratinée*. I'm all for getting rid of that ropy yellow toupee and opting for unbrowned onions and chicken stock instead of the brawny darkness of the classic. But I will not try to impose this taste on you (the recipe is classic but offers options that will lead to a lighter soup).

You might also want to think about making a complete Halles meal, a real blast from the past, starting out with what habitués called "*un demi, demi,*" a half dozen snails and a glass of beer (in theory a half liter but normally much less).

3 tablespoons butter	Salt
1 pound onions, peeled and finely chopped	Pepper
12 slices of French bread, lightly toasted	¾ pound grated Gruyère cheese
2 quarts boiling beef or chicken stock	

1. Melt the butter in a medium skillet and when the foam subsides, add the chopped onions and sauté slowly until they become a confit, browned and converted almost to a jam (or alternatively, stop cooking when they are soft but not browned).

2. Preheat the oven to 400 degrees.

3. In a medium soup pot whose bottom will hold three bread slices in a single layer, add the bread slices in four overlapping layers. Pour on the hot beef stock (or chicken stock if you are using unbrowned onions and serve as is, without continuing on with this recipe), season briskly with salt and pepper, and then cover with an even layer of the grated cheese. Place in the oven, uncovered, and cook until the cheese melts and browns.

Serves 4 to 6

Osso Buco alla Milanese
(Milanese Veal Shanks)

Osso buco is Italian for marrow bone (*osso* = bone, *buco* = hole), but it's best to leave it untranslated. "Milanese marrow bone" doesn't begin to do justice to the grand, hefty thick slices of veal shank customary in a proper osso buco. The other day, I watched one of the Ottomanelli brothers, my neighborhood butchers in Greenwich Village, tie the meat up tightly around a whole shank before he sawed it into 2- and 3-inch sections. That was the only hard part in making the dish—and I just watched.

The white wine and stock you cook the meat-encircled bones in turns dark but needs to be reduced quite a bit, so you should be prepared to array the bones on a serving platter and keep them warm in a low oven at the end. While you are attending to the saffron Risotto alla Milanese (page 178), which does not improve if held.

So there is more to osso buco than knowing a good butcher of Italian heritage. Fancier people than I will take the trouble to cut away the string, which is no longer necessary to hold the meat together, but I don't like the extra fuss, and I think it does guests good to get a sense of how the trick was done. Then they won't make fools of themselves as an NYU professor did watching Mr. Ottomanelli and telling his friend to watch how the butcher was wrapping meat around the bone.

If you make osso buco a lot, you might want to acquire the long thin forks purpose-built for pulling out the marrow from the *buco*. A normal fork will do (lobster picks are even better), and you will not need more than that to eat the very tender meat, cooked just to the point where it might fall apart, but juicy from cooking in its own juices and the sauce they have turned into.

The tenderness of osso buco is the genius of the dish. There really isn't much fat in the meat of such a young animal, but it does have a good amount of collagen, a component of connective tissue that decomposes into gelatin and gives the osso buco sauce its body and contributes to its rich mouth feel. The meat itself does not turn stringy as a similar cut of beef would. The remarkable tenderness and smoothness is what the Italians mean when they say something is *morbido,* meltingly soft. *Morbidezza* has nothing at all to do with our word "morbidity." Think of it as refinement verging on decadence but holding the line. Then again, at the end of a meal of morbid osso buco and risotto, morbid in an entirely different way, you may not be in a position to make fine distinctions between delicacy and enervation.

2 tablespoons butter

2 tablespoons olive oil

6 large veal shank sections, about ½ pound
   each

   Flour

1 medium carrot, scraped and finely
   chopped

1 stalk celery, trimmed and finely chopped

1 medium onion, peeled and finely chopped

1 cup white wine

1 tablespoon tomato paste

   Salt

   Pepper

1 quart veal stock or water

GREMOLATA

1 clove garlic, peeled and finely chopped

1 tablespoon finely chopped parsley

   Grated zest from ½ lemon

1. Melt the butter in the oil over high heat. Meanwhile dredge the shank pieces in flour and, without delay, brown them in the butter-oil mixture, in batches, unless you are using a very large pot. Return the browned shanks to the pot, lower the heat to medium, and add the carrot, celery, and onion. Let them brown.

2. Then add the wine, tomato paste, salt, and pepper. Add enough stock or water to barely cover the shanks. Cover and cook slowly over low-medium heat for around 2 hours. Every 20 minutes, turn the shanks and baste them. Add a little water or broth to keep the level constant.

3. When the veal is fork-tender, serve with Risotto alla Milanese. If the liquid is too thin, remove the shanks and reduce the sauce until it is thick enough. When the veal is on the serving platter, sprinkle with the garlic, parsley, and grated lemon zest (the gremolata).

Serves 6

Oysters have not always been a luxury food. In fact, they were once so plentiful that the poor could afford them. They were an essential component of public life in the Gay Nineties. The San Francisco Tenderloin was awash in them. Yes, they were cheap, but high livers like Diamond Jim Brady consumed them by the macho bushel, eating large.

Oysters Rockefeller

For once in a blue moon, we really know the origin of a dish, when and where it was first made, who invented it, and why. Oysters Rockefeller were created in New Orleans in 1899 by Jules Alciatore, son of the eponymous founder of Antoine's Restaurant. What was he thinking? All the authorities agree that he picked the name because John D. Rockefeller, the Standard Oil tycoon, was the very image of a Gilded Age, overnight millionaire, a flint-hearted Croesus in a top hat. But was there a connection between the absent honoree and the recipe that went beyond their names? I think so, but not the one I've read, namely that the dish was as rich as Rockefeller.

I think there's a better explanation. On top of every oyster Rockefeller, there's a dab of spinach puree. Green, like money.

There's more.

Oysters have not always been a luxury food. In fact, they were once so plentiful that the poor could afford them. They were an essential component of public life in the Gay Nineties. The San Francisco Tenderloin was awash in them. Yes, they were cheap, but high livers like Diamond Jim Brady consumed them by the macho bushel, eating large. So calling a fancy dish oysters Rockefeller was a sort of oxymoron, putting a silk shirt on a Dead End Kid.

Now the tables have been turned. Elaborately cooked oysters are out of fashion. Rockefellers cultivate a retiring civic-mindedness. No one would associate J.D.'s banker grandson David with raffish display. But oysters Rockefeller are still a rich experience; the acid, fibrous spinach and the fatty bacon balance the oyster's brine and slipperiness. The presentation on rock salt is poetic.

This isn't a dish you want to make for crowds. No person alone ought to think about opening more than two dozen oysters. And even if you can hire someone to stand by at dinner with an open the shells, shucking them only till they curl, so they won't dry out, is precision work.

Rock salt	Pepper
1 dozen Bluepoint or Pacific oysters	6 cups well-washed spinach
3 pieces bacon	1 slice of stale white bread, coarsely
White part of 2 scallions, minced	processed
Salt	3 tablespoons grated Parmesan cheese

1. Preheat the broiler. Pour a thin layer of rock salt on the bottom of an ovenproof pan large enough to hold all the oysters.
2. Shuck the oysters, leaving them on the half shell. Discard the other half of the shells and pour off the liquid from the oysters into a bowl. Reserve the liquid and arrange the half-shell oysters on the rock salt, leveling them in the salt.
3. Render the bacon in a skillet. When the bacon has browned thoroughly, remove and drain on paper towel.
4. Pour off all but 2 tablespoons of the bacon grease. Add the scallions, salt, pepper, and spinach. Stir-fry until the spinach wilts. Transfer to a processor. Pulse with the bread crumbs and cheese to form a green paste. Dab a tablespoon on each oyster
5. Broil for 8 to 10 minutes, about 6 inches from the heat. The oysters are done when they begin to curl away from their shells.

Serves 4

Paella Valenciana
(Valencian Rice Casserole)

Paella may be the most misunderstood and most often badly cooked of the world's great dishes. There are several reasons for this unhappy state of affairs, reasons that, as Lourdes March, daughter of Valencia, cookbook author and rice savant, says, spring from the history and nature of paella itself.

Although even Valencian traditionalists cook paella for large crowds, paella is not suitable for most restaurant kitchens because it should be cooked over a wood fire. And the tending of that fire requires the constant attention of the cook. In an à la carte restaurant, where many paellas are prepared at different moments for different tables and different diners, even if there were a wood fire, the fire would never be suitable for several different paellas at different stages of preparation. And if the restaurant were going to succeed at all, it would have to be making its paellas in individual pans, not one large one for all comers. Such a paella would have to be made ahead of time, and paella cannot be properly served except immediately after it is finished, when all flavors have mixed and been absorbed by moist, *a la diente,* individually separate grains of medium-grain rice.

The importance of the pan cannot be overstressed. The basic meaning of the word *paella* is in fact "pan." March traces the word back to Greek *pateras* and Latin *patella.* She argues that paella (the food) is a symbolic and actual merging of two great cultures that converged on the Iberian Peninsula and its peoples. The Romans brought the pan and the Moors brought rice. Valencians, at the confluence of both cultures and Spain's leading growers of rice, put the Islamic rice in the flat, two-handled Roman metal pan and took to cooking that rice with simple, available foods: vegetables and chicken and rabbit. To produce a perfect paella, the pan had to be the perfect diameter, just large enough so that all the liquid is absorbed at just the moment when the rice is fluffed and almost soft but still chewy.

Here are the standard relations between number of guests and paella diameters: for two to three people, 30 centimeters; for four to five people, 40 centimeters; for six to eight people, 50 centimeters; for 10 people, 55 centimeters; for 15 people, 65 centimeters; for 40 to 50 people, 90 centimeters.

All paella pans are shallow, from 1½ to 2¾ inches deep, to permit the rice to cook through evenly. In the old days, guests really did eat right out of the pan, with boxwood spoons.

March, I think correctly, sees this as proof of Moorish origins for paella. Round metal tables and wood spoons are survivals of medieval dining still prevalent in the Muslim world.

But it is in Spain that the peculiar combination of ingredients the world now knows as *paella Valenciana* came together and turned into a classic dish, the emblem of a nation. And the classic ingredients for the classic dish are remarkably simple—rice, rabbit, chicken, green beans, limas (of a large variety called *garrofón* in Spain), rosemary or rosemary-fed snails, tomatoes, saffron, paprika. They reflect the conditions of country life in the rice fields of Valencia, as does the classic paella fire, which responds in its modesty to the region's meager firewood supply. Vine cuttings and tree prunings are what you want for a paella fire in a paella barbecue (*paellero*), not big branches or logs. All of this specifically regional tradition can be duplicated with relative ease far from Valencia (except for the rosemary-fed snails!!), but rarely is, even in Spain. Lobster and shellfish urbanize and overwhelm a dish whose genius emphasizes rice, other plain ingredients, and the informality of a campfire cookout, as I learned from expert teachers some years ago.

"Please, no *troncos*," Alicia Ríos admonished me, no logs, as I tried to scrounge together a fire for a paella from a garden woodshed. Ríos is March's great friend and collaborator. She also lives in Madrid and is a food historian. So she knew that the bonfire I was assembling would be impossible to fine-tune, and a paella fire must be fine-tuned. Twigs and vine cuttings allow quick adjustments. Fortunately, the woodshed had vine cuttings. Ríos was pleased. She would have been even happier if there had also been apricot twigs, but the fire prospered anyway and she contented herself with teaching us the tongue-twisting Spanish word for apricot tree, *albaricoquero*. In a rudimentary way, our very mild disagreement over method pushed the paella a bit closer to Valencian tradition. The paella is a man's province, and its preparation is always a matter of discussion. Just remember to hold the lobster.

Very reluctantly, I will concede that it is possible to cook this dish indoors on a modern range. Simply regulate the burner heat to produce the results in the pan that the directions call for.

½ pound dried large lima beans, soaked in cold water overnight

6 quarts water

1 cup olive oil

One 3- to 3½-pound chicken, cut in serving pieces

One 2- to 2½-pound rabbit, cut in serving pieces

1¼ pounds green beans, trimmed

½ pound tomatoes, peeled and finely chopped

2 teaspoons paprika

2 sprigs rosemary or 12 snails fed on rosemary

Salt

Saffron

5 cups medium-grain rice (available where Hispanic ingredients are sold; Italian risotto rice will do; do not wash.)

1. Boil the limas in 1 quart of water for 1 hour. Drain, reserving both the limas and their cooking liquid.

2. Meanwhile, pour the oil in a paella pan 55 centimeters (approximately 21 inches) in diameter. Place over the barbecue where it will cook and level it securely. Light the fire. When the oil is hot, brown the chicken and rabbit pieces. Add the green beans and tomatoes. After a few minutes, pour in 5 quarts of water and the cooking liquid from the limas.

3. When the water boils, move the pan to the side of the fire so that the water simmers. Continue cooking for 45 minutes to an hour, until the meat is tender.

4. Add the paprika and the rosemary or snails. Taste the liquid and add salt if necessary. Add a few threads of saffron.

5. Check the water level. It should be just at the height of the paella's handle rivets. Remove excess or add boiling water if there is too little. Then move to the center of the fire or add more wood. Pour in the rice. Spread it as evenly as possible. Simmer for 10 minutes, then pull paella to the side of the fire and cook gently for 8 to 10 more minutes. Toward the end of this period, taste the rice. When it is al dente, remove the paella from the fire and let stand for 5 minutes, while the rice absorbs the remaining liquid.

Serves 10

Paris-Brest
(Cream-Puff Cake)

Every four years a sweaty band of elite amateur cyclists attempt to ride from Paris to the Breton city of Brest on the Atlantic coast and then back to Paris, covering 1,200 kilometers (about 750 miles) in ninety hours or less. The best riders do it in under fifty hours and none of them are professionals. Paris-Brest-Paris is the oldest long-distance cycling event there is. It began in 1891, only six years after the invention of the modern bicycle, as the brainchild of a journalist and cycling fanatic named Pierre Griffard. He promoted Paris-Brest shrewdly, so that it caught the imagination of France and later the world.

The excitement of the first "race" inspired a patissier (whose name seems to be lost) to create a wheel-shaped pastry consisting of a cream-puff-dough (pâte à choux, see below) torus stuffed with an almond-flavored pastry cream solidified with Italian meringue and called crème Chiboust.

An ordinary meringue is a silky, glistening foam of beaten egg whites amalgamated with sugar. An Italian meringue is a normal meringue beaten with liquefied sugar heated to the hard-ball stage, and therefore lightly candied. When this is mixed together with a yolky pastry cream and almonds, the cook has made one of the most sophisticated and tasty inventions in all cuisine. Piping it between the halves of the giant cream puff circle is the equivalent of pumping air into a bicycle tire.

This is a clever conceit, but the multilevel process that makes it happen, the culinary flow chart, shows in miniature why France took cooking to unrivaled heights in the nineteenth century. In the three generations between Carême and Escoffier, French chefs, acting very much in the spirit of the industrial revolution, organized their kitchens into brigades with special functions, feeder units for an assembly line. This way of thinking, a division of labor into rationally ordered, linked units, made it possible for a creative chef to invent new dishes by redirecting the flow of available materials into new permutations and combinations. Like an automobile plant in which thousands of parts and choices of color and accessories can be combined in dozens of ways, the nineteenth-century French restaurant kitchen was a machine of multiple potentials.

Whoever invented Paris-Brest conceived a way of making a large "cake" with a dough that normally got baked into small things, profiteroles (see page 164) or éclairs, by assembling three piped concentric rings of dough so that they would seep into each other and emerge from the oven as a single wheel. Then, building on the model of the éclair, he contrived a way of stuffing the wheel, by slicing it in half transversely at its middle, leaving a circular top and bottom. As for the cream filling, it is really two "creams" beaten together for a spectacular result, light and stiff and rich, something that inflates the pastry and gives it a reliable loft. When sliced, the Paris-Brest turns into eight or ten sandwiches, the final spectacular stage of many.

1 cup milk	**CRÈME CHIBOUST**
½ teaspoon vanilla extract	⅓ cup sugar
3 egg yolks	2 tablespoons water
½ cup sugar	3 egg yolks
2 tablespoons cornstarch	4 egg whites
⅔ cup Pâte à Choux (see below)	Confectioners' sugar
½ cup chopped blanched almonds	

1. Heat the milk until it foams. Reduce the heat to low, pour in the vanilla, cover, and let stand.

2. In a mixing bowl, whisk the yolks and ½ cup sugar together until they are smooth, thick, and light yellow. Gently whisk in the cornstarch.

3. Pour the milk into the yolk-sugar mixture. Whisk vigorously to blend. Then return to the stove and bring to the boil, whisking, and cook for 1 minute. Reduce the heat to low, cover, and keep warm.

4. Preheat the oven to 450 degrees.

5. On a buttered baking sheet, draw an 8-inch circle (use an inverted 8-inch pie plate and a round-ended table knife to mark the circle in the butter).

6. Fit a pastry bag with a half-inch nozzle and fill with the Pâte à Choux. Pipe out a circle of dough on the circle marked on the baking sheet. Pipe a second circle inside the first circle. It should touch the larger circle. Finally, pipe a third circle on top of the first two circles. Dust overall with the chopped almonds.

7. Bake for 30 minutes, keeping the oven door ajar with a wooden spoon. After 15 minutes, reduce the temperature to 400.

8. While the circle bakes, dissolve the remaining ⅓ cup sugar in 2 tablespoons water. Bring to a boil and cook until it reaches the hard-ball stage (248 degrees). This will take a few

minutes, during which you should beat the egg whites in an electric mixer until they form stiff peaks.

9. Mixing at high speed, pour the hard-ball-stage sugar syrup into the egg whites. Reduce the mixing speed to low. Return the yolk mixture to the boil and pour it into the white mixture. Beat only long enough to combine both mixtures. Then, without delay, scrape into a mixing bowl or a pastry bag to cool it. This is a crème Chiboust.

10. Cool the cake on a rack. Then, with a long, serrated knife, slice through the cake horizontally, about halfway up the side. Lift off the top slice and set it aside.

11. Spread the bottom half with the crème Chiboust. Replace the top slice. Dust liberally with confectioners' sugar. Refrigerate until ready to serve. The cream will not keep for more than a day.

Serves 8 to 10

Pâte à Choux

½ cup milk
½ cup water
¾ teaspoon salt
1 teaspoon sugar

7½ tablespoons butter, cut in pats
1 cup flour
1 cup lightly beaten eggs, about 4 to 5

1. In a heavy, nonaluminum saucepan, heat the milk with ½ cup water. While the liquid is coming to a boil, stir in the salt, sugar, and butter.

2. When the mixture boils, remove from the heat and beat in all the flour at once. Then return to the stove and continue beating the dough over medium heat to dry it out. When the dough comes away from the sides of the pan, remove from the heat and scrape into a mixing bowl.

3. Beat ⅓ cup of the eggs into the dough. Then another ⅓ cup, and finally the remaining ⅓ cup. Beat until smooth but no more.

About 4 cups dough

Pasta e Fagioli alla Pordenonense
(Noodles and Beans in the Style of Pordenone)

Aside from spaghetti, this was the first Italian dish I ever heard about. It was a big joke, or supposed to be. TV comics of the early fifties assumed they could always get a laugh by bringing up *pasta fazool,* a dialectal version of *pasta e fagioli* (pasta and beans). I didn't get the joke as a child, and I don't want to get it now. Of course, now nobody would dream of trying to get a yuck from saying something in peasant Italian, unless it was somehow connected to the Mob. Too many people still think organized crime and its alleged folkways are hilarious.

On an episode of *The Sopranos,* the mafiosi wives go to a lecture at their church in New Jersey to hear an advanced Italian-American woman give them a pep talk on how they'd all come a long way, baby. One of the speaker's self-esteem–building examples was gastronomic: "When they [people making fun of your lifestyle] say spaghetti and meatballs, you say eggplant parmigiana and broccoli rabe." It gets worse: "When they say your mothers wore black, you say we wear Armani."

The wives are furious. They think this woman is putting them down, that she is agreeing with the Italian-hating world that there is something embarrassing or low class about unreconstructed Sicilian-American food or other features of the world their immigrant ancestors created in America. I don't get it, because I don't believe that one recipe is classier than another—more complex, more expensive, sure, but intrinsically superior (when well prepared), not on your life.

The truth is that *pasta fazool* is a pan-Italian dish with many variations on the same idea: noodles cooked together with beans, starch on starch. There are four basic varieties of this dish: with lard, with olive oil, pureed, and not pureed. In all of these categories, the beans are cooked until quite soft.

This opulent recipe from Pordenone in the Friuli region of the extreme northeast of Italy, goes important and more in favor of the lard, adding potatoes, which are unusual for Italy but typical up there. I have tried *pasta e fagioli* with lard and prefer it that way. I am also amused by the belt-and-suspenders inclusion of unpureed beans with the puree.

When you serve it, if a guest, suppressing a giggle, says pasta fazool, you say . . . Actually, better not.

4 quarts water	4 potatoes, peeled and diced
Salt	1 bay leaf
1½ pounds dried cranberry beans (*borlotti*), soaked in cold water for 24 hours	3 pig's feet or 1 small hambone with some meat on it or 3 spareribs
1 medium onion, peeled and studded with 3 cloves garlic	¼ pound pasta: ditalini or tagliatelle
	Olive oil
1 small stalk celery, chopped	

1. Bring 4 quarts of water to the boil. Add salt and all the other ingredients except the pasta and the olive oil.
2. Simmer for 3 hours. Set aside about a third of the beans.
3. Remove the meat from the pork and discard the bones. Remove all the other solid ingredients (but discard the bay leaf) from the cooking liquid with a slotted spoon and run them through a food mill with the meat.
4. Return the pureed mixture and the reserved whole beans to the original cooking liquid. Return to the boil, add the pasta, and cook until tender, about 10 minutes: al dente texture is not desirable for this dish.
5. Remove from the heat and let stand for 10 minutes. Just before serving, stir in a soup spoon of olive oil.

Serves 6

Pâte Brisée
(Pie-Crust Dough)

This is the classic crust, both in contents and method, for French tarts and many other types of pastry. Except for the egg yolk, it is not very different from a standard American pie-crust dough. In other words, this is a short dough, heavy on the butter, but not so heavy on the sugar that it would qualify as a pâte sucrée. *Pâte brisée* means broken dough, probably because butter is broken into tiny pieces during the kneading and rolling processes. The result is a fairly smooth, "mealy" dough, mealy because it looks rather like cornmeal.

This is, self-evidently, a rich dough, but it is more than opulent. Prebaked (*à blanc*), it resists the soggy-making effect of "wet" fillings such as pastry cream. It is not the dough to use for top crusts (which should be less worked over and have no egg and a cruder "crumb," the size of peas, instead of cornmeal).

It would be much easier to make this crust with vegetable shortening or margarine, both of which require less caution in rolling out. But butter gives a superior taste. Of course, rancid butter will defeat this purpose utterly. Rancidity is that off-flavor you must have noticed when butter is left in the refrigerator for too long. Sometimes butter is already rancid in the market. Once you can recognize rancidity, you will be able to detect it through the paper the butter is wrapped in—before you buy it.

The method below is not the only way to make a crust with these ingredients, but it is the traditional French procedure and works nicely in the home. Instead of mixing the ingredients in a bowl, you work directly on the counter, starting with a circle of flour, the well or fountain (*la fontaine*), and then placing the other ingredients in its center. Proceeding with one hand (keeping the other clean for the telephone or for turning pages in a cookbook), you work together the ingredients you have just put in the center of the well and then work them into the flour, ending up with a ball of dough.

Thorough chilling relaxes the gluten, minimizing the toughness that glutinous elasticity would create.

Finally, the dough is rolled out into a circle, placed in a tart pan or flan ring, and, usually, prebaked briefly, for 10 or 15 minutes at a high temperature, say 450 degrees. Older cookbooks called this a fast oven. They also advised filling the crust with raw beans or metal "pie weights," to keep the crust from rising in waves off the pan during the early moments of baking.

There is a better way, at least if you are prebaking the crust in a pie pan or tart tin. Simply place a second pan on top of the crust. Then pick up this assemblage, invert it onto a baking sheet and bake. After a few minutes, turn the pans over together, replace on the baking sheet and remove the top one. This will let the crust brown during the final minutes it spends in the oven. Its color will tell you when to take it out.

The hardware specified here enables easy unmolding after the crust has cooled. Then it can be filled with pastry cream (*crème pâtissière*) or glazed with a heated, strained fruit preserve (classically apricot) and then covered with trimmed strawberries or raspberries, which can then be drizzled with the same preserve.

2 cups flour	1 egg yolk
¼ teaspoon salt	¼ pound cold unsalted butter
3 tablespoons sugar (eliminate for quiche)	Flour for the rolling surface
3 tablespoons ice water	

1. Form a wreath of flour on a wooden board (or marble slab) with the empty center about 5 to 6 inches wide.
2. Put the salt, sugar, and ice water into the central "well." Mix, in the well, with fingers until there is no trace of sugar or salt. Stir in the egg yolk and mix well.
3. Add the butter to the mixture in the well, little by little in small pieces. Work and mix until the butter is absorbed. Work in the flour.
4. Form a ball. With the heel of your hand, press and flatten the ball outward several times. Form the ball again and press the dough outward three times.
5. Flatten the ball to a thickness of about 1½ inches, keeping it round. Wrap it in foil and chill for 4 hours.
6. Roll the dough to a 12-inch circle on a lightly floured board or counter. Fit into a 9-inch tart tin with a fluted edge and removable bottom or a 10 by 1-inch flan ring set on a baking sheet. Trim excess.

One 9-inch tart or one 10-inch quiche crust

"Water boiled atop the charcoal fire. In and out of it went the duck; then it was dipped in honey. He wore no shirt, and I didn't like it that the other women in the *hutong* could see him half naked, even though I was sure most of them had seen more of him at other times."

—Aunt Tzipi

Peking Duck

After a series of nearly fatal adventures and hairbreadth escapes from the Nazis in the Vilna ghetto and then from the Soviets, my aunt Zipporah (always referred to as Tzipi in the family) reached safety in Shanghai wearing the same Russian army uniform she had taken from a drunken soldier in Magnetogorsk. All of this is described in unashamedly candid Yiddish in her unpublished memoir, which she kept in a red-covered school notebook with blue-ruled pages, now yellow and crumbling.

In Shanghai, Tzipi resumed her life as a socialist intellectual, within the community of Jewish refugees and also through a Chinese communist cell led by a man from Peking (as it was then called) named Chen Po. In his mid-forties and a notorious rake, he introduced Tzipi to opium and other less exotic forms of decadence, among them Peking duck, which he would make in a communal outdoor kitchen in his slovenly *hutong*. In between pipes and lovemaking.

My translation does not do justice to Aunt Tzipi's account of the preparations for Po's duck roast:

He would take the duck, stolen of course, and cut away the first two joints of the wings with his horn-handled razor. Water boiled atop the charcoal fire. In and out of it went the duck; then it was dipped in honey. He wore no shirt, and I didn't like it that the other women in the hutong *could see him half naked, even though I was sure most of them had seen more of him at other times.*

The most important part of the recipe is the drying of the duck. This separates the scalded, glazed skin from the meat and allows it to turn into delicious crispness, like grivenes *only a thousand times better. Po ran a bicycle chain under the wings and hung the bird from his window all night in the winter breeze. He put sticks between the wing and the torso, to let the wind reach every corner of the skin. He also told me that it was a tradition in the village outside Peking where he was born that a man, symbolizing the wind, had to touch a virgin's skin all over to ensure the complete success of the duck dehydration. He knew as well as anyone that I wasn't a virgin, but he said, lying back after a third pipe, I would have to do.*

1 quart water

1 duck, about 5 pounds

½ cup honey

1 cup hot water

4 cups flour

3 cups boiling water

2 teaspoons sesame oil

12 scallions, white parts only, julienned in
    2-inch matchsticks

1 cucumber, peeled, seeded, and julienned

Hoisin sauce

1. Boil a quart of water. Put the duck in a colander. Pour the boiling water over the duck, turning the duck as you pour so as to scald all the skin, which will shrink and turn shiny.

2. Let the duck drain; then put in a bowl. Dissolve the honey in a cup of hot water. Pour over the duck. Collect the excess from the bowl and repeat. Then brush the honey mixture over the areas of skin you have missed.

3. Now hang the duck in front of an electric fan or air conditioner. Run heavy twine under both wings for hanging the duck. Stretch the wings away from the body with short sticks. This process is crucial to drying the skin and preparing it for crisping. Hang the duck for at least 24 hours, until the skin is very dry and has started to pull away from the flesh.

4. Meanwhile make the pancakes: Put 3½ cups flour in a bowl. Beat in 3 cups of boiling water. Let cool until you can knead the dough briefly. Then let stand for a half hour in the bowl covered with a damp cloth.

5. Divide the dough in half and knead each half on a lightly floured board, for a few minutes. Roll each ball into a long cylinder. Cut each into twelve equal pieces. Roll each piece into a small circle. Brush half the circles with sesame oil. Put an unbrushed circle on each of the brushed circles. Then roll these "sandwiches" into thin pancakes.

6. In a seasoned but unoiled skillet, fry the pancakes for a minute or so on each side. They will puff and acquire brown spots. As you finish cooking a pancake, pull apart the two halves of the sandwich. Stack the finished pancakes on a platter and cover with a clean dish towel.

7. Preheat the oven to 325 degrees.

8. Set the duck breast up on a rack, in a roasting pan filled with an inch of hot water. Roast for 20 minutes. Then turn the duck over and roast another 25 minutes. Invert again, raise the oven temperature to 375 and finish roasting for 20 minutes. While it roasts, the skin will turn very crisp and red.

9. Ten minutes before the duck is done, steam the pancakes for 10 minutes in a covered steamer. Set the scallions, cucumber, and hoisin sauce in bowls on the table.

10. Carve the duck: Cut the skin into pieces that will fit in the center of the pancakes. Put on a serving dish. Then carve the meat into similar pieces and put on a separate platter. Bring to the table with the steamed pancakes. Let guests smear a pancake with sauce, then add a piece of skin, a piece of meat, some scallion, some cucumber, and then roll up the pancake and eat.

Serves 4 as a main course

Pho Bo
(Vietnamese Beef Soup)

As an American newspaper food editor during the Vietnam War, I made it my business to seek out Vietnamese food. Had I been in Saigon, this would have been easy, but in America it was something of a challenge. There were very few Vietnamese in the country and no Vietnamese restaurants in the New York area. I did manage to locate a cluster of them around Fort Bragg, the North Carolina home base of the 82d Airborne Division and the Special Forces (Green Berets). A former military language instructor ran the leading restaurant in the area, complete with Vietnamese waitresses in *ao dais,* the elegant traditional dress. It was there that I first tasted the fermented fish sauce that is the soul of Southeast Asian cooking (*nuoc mam* in Vietnam) and was introduced to Vietnamese spring rolls, *cha gio,* by a defrocked Green Beret from Arizona named Gustav Jung, who shared my eagerness to go to China, which was then closed to Americans. "I don't want to invade," he said. "I just want the air-conditioning franchise."

It was in New York, however, that I first tasted *pho,* the signpost dish of Hanoi. The Vietnamese wife of an American correspondent showed me how it was done. She never got her picture in the paper because the *New York Times* photographer somehow managed to fill an entire roll of film with shots of my feet. It was difficult in that Upper West Side apartment to conjure up how it would feel to be eating this thickly populated beef-based breakfast soup at a stall in its native place, the Communist capital Hanoi.

Pho is a bounteous dish, a strong broth strongly spiced with chili and aromatic saw-toothed coriander leaves, not to mention pungent *nuoc mam.* It is truly an eye-opener, but a major part of its appeal is its last-minute improvisational quality: raw beef cooked in the individual bowl when boiling stock is poured over it; condiments including chopped chilies, tossed in by the consumer. On its native ground, *pho* is slurped and eaten with chopsticks and a spoon simultaneously. Then, as I thought about it at the time, invigorated by your breakfast, you slip out into the jungle and set booby traps on trails where Green Berets would soon be stalking their Vietcong foe.

3 pounds beef shin or oxtail (with bones)

4 quarts cold water

1 medium onion, unpeeled

One 3-inch piece ginger, unpeeled

1 cinnamon stick

1 piece star anise

1 tablespoon salt

1 bay leaf

4 cloves

2 teaspoons fennel seeds

3 tablespoons bottled Vietnamese fish sauce (*nuoc mam*)

4 quarts water

Salt

1 bundle Chinese rice vermicelli

1 pound raw sirloin, very thinly sliced

3 scallions, trimmed and chopped (both white and green parts)

Fresh coriander sprigs (cilantro or, preferably, the more pungent variety with saw-toothed leaves called *ngo gai* in Vietnamese or *culantro* in Caribbean markets)

Lime wedges

Chopped fresh green chilies

1. Leave the beef to soak in 4 quarts cold water for several hours. Skim the surface and bring to a boil. Lower the heat and simmer for 3 hours, skimming occasionally.

2. Broil the onion and ginger over direct flame.* Hold them with a tongs or skewer them and rotate for 5 minutes. Some charring is desirable. Rub off the loose carbon.

3. Add the onion, ginger, cinnamon, anise, salt, bay leaf, cloves, fennel seeds, and fish sauce to the broth 15 minutes before it has finished simmering.

4. Meanwhile bring 4 quarts of water to the boil in another pot. Salt and add the rice noodles. Cook 8 minutes, dump into a colander. Refresh in cold water, and drain.

5. Divide the noodles into six portions and put one portion in each of six soup bowls. Divide the sirloin among the bowls, placing the slices over the noodles. Toss the chopped scallions and 3 sprigs of fresh coriander or *ngo gai* over the beef.

6. Strain the broth. Pour 1 cup into each bowl. It will cook the raw beef almost on contact. Serve immediately.

7. Pass the lime wedges and chilies separately.

Serves 6

* This can't be done on an electric stove.

Picadillo Boliviano

(Sautéed Chopped Meat with Shoestring Potatoes, Bolivian-style)

Picadillo **is Spanish for a chopped mixture,** usually with chopped beef as the central ingredient: compared to the gringo *picadillo,* or hamburger, this is one spicy meatball (actually, *picadillos* are not shaped but come to the table resembling our sloppy Joe). Within Latin America, there are a great many variations on the basic idea. This one comes from the Bolivian Andes, birthplace of the potato. So it should not be surprising that the Bolivian *picadillo* puts the French fries right into the burger, so to speak. Nevertheless, this combination, so familiar to us when the meat and potatoes are separate, may seem (it did to me at first) a bit weird when they are mixed together. On the plate and in the mouth, it seems utterly normal and brilliant in conception.

Be warned, however, that this dish is not only exotic but potentially dangerous. Deep-fat-frying involves large quantities of very hot cooking oil, into which you will be bringing cold, wet food. Too much food put into too much oil will cause explosive boiling as the suddenly heated moisture evaporates. In the worst case, the oil overflows, ignites and burns your house down. It was an out-of-control grease fire that closed down my friends George and Jenifer Lang's Café des Artistes for many weeks.

The way out of this is to leave plenty of headway at the top of the pot you use for deep-frying and to cook the potatoes in small batches. Say a generous handful. The two-stage frying is the classic method of obtaining crisp fries. Also, the thinner you cut the potato sticks, the crisper they will get.

If you don't want to bother with any of this, the basic *picadillo* will still be delicious, just not Bolivian. Serve this non-Andean variation with rice and add ¼ cup plumped raisins toward the end of step 3.

Vegetable oil

2 large Idaho potatoes, peeled and cut in
    shoestrings, soaked in water, and
    patted dry

2 medium onions, peeled and chopped

2 pounds ground chuck

1 to 5 dried red chilies, seeded and
    crumbled

1 teaspoon pepper

1 tablespoon ground cumin

  Salt

1. Heat oil for deep-frying.
2. Deep-fry the potatoes in batches until golden brown, at around 360 degrees. Drain on paper towels and let rest until the *picadillo* (see step 3 below) is well along toward done.
3. Heat 2 tablespoons of oil in a skillet and sauté the onions until translucent.
4. Add all the remaining ingredients and cook over low heat, stirring from time to time, until the mixture dries out and browns.
5. Heat the deep-frying oil until it begins to smoke. Refry the potatoes in batches until nicely browned. Drain in batches on paper towels. Stir the *picadillo* and potatoes gently together and serve with a green salad.

Serves 4

Pizza

It is possible that pizza is a Greek flat bread called *laganon.* The word is currently applied to pizza in Greece. And it is a fact that the epicenter of the planetary pizzaquake is Naples, established as a Greek colony in antiquity (Neapolis = new city in Greek) and evolved into Napoli, and that is why we call its people Neapolitans.

On the other hand, any definition of pizza must define it as a yeast-risen flat bread with a topping, to distinguish it from all the other untopped flat breads you can ferret out all over Europe and, indeed, in Italy (think focaccia). The exception, *pissaladière,* proves the rule. It is a dish of Nice, really an Italian city dumped by historical force majeure into France, but still called Nizza by those who take the long view.

What we now usually think of as basic pizza—tomatoes and cheese—was invented (or at least got its traditional launch) in 1889. Raffaele Esposito, a famous pizza maker, was invited to the palace of King Umberto I of Savoy and made three kinds of pizza for Queen Margherita, who loved the food of the people and was loved by them in return. She preferred Esposito's pizza topped with tomato, mozzarella, and basil, and gave it her name.

Today, it seems strange to think of pizza Margherita as a novelty that could divert the palates of royalty. To us, it is almost an innocent concoction, because when we encountered pizza it was already cut off from its roots in Italy and free to be hybridized to please local taste without the braking effect of a childhood experience with the dish's original simplicity or even the notion of it as a form of bread. So-called garbage pizza, an omnium-gatherum of animal, mineral, and vegetable toppings, was the showpiece of the culinary irrational exuberance of the fifties, perhaps a reaction against the drab conformity of the Eisenhower era.

Today, pizza has entered its elegant phase, swank and multiculti. It joins the Mexican tortilla and the pita of the Middle East as a universal bread that can embrace the foods and flavor of each cuisine. And unlike the croissant, pizza prospers in this wider world. It can handle more than anchovies and cheese. But that pizza of the fifties is the Italo-American classic. And here it is.

3 cups all-purpose flour, approximately

1 teaspoon salt

¾ teaspoon instant yeast

1 cup ice water

  Olive oil

  Cornmeal

2 cups chopped mozzarella cheese, 12 ounces

8 anchovy fillets, rinsed and roughly chopped

¼ cup grated pecorino cheese

1. Mix the flour, salt, and yeast together in a large bowl with a large metal spoon. Then stir in a cup of ice water. Continue to stir, vigorously, until the dough is smooth, springy, and sticky. It should pull away from the bowl but should not be so dry as to roll up into a ball. Add a bit of flour if it is too wet, or a bit of ice water if it is too dry.

2. Lightly flour a pastry board or the counter. Set the dough on the board; flatten and cut into four equal pieces. Flour your hands and form each piece into a ball.

3. Lightly oil and flour a cookie sheet. Put the dough balls on the metal sheet. Brush with oil. Put the pan with the dough into a plastic bag and seal. Refrigerate overnight.

4. Two hours before baking, remove the dough from the refrigerator and set on a lightly floured counter. Sprinkle the balls with flour. Press them flat, into disks about ½ inch thick. Brush the disks with oil and sprinkle with flour. Cover with plastic wrap and let rest for 2 hours.

5. Place a bake stone on the lower rack of the oven (or on the bottom of a gas oven) and preheat as high as possible for 1 hour.

6. Dust a cookie sheet with cornmeal.

7. Roll out one of the disks as thin as you can (or stretch it on the backs of your hands). Work it loose from the counter with a pastry scraper. Flour your hands and then carefully set a disk on them. Make a loose fist and bounce the dough on them. With each toss, stretch the dough a little and make it rotate a few degrees. After you have stretched the dough into a disk of 9-inch diameter (or more!), lay on the dusted sheet and top with ½ cup of the mozzarella, then a quarter of the chopped anchovies and finally with a tablespoon of the pecorino.

8. Slide onto the bake stone. Bake for 6 minutes or a little longer if the cheese has not melted and darkened. Remove the pizza and let rest a few minutes before cutting into slices. Repeat steps 7 and 8 with the three remaining disks.

Four 9-inch pizzas

Plum Pudding

Like the English horn, which is neither English nor a horn,* plum pudding has no plums and is not a pudding in the modern sense, either of dessert in general (British) or a custard (United States). The etymology is uncertain, but as best as can be told, "pudding" comes from a Middle English word for stomach or intestine. This fits with the culinary history of the term, since sausages were stuffed into animal intestine casings, hence blood pudding for the etymologically related *boudin* in France. The first steamed puddings in England, whether savory or sweet, were boiled in animal casings. Pudding cloths made this system more practical. The first recipe for a pudding-cloth pudding was published in 1617. The first reference to plum pudding appears in 1740.

Eventually the pudding cloth gave way to pudding basins, which are, to an American eye, like mixing bowls with ridged tops meant to facilitate sealing them with a cloth. Most plum puddings today are bought rather than made. In the United Kingdom, "plum" is archaic and the same dish is usually identified as Christmas pudding, although historically it was a dish eaten all winter.

"Plum" referred to the dried raisins and, by extension, to the other dried fruits. The use of suet, the rendered and purified, shredded hard fat around the kidney of beef animals or sheep, is still common in Britain. Shredded suet can be purchased in ordinary supermarkets. In the United States, perfectly usable suet cakes are most readily available at pet stores, for feeding to birds, but better butchers can easily save some for you or you can mail-order vacuum-sealed 3-pound cakes of pure beef suet for $3.25 per cake from Jackson Frozen Food Locker, 400 South High, Jackson, MO 63755 (573 243-4107); or from the Web site www.askthemeatman.com.

This pudding will keep for two years in a cool cellar or refrigerator, sealed in foil and then put in a Ziploc bag with the air squeezed out. When required, it is briefly resteamed, brought out hot and flamed with brandy as part of a Christmas pageant procession or just a winter dinner. If you haven't tasted one for some reason (perhaps you grew up in the Trobriand Islands), you have missed a treat. If you have, here is a way to make an even yummier one.

---

* It is a double-reed woodwind, like the oboe but with a lower, earthier range. Also called *cor anglais*, i.e., English horn in French, the origin of the name is unclear.

1½ pounds raisins	8 eggs, lightly beaten
½ pound dried currants or dried apricots	½ teaspoon salt
½ pound candied citrus peel, thinly sliced	1 tablespoon lemon juice
¾ pound suet, finely chopped (order in advance from your butcher)	1 cup stout
	Butter
¾ pound plain bread crumbs	1 recipe Hard Sauce (see below)

1. Roughly chop the raisins, currants or dried apricots, citrus peel, and suet by pulsating with the steel blade of a processor. Process these ingredients in separate batches. Mix them together with the bread crumbs in a large bowl. Then mix well with the eggs, salt, lemon juice, and stout. Let stand, covered, overnight.

2. Turn out the batter into a buttered 8-cup heatproof mold lined with cheesecloth. Press down. Cover the mold with a sheet of aluminum foil, pleated in the middle to allow for expansion. Tie the foil around the mold. Then set on a rack in a large pot. Pour in water to a 2-inch depth, bring to a boil, and steam for 5 hours. Keep an eye on the water and replenish as necessary.

3. Remove the foil. Loosen the pudding from the mold by tugging on the cheesecloth and unmold onto a cake platter. Pass Hard Sauce separately. It is traditional to slice leftover pudding and fry in butter.

Serves 12

Hard Sauce

This is called rum butter in England. Both names are accurate if slightly misleading descriptions of what is spirit-flavored, solid, but spreadable sweetened butter.

½ cup (1 stick) unsalted butter, softened	2 tablespoons rum or bourbon
1½ cups confectioners' sugar	

1. Combine all the ingredients in the jar of a processor. Process with the steel blade until it is very smooth and the sugar has lost its granularity.

2. Refrigerate, covered, until ready to use. Let return to room temperature and serve. Hard Sauce will keep for 3 days in the refrigerator.

About 1½ cups sauce

Poori
(Indian Bread Puff)

Indian breads are not breads in our sense at all. They are mostly made with wheat and some are leavened, but they are individual "slices," and don't come in loaves. Like pita and Mexican tortillas, many of them respond to a need for a "utensil" to bring food to the mouth in a cuisine without tableware to assist eating.

Pooris are no more typical of Indian bread style than any other, perhaps less so. But they are the most fun to make of all the basic types. You fight against the expanding balloon of dough with the spatula and it fights back.

2 cups chapati or whole-wheat flour, approximately	Salt
½ cup all-purpose flour	Pepper
½ teaspoon lovage seeds (*carom* or *ajwain*), crushed, optional	2 tablespoons vegetable oil

1. Stir together 1 cup of the chapati and all the all-purpose flour in a mixing bowl. Then stir in the lovage seeds, salt, pepper, and 2 tablespoons vegetable oil. When all these ingredients are well mixed, add cold water gradually until a dough forms and pulls away from the sides of the bowl. Cover and let stand for 4 hours (or refrigerate for as much as a day or two).

2. Working on a board or counter dusted with flour, divide the dough into 8 to 10 pieces and roll into balls.

3. Heat vegetable oil for deep-frying (quantities will vary according to the size of the container, but you will want oil to a depth of 3 inches) to 375 degrees.

4. Press one of the dough balls flat. Cover on both sides with flour and roll out to a 5-inch circle. Pick it up with a perforated spatula and set it warily into the hot oil. It will float. Press lightly on the top of the dough with the spatula. As it fills with air, it will "fight" with the spatula. Keep pressing until the *poori* turns golden brown. All this takes only a few seconds. Flip the *poori* over and brown the other side for a couple seconds. Remove with the spatula, drain on a paper towel, and continue with the rest of the dough until it is all used up. Serve immediately.

8 to 10 *pooris*

Pork Vindaloo
(Spicy Indian Pork Stew from Goa)

In just about any Indian restaurant, you will find some form of vindaloo. What makes a vindaloo? Menus tout it as fiery hot from chilies. So you might think that vindaloo means spicy. Indeed, since most of the restaurants in the Indian diaspora serving vindaloo are run by Bengalis, you could logically surmise that vindaloo is a regional dish of Bengal and that vindaloo means spicy-hot in the Bengali language. You would be wrong on all scores.

Vindaloo is a cooking method of Goa, the former Portuguese colony on the west coast of India, now famous for its beaches and tolerance for European youth-wanderers experimenting with nudity and cannabis. As for vindaloo, all evidence points toward a Portuguese origin. The basic dish uses pork, a meat little favored in India (lamb, beef, and chicken are frequently substituted). Vinegar and garlic are also crucial. Pork, vinegar, and garlic are a common Portuguese combination. The Portuguese also brought chilies to south Asia; so it makes sense that India's spiciest dish should be an adaptation of ingredients brought there in the early sixteenth century by Portuguese colonists.

Indian cooks then naturalized the dish by marinating the pork in their own spices and souring it further with indigenous souring agents, tamarind and the rind of the kokum fruit (*Garcinia indica*). They also took to stir-frying the dish in mustard oil, a powerfully aromatic substance. Indians don't like the smell; so they cook it to the smoke point, where it starts to break down and loses its odor.

The name vindaloo is said to be an indicized form of the Portuguese words for vinegar and garlic, *vinagre* and *alho*. But isn't it just as plausible to think that the *aloo* part of the word is the Hindi word meaning potato? Vindaloos sometimes include potatoes, and the Portuguese could easily have been the ones to bring potatoes to India from South America.

Perhaps you will think me perverse for including an Indian dish that was adopted from European interlopers. But aside from its complete assimilation into Indian foodways from Goa to Bangladesh, not to mention London, New York, and Sydney, vindaloo is typically Indian in its foreign origin. Indians, more than the people of any other ancient civilization, have absorbed exotic foods and made them their own, from New World tomatoes and potatoes and chilies to African black-eyed peas. Over the centuries, vindaloo has evolved into something no longer recognizable as Portuguese pork with vinegar and garlic—especially when it is made with lamb, tamarind, kokum rind, garam masala, and mustard oil.

1½ pounds pork shoulder or 6 pork chops	4 cloves garlic, peeled and finely chopped
1 medium onion, peeled and chopped	2 tablespoons vegetable oil
2 teaspoons chopped coriander leaves	½ cup vinegar
One 1-inch piece fresh ginger, peeled and chopped	1½ teaspoons turmeric
	3 medium tomatoes, sliced
½ teaspoon cayenne	1½ cups hot water
1½ teaspoons garam masala (see Note)	1 tablespoon salt

1. Debone and cube the pork.
2. Combine the onion, coriander leaves, ginger, cayenne, garam masala, and garlic. Stir half of this mixture together with the pork pieces. Let stand for 2 hours, unrefrigerated.
3. Heat the oil in a skillet and stir-fry the onion-spice mixture in it over medium heat until the onion stops steaming and begins to brown. Add the vinegar, turmeric, and tomato slices and stir-fry for a couple of minutes longer.
4. Add the pork. Stir-fry with the onion/tomato mixture for 10 minutes.
5. Pour in 1½ cups hot water, bring to a boil, and simmer, covered, for 30 minutes or until the pork is cooked through. Add salt to taste.

Serves 6

Note: *Garam masala is available in Indian food stores, but homemade is far better and can be very simple to make. For example: Take 2 tablespoons black peppercorns, 2 tablespoons coriander seeds, 1 tablespoon caraway seeds, 1 teaspoon whole cloves, and the seeds of twenty-five large cardamom pods and pound them to a powder with a mortar and pestle or grind in a clean coffee grinder. Blend in 1 teaspoon ground cinnamon and store in a jar.*

Profiteroles au Chocolat
(Small Cream Puffs with Chocolate Sauce and Vanilla Ice Cream)

The duchess lived in quiet exile in the posh sixteenth arrondissement in Paris and did not seem too busy, even at short notice, to receive a young American couple dimly connected to her much livelier brother in Michigan. Lunch was decorous and restrained. Served by a maid in a black-and-lace uniform I would never see again except in pornographic videos, the food arrived on faded Italian china the old lady must have brought with her as a young bride from Florence. It began with clear consommé, moved on to nondescript white fish in a lukewarm and therefore gluey Mornay sauce, salad, and then various silver bowls, all set in front of me, evidently for dessert. By this point, I wasn't expecting much.

"Could you serve the profiteroles, please," she said to me. "My hands are too stiff today."

In one bowl was vanilla ice cream. In another, molten chocolate. In the largest of all was a pile of little tan orbs. I distributed them and by the time I finished, I knew that I was facing tiny cream puffs. They were delicious, so pleasurable that I couldn't believe the same kitchen had produced them. The name comes from an antique French expression for a little bit of *profit,* a sort of extra favor a valet got from his master. There is no such place or person as Profiterole.

Profiteroles themselves have lost ground in modern times. A whole category of dishes once employed the little plum-size choux paste balls. Glazed with sugar and crackly, they showed up on gâteaux St. Honoré until the nouvelle cuisine replaced showy pastries with showier tablefuls of labor-intensive goodies. And they were the building blocks of the conical cake called *croquembouche* (crunch-in-mouth). I ate some of that for the first time on the S.S. *France,* to test the idea that you could order anything you wanted in the first-class dining room. So I asked for a *croquembouche* one night. And out it came, with not an eye rolled. Not by the staff, anyway. But French people at neighboring tables giggled and asked us if we'd just got married. *Croquembouche* is a wedding cake in France. Or was.

If profiteroles survive in desserts, they have all but vanished in their once common unsweetened form. As such, they used to be common additions to soup. Grimod de la Reynière, the first foodie, mentions (in his *Manuel des Amphitryons,* 1808) a menu that included *filets de merlans en profiteroles,* which were presumably savory profiteroles stuffed with bits of whiting fillets.

"Could you serve the profiteroles, please," she said to me. "My hands are too stiff today."

In one bowl was vanilla ice cream. In another, molten chocolate. In the largest of all was a pile of little tan orbs. I distributed them and by the time I finished, I knew that I was facing tiny cream puffs. They were delicious. . . .

Perhaps the moment has come to revive the unsweetened profiterole. It could be stuffed with almost anything. If the croissant can be distorted into an all-purpose food holder, why not redeploy the profiterole as the versatile, main-course vehicle it once was?

4 ounces semisweet chocolate

6 tablespoons milk

1 tablespoon heavy cream

2 tablespoons sugar

1 tablespoon butter

1 recipe Pâte à Choux (page 144)

Confectioners' sugar

1 pint vanilla ice cream

1. Melt the chocolate in a double boiler.
2. Meanwhile heat the milk in a saucepan until it starts to foam. Add the heavy cream, return to the boil, and then remove from the heat.
3. Whisk in the chocolate, the sugar, and the tablespoon of butter and return to the boil briefly. Keep warm in a bain-marie.
4. Preheat the oven to 425 degrees. Butter and flour a baking sheet.
5. Put the dough in a pastry bag fitted with a circular nozzle. Pipe out a dozen cream puffs around 1½ inches across on the baking sheet. Dust with confectioners' sugar.
6. Bake for 15 minutes in the middle level of the oven with the door held ajar with a wooden spoon. As soon as the oven is loaded and the door propped open, reduce the temperature to 400 degrees to prevent the puffs from splitting.
7. Cool on a rack.
8. Make two more batches of 12 profiteroles in this manner, preheating the oven to 425 degrees each time and then reducing the temperature to 400 degrees when you put the fresh batches in. The puffs will keep nicely in plastic bags in the refrigerator for a week or in the freezer for a month. Defrost in the refrigerator over 24 hours.
9. The sauce in this recipe is meant to cover a dozen profiteroles, which will serve four people. For the final assembly, make an incision in each puff. Fill with a dessert spoonful of vanilla ice cream. Pour hot chocolate sauce over the puffs. Serve immediately.

Around 36 profiteroles

Quenelles de Brochet, Sauce Nantua
(Lyonnais Pike Dumplings with Crayfish Sauce)

The hit of the 1939 New York World's Fair, gastronomically speaking, was the French pavilion. Its restaurant offered fairgoers a taste of what they might find in an important restaurant of the day in Lyon. Lyon was the hometown of Henri Soulé, the mastermind of the pavilion, but he never went back. At least not for long. Hitler began marching into Poland that summer. The rest of Europe fought back by sitting still. Soulé had no intention of leaving safe America for the nail chewing of the Sitzkrieg.

Instead he capitalized on his newfound American fame and opened Le Pavillon in Manhattan. While the Germans were breaching the pathetic Maginot Line and overrunning France, Le Pavillon was creating a crystallized vision of France for affluent and socially prominent Americans through fancy food. This vision, distorted as it inevitably, even purposely was, stood for the real, the unvisitable France and its legendary glories of the table well through the war and on into the fifties and sixties. Cheap air travel to Europe let too many people see that Le Pavillon wouldn't have competed well with serious restaurants on its home ground, that its snobbery was not at all an intrinsic part of fine dining in the mother country, and that Soulé's menu itself was a very specific and calculated reduction of a cuisine into a group of dishes marketable to a provincial clientele.

And on that menu, the trademark dish was *quenelles de brochet*. These pike dumplings of a preternatural lightness became the heraldic emblem of French haute cuisine for Americans who ate in Le Pavillon or its clones, La Caravelle and La Côte Basque. As late as 1999, a veteran of those days took me to La Caravelle, persuaded me to try the quenelles, and asked if I thought they weren't the best around. Actually, I couldn't think of another place that served them still. *Sic transit . . .*

Well, not quite. Quenelles are a paragon of delicacy. Light as air. Gefilte fish raised to another level.* And a perfect exemplar of the penchant for pureeing in high-style classic French cooking. Sauce Nantua fits them perfectly in spirit. It is the epitome of the flour-bound sauce turned out easily by a restaurant kitchen that produced crayfish butter each day for its morning *mise-en-place*.

---

* I've often wondered if Soulé hadn't put them on his menu with a bit of malice aforethought, showing a city where many people had gefilte fish in their food heritage what a really refined French fish dumpling was.

The pureeing of the fish and the crayfish tails reduce them to pure messengers of flavor. What is essentially an unsweetened cream-puff dough gives an ethereal body to the fish. The sauce gives intense color and a strong flavor counterpoint to the bland and pale dumplings.

Nantua is a small town not far from Bourg-en-Bresse, the Burgundian chicken capital, and surrounded by rivers and streams presumably choked with crayfish.

¾ pound fillet of any white, fleshy fish such as pike, flounder, or halibut

2 cups milk

½ pound (2 sticks or 16 tablespoons) plus 3 tablespoons butter

1 cup minus 2 tablespoons flour plus 3 tablespoons flour

5 whole eggs

Pinch of salt

3 egg whites

6 tablespoons chilled heavy cream

White pepper

Grated nutmeg

¼ cup unshelled crayfish tails

2 tablespoons oil

Domestic paprika, optional

1. Put the fish through a meat grinder or Mouli fitted wih its finest blade, three times. Knead until very smooth.

2. Bring 1 cup of the milk to the boiling point with 2 tablespoons of butter cut in small pieces. Just as the milk begins to foam, add 14 tablespoons (1 cup minus 2 tablespoons) flour all at once. Stir vigorously until the mixture gathers into a smooth dough. Remove from the heat and beat in 1 whole egg and a pinch of salt. Return to the stove and stir over low-medium heat for a few minutes to dry out the dough. Push through a fine strainer and then beat into the fish.

3. Melt 14 tablespoons butter (the remainder of 2 sticks of butter from which you have previously taken 2 tablespoons) and beat into the fish-dough mixture.

4. Now, in succession, beat in four whole eggs, three egg whites, and 6 tablespoons heavy cream. Season with salt, white pepper, and nutmeg.

5. Chill for several hours, until quite stiff.

6. On a lightly floured board, roll the dough into ten cylinders 4 inches long. Place them on a cookie sheet between two pieces of wax paper and refrigerate.

7. After an hour, bring 6 inches of lightly salted water to a boil in a fish poacher or other pan large enough to hold all the quenelles. Reduce the heat so that the water barely quivers, carefully slip the quenelles into the water, and poach them for 15 minutes or until they have solidified. After 10 minutes, shake the poacher or pan so that the quenelles roll over.

8. Remove the quenelles from the poaching liquid with a slotted spoon and let them cool and drain on a dish towel. When they are at room temperature, either freeze them in a tightly sealed container or proceed to the final stage of cooking.

9. Preheat the oven to 350 degrees.

10. Make the sauce Nantua: Melt a tablespoon of butter in a small heavy skillet. Whisk in 3 tablespoons of flour all at once to make a roux. Continue whisking over medium-low heat until the roux has lost its raw taste, but do not let it color. Scrape into a bowl and let cool.

11. Meanwhile, sauté the crayfish tails, with shells on, in the oil until opaque. Drain them. Melt the remaining two tablespoons of butter. Put the crayfish tails in a blender and puree with 2 tablespoons of melted butter. Push the resulting crayfish butter through a fine strainer and reserve. Next, bring the remaining cup of milk to the boiling point in a nonaluminum saucepan. Reduce the heat and whisk in the room-temperature roux. Continue whisking until there are no lumps. Strain and season with salt and white pepper. Whisk in the crayfish butter. If the color of the sauce is not pink enough, add a little paprika. Hold the sauce in a bain-marie until ready to serve.

12. Bring the salted water in the poacher or pan back to the boil. Remove from the heat and slip the quenelles into the liquid. Set the pan in the middle level of the oven and cook for 10 minutes or until the quenelles have swelled noticeably. Remove them from the poaching liquid with a slotted spoon and transfer to a serving platter.

13. Pour the sauce over them and serve.

Serves 4 to 5

Quiche Lorraine
(Savory Custard Pie from Eastern France)

Craig Claiborne's recipe for quiche in the *New York Times Cookbook* (1961) starts with a pie crust that is baked empty, for 5 minutes, in a nine-inch pie plate. No directions and no list of ingredients are given for the crust, but any American reader would assume that Claiborne meant a conventional American crust and a conventional, sloping-sided pie plate. (Sophisticates might ask themselves whether to fill the crust with beans to weight it down while baking, but this is a detail.) Then he directs us to sprinkle the bottom of the crust with crumbled cooked bacon, sautéed onion, cubes of Gruyère cheese, and grated Parmesan. Over this we are told to pour a custard mixture of cream, whole eggs, nutmeg, salt, and white pepper.

This is a fine recipe: it will produce a delicious pie. But it is very different from the recipe for quiche Lorraine in that other classic American primer published in the same year, *Mastering the Art of French Cooking* by Julia Child, Simone Beck, and Louisette Bertholle. Julia and company state unequivocally that the "classic" quiche contains "no cheese." They blanch their bacon to remove its powerfully smoky taste and to make it approximate the flavor of the classic French ingredient, an unsmoked bacon called *lard de poitrine*. Their extremely short crust is made from a classic Pâte Brisée dough (page 147) and is weighted down with beans while it parbakes. Instead of sprinkling the bacon on the bottom of the crust, they press it into the crust. And they don't crumble the bacon. They cut it into pieces an inch long and ¼ inch wide. There is no onion in their quiche and, of course, no cheese.

Who is right? Craig or Julia *et aliae?* If we consult standard French sources and use them as our test for authenticity, the Child recipe comes closest to being the real thing. Austin de Croze, in *Les plats régionaux de France* (1928), prefers a fluted mold for the crust, the kind widely sold here as a quiche pan, but he permits a flan ring "*à défaut.*" Child settled for a flan ring or a standard, unfluted, straight-sided American cake pan. De Croze says nothing about parbaking, but the informant whose recipe he reprints was a restaurant chef likely to have thought the necessity for parbaking too obvious to bother mentioning. At any rate, de Croze garnishes his crust with blanched, lightly browned *lard,* and he permits onion and herbs as optional additions. He does not advise pressing the *lard* and other garnishes into the crust.

In another Bible of French cooking, *La Cuisine de Madame Saint-Ange* (1925), the very detailed recipe for quiche Lorraine resembles the Child recipe in most respects. There is no cheese and no onion. The crust is Pâte Brisée. But Madame Saint-Ange tells us to put thin slices of butter on the bottom of the empty crust. Then she says to press the slices of *lard* to the butter "so that the pieces stick to the bottom and don't float to the surface of the custard mixture when it is poured over them."

I have tried this, and it worked fairly well for me, although I wasn't sure why Madame Saint-Ange cared if the *lard* surfaced. I read her text again and noticed that her researches into antique recipes had revealed that old-fashioned quiches had crust made from bread dough. Could it be that by keeping the *lard* in contact with the crust, she was preserving the taste and texture of a folkoric bread resembling, perhaps, the Italian bread that contains bits of prosciutto? This is pure speculation. It may simply be that this distinguished teacher of cooking preferred to hide the *lard* slices like buried treasure beneath a surface of ungarnished golden custard. This makes sense because Madame Saint-Ange considers *lard* to be an optional ingredient. For her, the essential quiche Lorraine is nothing more nor less than a richer version of a milk flan (*flan au lait*), a pie filled with a milk-and-egg custard. For the quiche Lorraine, one substitutes cream for milk.*

I like this idea: the naked quiche. It has a lovely simplicity about it, and I am convinced, both by Madame Saint-Ange's authority and by common sense, that our bacon-garnished quiche is really a fancified version of a cream custard pie, which itself is a luxurious descendant of a milk flan.

It certainly tastes wonderful. But the question on the table is: Is it better because it is authentic? Well, of course not. The Claiborne quiche and the Child quiche and dozens of other variously garnished quiches make splendid eating. The trouble is that you and I are tired of eating quiche because we have been fed too many of them. And most of those quiches have been poorly made.

You will be pleasantly surprised if you take the trouble to try your hand again at this old standby. It is essential to prebake the crust. Otherwise it will turn out sodden and loathsome. And you will get a remarkably delicate and authentic result if you make the custard with pure cream.

---

* Why is this given the epithet *Lorraine*? Does the extra richness of the cream really connect it somehow with France's eastern border province of that name, or its Germanic cities, Nancy and Metz? For once, the geographic connection is persuasive. *Quiche* is an Alsace-Lorraine dialectal reflex of standard German *Kuchen*, cake (just as the Alsace-Lorraine word for the dark blue plum is *quetsch*, pronounced as in *kvetsch*, the Yiddish for whinge, which (*quetsch* not *kvetsch*) derives from standard German *Zwetschgen*). Why does the richer version of the flan get the Lorraine tag? Now there is a question lost to the ages, along with the name Achilles used when dodging the Greek draft while disguised as a woman, or the details of Sherlock Holmes's never-recorded case of the giant rat of Sumatra.

1 recipe Pâte Brisée (page 147)   ½ teaspoon salt

  Butter   1 pinch white pepper

2 whole eggs plus 2 yolks   1 pinch ground (or preferably grated)

2 cups heavy cream   nutmeg

1. Preheat the oven to 400 degrees.
2. Butter one side of a sheet of aluminum foil. Set it into the crust, butter side down. Fill with dried beans or rice. Bake for 9 minutes. Remove the foil and its contents (the beans or rice can be reused for this process but don't try to eat them). Set the empty crust back in the oven for a few minutes, until the crust browns slightly and starts to pull away from the pan.
3. Cool the crust on a rack. Reduce the oven to 375 degrees.
4. Beat together the eggs, cream, and seasonings in a bowl until well blended.
5. Pour the mixture into the crust and bake for 30 minutes. Unmold and serve while still warm.

Serves 6 to 8

Ribollita
(Tuscan "Reboiled" Bean and Greens Soup)

In the food counterculture, the well-heeled rabble that militates against fast food and overprecious chefs, Frankenfoods and pesticides and antibiotically tampered meat, *ribollita* is the poster dish. What more could Slow Foodies ask for than a peasant soup "reboiled" from yesterday's leftovers? Devotees of *cucina povera,* the cooking of the poor, could hardly invent anything "poorer" than this celebrated and adored member of a whole, hearty Italian family of "poor" soups and peasant *minestre.* And there is the added touch of poignance that this is a *Tuscan* peasant soup, now that rural Tuscany is mostly populated by expatriate Germans and with Brits who jokingly call it Chiantishire.

Far be it from me, however, to vie with my betters over who is more down to earth. I like a peasant soup as much as the next college graduate, and *ribollita* is a great peasant soup, but it has inspired the kind of dogfight over authenticity among its nonpeasant fans that peasant food so often does.

After all, the point of getting back to a preindustrial, uncontaminated style of eating has to be that we decadent urbanites can find a path back to a Rousseauian simplicity, to a real, viz., an authentic, country table. No microwaves need apply. And the ingredients must be precisely the ingredients traditionally used for each dish in the age of horse-drawn plows.

If you scan the list of ingredients below, you will be struck by one item that you didn't grow up with in Akron. *Cavolo nero,* literally black cabbage, is the equivalent for this recipe of what mountain climbers call the crux of a climb, the one place on a pitch that has to be overcome if you are going to succeed in moving upward to the next pitch or finishing the ascent. Put simply, no *cavolo nero,* no *ribollita.*

I had been told by dyed-in-the-homespun *ribollitistas* practicing their religion in Manhattan that *cavolo nero* was unavailable on this side of the Atlantic. I'd have to rent a villa in Radda near from if I wanted to make *ribollita* myself. Then I opened Benedetta Vitali's *Soffritto, Tradition and Innovation in Tuscan Cooking* (2001) and discovered that *cavolo nero* was actually sold in the New World as elephant kale or lacinato kale.

Although Ms. Vitali is a real Tuscan and runs a restaurant in Florence, she took the trouble to find out how American readers could find what they needed to duplicate her food. No longer did I have to decide whether to cross the Atlantic or make do with ordinary kale if I was going to purify my toxic soul with *ribollita.*

THE COOK'S CANON   **173**

One place that sells elephant kale (in season, of course), is a CSA (community-supported agriculture) farm co-operative near Ithaca, New York. Their Web site has banjo music and plenty else to offer. But don't get me wrong, I would be happy to make this soup with the traditional, crux ingredient, but I've tried it with kale and even plain green cabbage and the idea was strong enough to survive the substitution. This is life in the big city. Get used to it. But eat more *ribollita*.

2½ cups dried cannellini beans	10 leaves *cavolo nero* (black cabbage sold as elephant kale or lacinato kale) or ordinary kale
5 cloves garlic, peeled and minced	
5 sage leaves	
2½ cups olive oil, approximately	6 leeks, trimmed and sliced (green and white)
2 onions, peeled and chopped fine	
5 carrots, peeled and chopped fine	6 cups beef stock
3 stalks celery, trimmed and chopped fine	4 sprigs thyme
5 potatoes, peeled and chopped fine	Salt, if needed
3 zucchini, peeled and chopped fine	Tuscan or other sourdough bread, sliced about ½ inch thick
½ Savoy cabbage, cut as for slaw	

1. Soak the beans overnight in enough cold water to cover them by 2 inches. The next day add 2 cloves garlic and the sage. Bring to a boil and simmer very slowly, covered, for about an hour. Do not stir. The beans are done when they are just tender. Reserve with the cooking liquid.

2. Heat ¾ cup olive oil in a skillet and sauté the onions, carrots, and celery until lightly browned. Then add the potatoes, zucchini, cabbage, *cavolo nero* or kale, leeks, remaining garlic, and the beans with their liquid. Add beef stock to cover and the thyme.

3. Bring to a boil, reduce the heat, and simmer gently for about a half hour.

4. Stir in the remaining oil. Add salt if necessary.

5. In a clean pot you can serve the soup from, pour in an inch of soup. Cover with a layer of bread slices. Alternate layers of soup and bread until the soup is used up. Finish with a layer of bread. Then add additional beef stock to saturate the bread.

6. Let rest for several hours. Before serving, reheat over low heat, stirring gently.

Serves 10

Rice Pudding

Rice pudding is comfort food par excellence. It is soft, rich, and white. It is also comforting for the cook, because it takes about 5 minutes, maybe less, to mix together the ingredients before putting them in the oven. You do have to stick around for the two and a half hours it takes to finish baking in the oven.

If you are worried about cholesterol, rice pudding can be made with skim milk (though it will be less "comforting" to the mouth). If you are holding down on starch, please note that, although this is undeniably a *rice* pudding, it has very little rice in it—¼ cup divided among six portions. How can this be? How can so little rice absorb so much milk? The ratio of volumes is 16 to 1. But in the course of the slow cooking, the milk gradually evaporates at the same time that the rice swells from absorbing what is left. At the end, the rice grains are still intact (they will break down completely if you keep on cooking them, as in the Chinese eight-jewel rice pudding, in which eight different honeyed fruits cover a solid mass of steamed glutinous rice.)

Every culture that eats both rice and milk seems to have its own rice pudding. In the Middle East, aniseed, rosewater, and mastic give the dish a pungent regional flavor. In India, *kheer* (in the recipe Madhur Jaffrey gives in *An Invitation to Indian Cooking* [1973]) starts out with a quart of milk and a tablespoon of rice (64 parts milk to 1 part rice!), but very slow simmering reduces the volume to 2 cups of thickened milk. Cardamom seeds (discarded later) infuse the milk with their typically Indian flavor during this process.

My simple recipe for rice pudding is basically English. Many people prefer it baked without the stirring, so that a skin does form on the top, a skin they claim to love. Nanny made them eat it, and they don't get the full, chilly blast of nursery nostalgia if the "hide" isn't there to remind them of their childhood.

In France, as you might guess, they have taken rice pudding a few steps beyond its humble origins. The French kitchen mentality views rice steamed in milk not so much as a dish in itself but as an *appareil,* a prepared material for use in a more complex dish. There are molded rice puddings, rice pudding cakes, and for a truly snazzy occasion, *riz à l'imperatrice,* in which what we would call rice pudding is mixed with chopped kirsch-soaked fruit, then combined with a stiff crème anglaise custard and whipped cream. This goes into a charlotte mold

My simple recipe for rice pudding is basically English. Many people prefer it baked without the stirring, so that a skin does form on the top, a skin they claim to love. Nanny made them eat it, and they don't get the full, chilly blast of nursery nostalgia if the "hide" isn't there to remind them of their childhood.

whose bottom has been coated with a centimeter of gooseberry jelly. Very well chilled, the dessert is unmolded before service. Then there are subrics. . . .*

¼ cup raw long-grain rice	½ teaspoon vanilla extract
1 quart whole milk	¾ cup raisins
Pinch salt	Grated nutmeg or cinnamon
¾ cup sugar	

1. Preheat the oven to 300 degrees.
2. Stir together the rice, milk, salt, and sugar in a greased, 6-cup soufflé mold (or other oven-proof dish of this volume). Set in the oven and bake for 2 hours, stirring occasionally, to work the "hide" that collects on top of the pudding back into the rice.
3. After 2 hours, stir in the vanilla and raisins. Return to the oven for 30 minutes.
4. Sprinkle with nutmeg or cinnamon. Serve lukewarm or cold.

6 Servings

* Since you insist. For a subric, mix the rice pudding fresh from the oven with liqueur-soaked, chopped glazed fruit. Spread this mixture out on a buttered baking sheet in a layer about 1¼ inches (3 centimeters) thick. Butter the top of the rice mixture to keep it from drying out. When it cools, cut the mixture into disks with 2-inch diameters. Dip them in flour and then fry them in hot clarified butter to color them on both sides. Arrange them on a platter in a large circle and spread their centers with gooseberry jelly or any other firm conserve.

Risotto alla Milanese
(Milanese Boiled Rice)

You can make a pretty good risotto with water instead of stock, but you can't make it at all without the kind of medium-grain rice they grow in the Po Valley in Italy near Genoa. That's because long-grain rice, the variety we grow here, or that is sold as Carolina rice, will turn to mush long before it absorbs all the liquid and fat that risotto rice will slurp up. And so you won't get the rich and creamy result that the right kind of rice will give.

Risotto just means a rice (*riso*) dish made in this very simple way: Coat the rice in hot butter and then start adding liquid and other ingredients until you reach the perfect point of chewy tenderness called al dente, on the tooth.

There are whole cookbooks devoted to the many possible varieties of risotto, and even they haven't exhausted all the possibilities of throwing special ingredients in with the basic risotto. But *risotto alla milanese* is the most famous risotto, because it is usually paired with Milan's other "greatest" dish, Osso Buco alla Milanese (page 134), also because it is elegantly simple and yet earthily delicious, and because the tiny amount of precious saffron, the dried sex apparatus of a special crocus cultivated in Spain, adds a unique flavor and a deep yellow color.

The marrow this recipe tells you to add may strike you as overkill in the unctuous department if you are serving this risotto with osso buco, braised veal shanks whose own marrow is a highlight of that dish. Marrow is less if there is too much of it. But if you are making this risotto by itself, then some marrow will be very nice indeed, and will remind people in the know that they are having a supremo Milanese dish: a kind of subtle reminder of osso buco, without the extra calories.

Something no Milanese will tell you is that this risotto shows all the earmarks of Spanish influence. Well, two earmarks. The first is the saffron, not exclusively a Spanish product but closely identified with Spain, which picked it up from the Moors and ran with it. (The Spanish word for saffron is taken right out of Arabic, *azafrán,* and the Italian cognate, *zafferano,* is a likely offspring.) Second, in Italian recipes for risotto, you will notice that the action of stirring in the quite large amount of grated Parmesan cheese at the end is expressed by the verb *mantecare,* which is usually defined as making something smooth and homogeneous, buttery. Sometimes Italians say an ice cream is *mantecato.*

In any case, this is a word with an obvious Spanish origin and no obvious connections in

Italy except itself. In Spanish, the word for lard is *manteca,* butter is *mantequilla,* i.e., a little or more delicate "lard." My speculation is that risotto arose during the later sixteenth century when Italy was essentially a Spanish province and Milan was governed by a Spanish viceroy. Cross-cultural fertilization between the two peninsulas was routine.

6 cups Light Meat Stock (see below)	3 ounces beef marrow, chopped, optional
6 tablespoons butter	Salt
1 medium onion, peeled and finely chopped	Pepper
2 cups medium-grain risotto rice	1 cup grated Parmesan cheese
²⁄₃ teaspoon saffron threads	

1. Bring the stock to a boil in a 2- to 3-quart saucepan, reduce the heat to medium-low, and simmer.
2. Melt all but 1 tablespoon of the butter in a heavy 4-quart saucepan over medium heat. When the foam subsides, add the onion. Sauté until translucent. Then pour in the rice all at once and stir in the butter until the grains are coated.
3. Add 1 cup of simmering stock, raise the heat a bit, and simmer vigorously. Stir continuously until the liquid has almost all evaporated. Add another cup and continue as before. Keep adding more stock until the rice is al dente. This will take about 20 minutes. If you run out of stock, use boiling water.
4. While you are cooking the rice, pulverize the saffron with a mortar and pestle, dissolve it in a bit of hot stock and then stir it into the rice after it has been cooking for 10 minutes. Stir in the marrow. Taste and add salt and pepper if necessary.
5. When the rice is cooked, stir in ¾ cup Parmesan and the remaining butter. Pass the remaining Parmesan.

Serves 6

Light Meat Stock

4 pounds beef scraps

4 stalks celery, chopped

2 medium onions, peeled and quartered

2 carrots, scraped and cut in rounds

1. Put all the ingredients in a large, heavy pot. Do not brown the meat. This is a *light* stock.
2. Add cold water to cover. Bring to a boil, lower the heat, and simmer very slowly for 3 hours, adding more water as necessary to keep the solid ingredients covered.
3. Strain the stock and discard the solid ingredients. After it cools in an uncovered bowl, the stock can be refrigerated for 2 days (covered) or frozen for 2 months.

3 to 4 quarts

Ropa Vieja
(Cuban Beef Casserole)

Ropa vieja literally means "old clothes." Maybe tatters would be an even better translation, because the beef is cooked until it can be easily shredded. So far this may not sound like something you want to try, but the end result is a delicious thing, the most famous Cuban dish, with a misleadingly ironic name. When I was in Havana in 2002, each of the *paradores* (licensed private restaurants) I ate in served its own variation on *ropa vieja*. This recipe is inspired by the one I liked best.

1 pound skirt or flank steak	2 dried red chilies, stems and seeds removed
1 red bell pepper	
2 tablespoons vegetable oil	3 cloves garlic, peeled and chopped
1 large onion, peeled and chopped	One 6-ounce can tomato paste
	½ teaspoon pepper
	Salt

1. Put the meat in a small saucepan. Add water to cover generously. Bring the water to a boil, reduce the heat, and simmer for 1½ hours or until very tender. Add more boiling water if necessary to keep the meat submerged while it cooks.

2. Impale the red pepper on a long-handled fork and rotate over an open flame until the skin blackens.* Let cool in a paper bag. Pull away the skin, trim, remove the seeds, and julienne. Reserve.

3. Drain the meat and pull apart into shreds. If this is not easy to do, cook it some more.

4. Heat the oil in a skillet. Sauté the onion until translucent. Then add all the other ingredients except the red pepper strips. Stir-fry until well mixed and heated through. Arrange the pepper slices on top of the meat mixture and serve with rice and black beans.

Serves 4

* This can't be done on an electric stove.

Saltimbocca alla Romana
(Roman Breaded Veal and Ham)

As the name implies this is a Roman specialty, but you will find it everywhere in Italy. Also, as the name implies, it is delicious, literally it "jumps in your mouth." This jokey kind of recipe name that includes a comical action is a special category in world cuisine. Italian menus also include *tiramisu* or pull me up (from a heavy meal?) for a cakey cheese tart; *strangolapreti* or *strozzapreti* (strangle or throttle priests, for gnocchi or other pasta that priests couldn't swallow). In Mexico, you will find *manchamanteles* (stain your tablecloth, a stew).

Whether or not you feel so high on saltimbocca that you do think it might jump into your mouth, you have to admit that it is a very clever light dish that exploits two of Italy's best ingredients, veal and prosciutto, with deft simplicity. Don't even think about making this unless you have fresh sage leaves, because the whole point of the dish is to have a real leaf lurking inside releasing flavor. The toothpick also matters; stitching it through the three main ingredients so that it lies flat is essential to the successful cooking of the dish.

6 veal scallopine, about ¼ pound each	6 slices prosciutto
Salt	Flour
Pepper	3 tablespoons butter
6 sage leaves	½ cup dry white wine

1. Line up the scallopine on a counter. Salt and pepper them lightly on both sides. Put a sage leaf in the center of each. Top each with a slice of prosciutto. Fasten each with a toothpick: Push the toothpick through the package twice, like a needle so that it lies flat and holds the sage leaf between the veal and the ham, and so that the package can be browned on both sides.
2. Dredge each saltimbocca in flour and shake off excess.
3. Melt 2 tablespoons butter in a large skillet. Add the saltimboccas, raise the heat, and brown on both sides. Remove from the heat to a serving platter. Remove the toothpicks and discard.
4. Deglaze the pan with the wine, and reduce the liquid almost completely. Melt in the remaining tablespoon of butter, pour over the saltimboccas, and serve immediately.

6 servings

Sauerbraten
(German Marinated Pot Roast)

Sauer **is for the vinegar in the marinade.** *Braten* is the roasting that follows 5 days of marination in the vinegar, red wine, vegetables, and spices. If it weren't for the vinegar and the long marination, with its mild pickling effect, this could be just another pot roast, a big piece of not-so-tender beef stewed in a pot until tender. But with sauerbraten, the stewing (really braising) liquid is the marinade; so the flavors intensify further, and the resulting liquid turns into a sweet-and-sour sauce at the end when it is thickened with gingersnaps crushed in a mortar or in a blender and raisins, the addition of which makes it officially a Rhenish sauerbraten.

Eliminate step 6 if you'd rather not have a traditional, roux-thickened sauce. And don't feel bad about leaving out the gingersnaps or otherwise departing from tradition. No German gastronomic police are circulating in the land, and even the most *echt* German cooks have departed radically from sauerbraten tradition, if it is true that the dish started out as a way of dealing with horsemeat.*

The grandest piece of sauerbraten lore goes back to the ninth century, when Charlemagne (Karl der Grosse in this context, and he was crowned at Aachen) decided to use fresh meat instead of the leftover roasts favored at the court of Albrecht of Cologne. I wouldn't swear to it.

---

* Horsemeat has been sold legally in France since 1811. Special butchers, identifiable by the horsehead "busts" hanging in front of their shops and the phrase *boucherie chevaline,* still operate in France but less widely than a few years ago. The meat is said to be sweeter than beef, appropriate for all dishes normally prepared with beef and particularly recommended for steak tartare because, according to Larousse Gastronomique (1961), horses do not suffer from tuberculosis or tapeworm (or presumably mad cow disease).

In America, there is a small vocal underground of gourmands who favor horse fat for frying potatoes. I have not tried this but it may be so, since horse fat was used to fry potatoes at the most spectacular of all recorded horse banquets. In 1865 in Paris, Flaubert, Dumas, and the revered epicure Dr. Véron tied into a meal composed entirely of horse dishes, from horse consommé with vermicelli to filet of horse with mushroom salad in horse oil to a rum cake with horse bone marrow. Edmond Goncourt did not enjoy himself.

During World War II, to supplement the limited supply of beef, the Harvard Faculty Club put horsemeat on its menu. It was so well liked that it remained a club standby for many years after the war.

2 medium carrots, scraped and cut in
  rounds

2 celery stalks, trimmed and cut in rounds

2 medium onions, peeled and finely
  chopped

4 cloves

8 juniper berries

2 bay leaves, crumbled

1 bottle red wine

1 cup red wine vinegar

1 cup water

3½ pounds top round of beef

2 tablespoons lard or butter

1 cup crumbled gingersnaps

1 cup raisins

1 tablespoon lard or butter

1 tablespoon flour

Salt

Pepper

1. In a medium saucepan, combine the carrots, celery, onions, cloves, juniper berries, bay leaves, red wine, vinegar, and 1 cup water. Bring to a boil, reduce the heat, and simmer for 5 minutes. Transfer to a large bowl, add the beef, cover, and refrigerate for 5 days. Turn the beef twice a day.

2. Remove the beef from the marinade and rinse. Strain the marinade and reserve the solid ingredients as well as the strained liquid.

3. Melt 2 tablespoons lard or butter in a large, heavy pot. Brown the meat in the hot fat on all sides.

4. Remove the meat to a plate. Deglaze the pot with the marinade liquid. Add the solids (discarding the bay leaf), simmer for 5 minutes. Then put in the meat. Hermetically seal the pot, either by placing a clean dish towel around the rim and then putting the lid on top of it or by stretching a piece of aluminum foil across the pot and then putting on the lid. Simmer for 1½ hours or until the beef is tender. (At this point, you can refrigerate the beef for 2 days before serving. Let it cool with the lid ajar.)

5. Remove the beef. Puree the cooking liquid in a blender with the gingersnaps. Return to the boil, add the raisins, and simmer for 15 minutes.

6. Optional roux: As soon as you have started this final cooking stage, melt 1 tablespoon lard or butter in a small skillet and stir in the flour. Continue stirring over low heat until you have a smooth brown roux. Stir in ½ cup of the cooking liquid or a bit more, to produce a smooth slurry. Whisk this into the liquid in the main pot. Add salt and pepper.

7. Remove the beef to a platter, slice and nap with some of the cooking liquid. Pass the rest of the cooking liquid separately.

Serves 6 to 8

Savarin Valaisanne
(Yeast-Risen Ring Cake Soaked with Swiss Pear Brandy from the Valais Region)

Jean-Anthelme Brillat-Savarin (1755–1826) is the author of the most admired book on food ever, *La Physiologie du goût* (1825), *The Physiology of Taste*. Its most famous passages are a series of highly quotable maxims (A meal without cheese is like a beautiful woman with only one eye; the invention of a new dish is like the discovery of a new star).

During the early years of the Revolution, he fled through Switzerland to New York, where he gave French lessons, played the violin in the John Street Theater, and spread the good word about scrambled eggs and that new invention, ice cream. Rehabilitated, he returned to France and cut a wide swath in the burgeoning post-Napoleonic food scene dominated by the chef Carême and the first food journalist Grimod de la Reynière. Brillat-Savarin died after catching cold at a memorial service for Louis XVI in 1826. His name, which he had augmented with Savarin in order to qualify for an inheritance from an aunt of that name, was attached by an admiring posterity to a variety of dishes and garnishes.

The round Norman triple-cream cow's milk cheese called Brillat-Savarin was invented in the twentieth century by the master *fromagier* Androuet. The most famous commemorative dish is the large, yeast-risen, alcohol-soaked toroidal cake, created in Paris during the Second Empire by those great pastry chefs the Julien brothers. Our hero had taught Auguste Julien how to make the alcoholic syrup in which this enlarged baba is traditionally soaked.

There are many variations on the basic savarin idea. This one substitutes pear brandy for the classic rum syrup, in memory of Brillat-Savarin's escape to Switzerland, where pear brandy is a specialty of the canton of the Valais. Should you wish to honor his American sojourn, substitute bourbon for the pear brandy.

Savarin, the gâteau, is a bit of a production but it is worth it. The unusual shape, the moistness (guaranteed by the imbibition of all that boozy syrup), and the potential for further decoration—filling the center with whipped cream and/or glazed fruits (pear suggests itself here)—all assure the continuation of the Brillat-Savarin legend at your table.

1 package active dry yeast

½ teaspoon salt

1 cup plus 1 tablespoon sugar

½ cup lukewarm milk (around 110 degrees)

4 eggs, lightly beaten, at room temperature

2 cups flour, approximately

11 tablespoons butter, softened

1½ cups water

½ cup pear brandy

¾ cup apricot preserves

1. Dissolve the yeast, the salt, and 3 tablespoons of the sugar in the milk.
2. Stir the eggs and then the flour into the yeast mixture. Beat for several minutes with a wooden spoon in order to produce a smooth, soft dough.
3. Let the dough rise in a warm, draft-free place until it doubles in bulk. This may take anywhere from 40 minutes to 2 hours. The ideal room temperature is 80 degrees. Somewhat lower room temperatures slow but do not cut off the growth of the yeast, which gives off carbon dioxide that makes the dough rise. In any case, cover the bowl. One of those elasticized soft plastic "shower cap" bowl covers is ideal.
4. Beat the butter into the risen dough (reserving ½ tablespoon).
5. Preheat the oven to 400 degrees.
6. Grease the inside of a 6-cup savarin mold with the reserved butter. Pack the dough into the mold as evenly as possible, and smooth the surface with a flat wooden spatula. Cover with a moist dish towel and let rise until the dough almost fills the mold.
7. Bake the savarin for 10 minutes in the middle of the oven. Then reduce the heat to 350 degrees and continue baking for about 10 more minutes, at which point the cake should be nicely puffed up, browned on top, and cooked (so that a trussing needle will pass through it and come out clean). Remove from the oven and cool on a rack.
8. While the savarin cools, prepare the syrup: Dissolve 11 tablespoons of the sugar in 1½ cups of water and bring to a boil. Then pour in the pear brandy, remove from heat, and let cool.
9. Unmold the savarin onto a flat platter. Invert it onto another platter so as to leave the top (the flat, browned side) up. Then slice off a thin horizontal layer (in effect, the top crust) and discard (this facilitates the absorption of the syrup).
10. Pour the syrup into a skillet just large enough to hold the savarin. Invert the savarin once more, so that the cut side is down, and slide it gently into the skillet. Let it stand in the syrup for 30 minutes.

11. Meanwhile, sieve the apricot preserves and combine with the remaining 3 tablespoons of sugar in a saucepan.

12. Pour off the excess syrup, if any, from the skillet. Invert the savarin onto a flat platter and then invert a second time onto a circular serving platter. The cut side should be down, the curved side up.

13. Heat the apricot-sugar mixture until it comes to a boil. Then, working quickly and gently, cover the savarin with apricot glaze. Fill the central cavity, if you wish, with berries or whipped cream.

10 servings

Shepherd's Pie

You don't have to be a genius to figure out that a dish called shepherd's pie would have lamb in it. Nor do you need to be a food historian to deduce that this homely but immensely beloved "pie" in which mashed potatoes top the lamb below could not have arisen until potatoes had become a staple in Britain in the early nineteenth century. In fact, shepherd's pie in its modern form—mashed potatoes on top of ground lamb—came along later in the century, after the invention of meat grinders.

Today, you are just as likely to be served a "shepherd's pie" made with hamburger, although the real name for this beefy cousin is cottage pie. Worse still, the thrifty, labor saving soul of the Ur-pie made from leftover roast lamb is often corrupted with purpose-bought meat that has to be specially cooked. And people who will do that won't stop at working in wine and a variety of vegetables and grated cheese. Why stop there? Truffles might dress things up to the point where you could give the dish its French name, *Hachis Parmentier*.

2 pounds leftover lamb, ground

1 cup meat broth

2 tablespoons butter

1 onion, peeled and finely chopped

1 recipe Mashed Potatoes (page 118)

1. Mince the lamb in a processor with the meat broth, which should be composed of drippings from the lamb roast—as much as possible.
2. Melt the butter in a skillet. Sauté the onion until translucent. Stir in the ground lamb. Continue sautéing over medium-high heat so as to brown the meat. Stir every few minutes. This should take about 10 minutes.
3. Put the lamb mixture in an ovenproof casserole. Spread the mashed potatoes over the top and decorate the top by dragging a fork over it to make a pattern of lines. Cover and keep warm for as much as an hour in a low oven, if necessary.

Serves 6

Shrimp, Crab, and Okra Gumbo

Okra and *gumbo* **are both words from West African languages** imported by slaves to this hemisphere along with okra itself (in French okra is *gombo,* its botanical name is *Abelmoschus esculentus*).* On this side of the Atlantic, the okra belt stretches from Brazil to the American Old South, where slavery flourished and left behind a bitter legacy, bitter except in its musical and culinary contributions to the larger culture. From New Orleans to Salvador da Bahia, African recipes adapted to the New World are code-named Creole.

The word originally referred to people of European stock born in the colonies. But it has come to mean African-American. In each place, Creole cooking developed a local style and local recipes. In New Orleans, okra, which turns gluey when thoroughly cooked, gave its name to a soup of seafood, rice, and sausage, which it thickens.

Not all the elements of a New Orleans Creole gumbo are African by any means. The brown roux the recipe begins with is typical of New Orleans Creole dishes but it must have arrived with the French refugees from eastern Canada, the Cajuns, so-called because, under French control, what are now the Maritime Provinces and the U.S. state of Maine were called Acadie (as they still are by resident francophone cultural loyalists—see, for example, the Web site acadie.net) or Acadia, hence Acadians, hence Cajuns.

There is also an Amerindian gumbo tradition. Or perhaps I should say that Creoles and Cajuns learned to use the ground leaves of the sassafras tree as an alternative thickener for gumbo from Choctaws in Louisiana. Called filé (from a French word meaning threadlike or ropy, perhaps from its coagulating effect), this substance is now illegal in commerce because of its demonstrated carcinogenic danger. Sassafras also used to be the prime flavorant in root beer but it has been replaced by a birch extract, also for medico-legal reasons. So I have used okra in my recipe below.

I still have a supply of filé acquired in an introuconco in New Orleans long before the ban. It is turning out to be a lifetime supply. I keep it in my spice rack as a souvenir of a working trip to centers of Creole gastronomy, starting in New Orleans and then passing through the French Antilles. Returning through customs in 1972 with three bottles of greenish powder, I had an awkward job explaining that they contained sassafras and not *cannabis.*

---

* Other African plants naturalized here are black-eyed peas, the true yam, the oil palm, and the watermelon.

½ cup vegetable oi

½ cup flour

3 cloves garlic, peeled and minced

½ cup chopped green bell pepper

1 medium onion, peeled and chopped

2 tablespoons chopped parsley

2 scallions, chopped (green parts only)

2 canned Italian tomatoes, seeded and chopped

1 kielbasa, sliced

4 cups water

1 pound fresh blue crabs, smashed with a cleaver

1 pound okra, topped and tailed

6 sprigs thyme

1 crumbled bay leaf

Salt

Cayenne

1 tablespoon vinegar

4 cloves

½ teaspoon ground or, preferably, grated nutmeg

5 whole allspice

1 pound peeled shrimp

2 cups rice, boiled until al dente

1. Set the oil over low heat in a 6-cup saucepan. Whisk in the flour and continue whisking until it turns a light brown. Add the garlic, bell pepper, onion, parsley, and scallions. Continue stirring until the green pepper has softened.

2. Add the tomatoes, kielbasa, water, crabs, and okra. Bring to a boil. Add all the remaining ingredients except the shrimp and rice. Bring to a boil and simmer for 15 minutes, stirring.

3. Add extra water as necessary to keep the soup from turning into a solid mass.

4. Add the shrimp and simmer until they turn pink, 3 to 4 minutes. Remove from heat. Put the cooked rice in individual serving bowls and pour the gumbo over it.

Serves 4 to 6

Sole Meunière
(Sole Miller-Style)

Meunière is literally miller-style. This may be one of the rare instances where a classic menu code word may spring from a meaningful reality. Millers live by millstreams, in which fish might be swept along by the man made force of the millrace as it drives the wheel of the mill. Yes, I know that sole are sea fish—flat sea fish with a single eye looking up at anyone looking down at them. But *meunière* is a style not necessarily tied to sole alone (no pun intended). Escoffier gives a recipe for trout *à la meunière.* No doubt the ideal fish to be prepared this way—dredged in milk and flour, pan-fried in butter, and sauced with more butter, lemon juice, and parsley—is the chub or shiner (*Cyprinella* spp.) They're nicknamed *meunier* in French (formal name *chevesne*), because they live near mills, presumably to feed on spilled grain.

The grain itself provides a second possible derivation for *à la meunière:* the fish is dredged in flour, flour that comes from a mill!!

The third, and most likely, source for *meunière* is that the chefs who gave French dishes their standard names ran out of arbitrarily chosen place names—*lyonnais, maltaise*—and turned to the professions and trades. Just as they could invent birthplaces for dishes, they could also assign them to various lines of work. So we have *financière, forestière, menagère, cardinal, paysan provençal, chasseur,* and *meunière.**

Why, you ask, is this straightforward method of cooking fish any different from what ordinary fishermen do with their catch? The special *meunière* touch—not that it is beyond the reach of fishermen who can't boil potatoes—comes at the end. Just before it is brought to the table, the fish is sprinkled with lemon juice. At the table or within view and hearing of the diner, melted butter is poured over the fish and sizzles alluringly on contact with the acid lemon juice. If you think it is a trivial stunt, you haven't had it done for you. A small thing but elegant, and it creates a simple, cleverly executed lemon-butter sauce.

* There are two other main categories of recipe names. Famous and powerful men: Richelieu, Suvarov, Rothschild, Henri IV, Byron, Victor Emmanuel, Rossini. And famous women, usually actresses or singers: Melba, Caroline (La Belle) Otero, Adelina Patti, Comtesse Marie, Empress Josephine, Mary Garden. If any of these luminaries ever cooked any of these dishes, I will eat grass like oxen.

Salt

Four 6-ounce sole fillets

1 cup milk

1 cup flour

3 tablespoons butter

Juice of 1 lemon

1 tablespoon chopped parsley

1. Salt the fish lightly. Moisten the fillets in the milk and then dredge in the flour, coating them evenly. Set on wax paper and let rest for a half hour.

2. Heat 2 tablespoons butter in a skillet large enough to hold all four fillets. Sauté the sole over medium-high heat. Turn the fish so as to brown nicely on both sides. Sole is a thin, flat fish and will cook rapidly. It is done when it offers gentle resistance to a finger probe. Remove to a warm serving platter.

3. Add a tablespoon of butter to the butter in the skillet. While it melts, squeeze the lemon juice liberally over the sole. Sprinkle with the parsley.

4. When the butter foams, bring it to the table with the fish and pour the butter over it. When it hits the lemon juice, it will sizzle. This is the humble glory of sole *meunière*.

Serves 4

Soufflé

Orson Welles once pretended to lock me inside Jean-Pierre Melville's shooting set in Paris, cackling in his most resonant Lamont Cranston voice about "the Cask of Amontillado," a Poe story in which the hero is immured. Then we went to lunch at La Truite and he tried to order an almond soufflé although there wasn't one on the menu. He did it all the time but hadn't found one in many years.

I can't tell you why the almond soufflé has slipped from view, but I can tell you the trick of making one. You can't do it with almonds; they would sink the soufflé. And almond extract is not something you'd want to flavor a delicate dessert. The answer is *orzata,* an almond-flavored syrup from Italy. If you can't find it, substitute Grand Marnier, the French orange liqueur, not really a substitute but a standard soufflé ingredient in its own right.

Restaurants make a great fuss about soufflés. You have to order them in advance and they tend to add a surcharge, to cover the last-minute effort and attention in the kitchen. At home, the soufflé is a piece of cake. The labor is free and you can time the whisking so that you don't have to be away from the table for more than a few minutes.

A soufflé is a trick done with eggs and a béchamel sauce. "Soufflé" means blown or inflated and that's exactly what happens. The air whisked into the whites expands in the oven and the custard/béchamel medium the whites have been folded into holds them there just tightly enough to let you bring an airy confection to the table and serve it before it collapses.

A word about beating egg whites to stiff peaks: traditionalists did it in copper bowls. Modern cooks with powerful, electric mixers with balloon whisk attachments add a bit of cream of tartar to keep the whites in line. Scientific experiment has shown that the copper really does react with the whites in a helpful way, and that cream of tartar supplies a similar effect. I love my round-bottomed copper bowl with its copper ring handle. The whisk zooms lightly along the curved surface, and I can use it for zabaglione, too (page 231). But I also like my K5-A mixer, which does clean work when I don't feel like spending 5 minutes twirling a whisk.

This recipe is for a molded soufflé. The mold gives it a shape. That is the French way, beauty through control. In Austria, there is a more relaxed alternative, an unmolded soufflé called Salzburger Nockerln. In fact, it looks quite under control when served, like a cloud. Because it has been baked in a flat pan, it cooks faster and is easier to serve than a molded soufflé.

On the other hand, the molded, French-style soufflé comes with a runny center, stands up tall, and makes people say, "Wow."

Butter and sugar for the soufflé mold

1 cup milk

½ cup sugar

⅓ cup flour

1½ tablespoons butter

4 eggs, separated, plus 2 egg whites

¼ cup *orzata* or 1 tablespoon almond extract or ¼ cup Grand Marnier

Confectioners' sugar

1. Preheat the oven to 350 degrees.
2. Butter the insides of a 6-cup soufflé mold. Then sprinkle the insides with granulated sugar.
3. Hold back 3 tablespoons of milk and put the rest in the saucepan and bring to a boil. Remove from the heat as soon as the milk begins to foam up.
4. In a mixing bowl, whisk together ½ cup sugar, the flour, and the remaining 3 tablespoons milk. Whisk in a bit of the boiled milk and then pour the mixture in the bowl into the saucepan. Heat this thick béchamel over low-medium heat for 2 minutes, stirring constantly. Then remove from heat.
5. Add the butter, cover the saucepan, and let cool for 15 minutes. Stir in the egg yolks with a wire whisk. Add the desired flavoring.
6. Beat the egg whites until they form soft peaks. Along the way, beat in the remaining sugar.
7. Fold the egg whites into the yolk/milk mixture. Pour into the prepared mold. There should be ¾ inch of leeway at the top. If you cover the mold and keep it warm you can hold the soufflé for a half hour.
8. Dust with confectioners' sugar and bake for about 20 minutes. The top should be lightly browned and the sides of the soufflé should be pulling away from the mold. The soufflé will have risen to the top of the mold or slightly higher. The outer part of the soufflé will be solid, the center creamy.

Serves 4

Southern Fried Chicken

Millions have been made on chicken pieces fried in deep fat. And millions of Americans care deeply about their notion of where it came from and how it should be cooked. We can probably all agree about a few basic things in this otherwise contentious area. It comes from the South. It is always dredged in some kind of flour or other starch. It is chicken.

Of course, there are many other foods that are "southern-fried." I have eaten southern-fried quail and southern-fried eggplant. I have even tried to eat southern-fried bacon in a downtown Atlanta cafeteria. I love southern-fried catfish and hush puppies, which are balls of southern-fried cornmeal. The trouble is that I think while I eat. I know that the southern part of "southern-fried" is a polite way of claiming for Dixie what came to the prebellum South in the minds of slaves from West Africa. Saying this is almost as inflammatory as telling Mexicans that their national saint, the Virgin of Guadalupe, takes her name from a shrine devoted to the Virgin Mary in Spain, in a place called Guadalupe.

How do I know for sure that southern frying is really African frying? Because I have seen and tasted "southern-fried" food all over the Caribbean and in parts of South America with significant black populations descended from slaves. The hush puppy is only the northern extension of a Yoruba fritter made in the United States with cornmeal instead of with the black-eyed pea flour black women street vendors use to make what they call *acaraje* in Brazil's Bahia province. Black-eyed peas are imports to the West Atlantic rim from Africa, and Bahian *acaraje* are identical to fritters of the same name that are still a popular food in Nigeria. And they are first cousins of the *acrats* eaten in Martinique and Guadeloupe.

Someday, an ambitious person will gather all these post-African recipes and assemble them in a book of West Atlantic Creole food, the food of the Americas-born children of slaves. Then we will really understand the full splendor of the tradition that southern-fried chicken belongs in.

This is not to attack Colonel Sanders or Sarah Rutledge, the Charlestonian daughter of a signer of the Declaration of Independence, who included a recipe for southern-fried chicken in *The Carolina Housewife* (1847). Her recipe does not differ from a dozen others published since by cooks both white and black. If the method is undoubtedly African, there is much in it that evolved here and that affects the taste of the dish. In particular, lard is the "authentic" local substitution for the African palm oil (which was successfully transplanted to South

America and is what those street cooks in Bahia use). The spice is another important indicator. Black cooks, or commercial purveyors who want to attract a black clientele, put in red pepper, lots of it.

But in the United States of America every group can enjoy the style of living it prefers, even if that means buying Colonel Sander's, uncrisp, blandly seasoned "original" Kentucky-fried chicken.

2 cups flour

1 tablespoon salt

2 teaspoons black pepper

1 teaspoon cayenne

2 small chickens (3 pounds or less) cut into 8 pieces each, or 16 precut chicken pieces, rinsed and patted dry

1 cup lard, at room temperature, or 1 cup vegetable oil, approximately

1. Put the flour, salt, pepper, and cayenne in a large paper bag. Shake the bag to mix the ingredients.
2. Put a few of the chicken pieces in the bag, Shake well to coat the chicken with the flour mixture. Remove from the bag to a sheet of wax paper with tongs. Shake the excess flour back into the bag. Continue until all the chicken pieces are coated with the flour. Cover with a second sheet of wax paper and let stand at room temperature for an hour, so that the flour will adhere to the chicken.
3. Heat a skillet large enough to hold all the chicken pieces and put in the lard. When the lard melts, slide in the chicken pieces. Cover and cook over medium-high heat. The lard should come halfway up the chicken. Turn at least once with tongs, so that the chicken pieces are golden brown on all sides. About 10 minutes per side.
4. Remove the chicken and drain on paper towels. Serve immediately.

Serves 6

Spaghetti alla Carbonara
(Spaghetti with Unsmoked Bacon and Eggs)

The oldest myth in gourmet mythology is the heroic tale of Marco Polo, intrepid Renaissance Venetian traveler, and how he imported pasta from the court of Kublai Khan in Cathay. Evidence for noodles in Italy before Polo is abundant. But if pasta is primordial in Italy, why does it also predominate in the national culture? One hardly needs to point out how pervasive this form of quick bread, whether extruded, rolled, or stamped out, is in the alimentary universe of the descendants of the Romans. No clear evidence exists to explain this decisive dietary choice. But it is inarguable. Italians even boil special pasta for their dogs. For themselves, the choice is almost infinite. So it would be foolish to single out a single noodle, and yet spaghetti is clearly the poster bambino of the category.

Most American recipes substitute our smoked bacon for unsmoked Italian pancetta. Why bother making the dish with an ingredient that so radically changes its taste? There are so many other ways of dressing pasta. Perhaps the *baconisti* are willing to forgive themselves this barbarism because they are too besotted with the way the hot noodles cook the eggs in the serving bowl to give up the dish just because of a quibble over pancetta.

6 quarts water	4 eggs
Salt	Pepper
1 tablespoon olive oil	1 pound spaghetti
½ pound pancetta (unsmoked Italian bacon), or U.S.-style smoked bacon, diced	1 cup grated Parmesan cheese

1. Boil 6 quarts lightly salted water.
2. Heat the olive oil in a skillet. Sauté the pancetta or bacon until it is very lightly browned but not crisp. Drain and reserve.
3. Meanwhile beat the eggs with salt and pepper until the yolks and whites have blended.
4. Put the spaghetti in the boiling water. Stir once and cook at a full boil until al dente, about 10 minutes. Drain briefly and transfer to a warm serving bowl.
5. Stir in the cheese, then the pancetta or bacon and, finally, the eggs. The heat of the noodles will cook the eggs. Serve immediately.

Serves 4 to 6

Standing Rib Roast
with Yorkshire Pudding

In the Middle West when I was growing up in the fifties, young—and sometimes even older—brides often succumbed to a malady known as hostess heat. This was a fever brought on by panic over the prospect of preparing dinner for guests. What if the rumaki were cold? What if the hollandaise curdled? What, worst of all, if the Yorkshire pudding came out greasy and flat, instead of as nicely browned and puffy pastries baked at the last minute in the drippings of that most canonical of roasts, the standing rib?

Because of its size, a standing rib roast was invariably company food. All by itself, it made for a festive dinner party, but some anonymous villain in Yorkshire had saddled the American housewife in a society still dominated by Anglo-Saxon attitudes with the ticklish problem of turning out a so-called Yorkshire pudding at the last minute, when hostess heat burned highest.

Following the lead of C. Anne Wilson in *Food and Drink in Britain, from the Stone Age to the 19th Century* (1973), it is possible to sketch a rough history not only of Yorkshire pudding but of roast beef itself. From the end of the Middle Ages, Yorkshire was a cattle-raising center, its pastures and cow barns then known as vaccaries. The demand for beef increased and stayed steady during and after religious meatless days were abolished during the Cromwell Commonwealth. But spit-roasting remained the normal method for roasting meat until the nineteenth century, and the mechanical spits of the day had a dripping pan (in France, *lèchefrite*).

When wheat came into general use in the eighteenth century, thrifty cooks in the north of England, including Yorkshire, started making batter "puddings" directly in the dripping pan while the roast turned. Ms. Wilson notes that in 1737, a recipe was published in the anonymous cookbook *The Whole Duty of a Woman* for a "a dripping pudding" made under a roasting piece of mutton with a batter like those made for pancakes. Then, in 1747, Hannah Glasse published the first edition of the most important of all British cookbooks, *The Art of Cookery, Made Plain and Easy, by a Lady,* which contained the first printed recipe for "Yorkshire Pudding."

This was really hard work, and chancy, what with all that stooping in front of a hot fire, as well as the uncertainty of timing with a spit. So when you try to make Yorkshire pudding (for a discussion of "pudding" in British usage, see page 159) in your modern oven, think of how much easier your whole duty as a woman or man is than it was for the cooks who first tried their hands at this fine thing. They also liked to serve raspberry vinegar with their dripping puddings and beef. Vinegar went out of fashion for two centuries and a half but returned to chic with the nouvelle cuisine. Try some with your roast and Yorkshire pudding.

1 tablespoon plus 1 teaspoon salt	2 cups milk
1 tablespoon pepper	4 eggs
2 tablespoons olive oil	2 cups flour
One 8-pound (3-rib) standing rib roast	½ cup drippings from the roast

1. Preheat the oven to 450 degrees.
2. Whisk together the salt, pepper, and olive oil to make a paste. Rub the meat liberally all over with it. Then put the roast in a roasting pan, fat side up.
3. Set on a rack in the lower third of the oven.
4. After 20 minutes, reduce the temperature to 325 degrees. For rare meat, cook another hour and a half. Test with a meat thermometer. Rare is around 115 degrees. Medium-rare 120, medium 125, and well done 130.
5. Remove the roast from the oven and let it stand for 20 minutes before carving. Meanwhile, raise the oven temperature to 450 degrees.
6. Warm a medium baking pan in the oven while you prepare the Yorkshire pudding for baking.
7. Working quickly, whisk the milk and eggs together until smooth. Then whisk in the flour and the remaining 1 teaspoon salt.
8. Pour the drippings over the heated pan so that they cover the bottom completely. Then pour the egg-flour batter over the drippings, covering them completely.
9. When you are sure the oven temperature is 450 degrees, bake 10 minutes. Reduce the temperature to 350 degrees and bake another 15 minutes or until nicely browned. (The roast should be ready to carve after about 5 minutes of this final pudding-cooking stage. So if all goes well, you will be ready to bring out the Yorkshire pudding right after the meat and vegetables have been served.) Cut into squares and serve.

Serves 10 to 12

Steak au Poivre
(Steak with Pepper Sauce)

In every bistro in the world, you can order this pan-fried, flamed steak with its simple but sinus-clearing pepper-and-cream sauce. Served canonically with a daunting pile of crisp *frites* (French fries to you and me), this is a standard item in French cooking in the real world of brasseries and no-star country inns. But in the literature of haute cuisine, it gets no respect.

There is no reference to steak au poivre in *Larousse Gastronomique* (1938), and none either in Escoffier's handbook for home cooks, *Ma Cuisine* (1934) or in his professional summa gastronomica, *Le Guide Culinaire* (1921). This cannot be an oversight. Well, then, is it snobbery or pride of craft? A bit of both, I think. A great chef can't be bothered with plebeian dishes.

A far lesser light than Escoffier, a martinet named Fayet, used to operate an expensive restaurant in midtown Manhattan called Lafayette. The similarity between its name and his was not accidental. Just as the Marquis de Lafayette had deigned to help the American colonists with their little revolution, Fayet was going to show us that the highest French standards could be maintained in this desert of fast food and grotesque informality. One day a Rothschild came in and tried to order a grilled steak. Fayet wouldn't serve him. Ditto for Alfred Knopf the publisher, who asked in vain for iced coffee on a July day.

Steak au poivre is a serious step up from *entrecôte grillé,* but too associated with mundane eating to get even a nod in a grand cookbook. The word steak may have also caused a problem. Although it has been completely absorbed into French, it still carries an English taint, as does the risible earlier borrowing *bifteck.*

To the unprejudiced palate, which includes millions of its French admirers, steak au poivre is a splendid gustatory event that begins with a flash in the pan and ends with a sauce thrown together *à la minute,* at the last moment. Somehow, even noncooks sense the rapid volley of events that preceded by seconds the arrival of the steak at the table. And if they think about it, they will realize that the pepper in the name of the dish is not just a whim. Coarsely cracked peppercorns, well heated, give off a strong flavor. In this dish, that aroma challenges but does not overwhelm the deeper flavor of the meat. The cream tames the heat of the pepper and the emulsifying mustard but gives them their heads nonetheless.

2 tablespoons black peppercorns, coarsely
crushed with a mortar and pestle

One 4-pound sirloin steak, 3 inches thick

2 tablespoons butter

2 tablespoons cognac

Salt

1/3 cup heavy cream

1 1/2 teaspoons Dijon mustard

1. Press the cracked peppercorns into the steak on both sides.
2. Melt the butter in a skillet just large enough to hold the steak. When the foam subsides, put in the steak and pan-fry at medium-high heat, turning from time to time in order to brown both sides and cook the thick piece of meat evenly. When both sides are browned and the meat is slightly firmer than it started out, you have a rare steak. Test this if you aren't sure by cutting into the meat at its thickest point.
3. Remove the skillet from the heat and put the steak on a carving board. Cut into four pieces or into strips cut against the grain of the meat. Reassemble the steak on a serving platter. Then degrease the liquid in the skillet.
4. Add the cognac to the degreased liquid. Heat until it vaporizes. Then light it with a match and let it burn until it stops flaming. Stir in the salt, heavy cream, and mustard. Whisk together and pour over the steak.

Serves 6 to 8

Strawberry Preserves

If all goes well and you pay close attention to the temperature and behavior of the sugar and the syrup as you cook this recipe, you will have preserved the strawberries, literally and figuratively. They will be stabilized by cooking and by the absorption of the syrup—and they will be preserved as whole fruits that look like—and are—strawberries, glistening red and with a subtly altered but entirely recognizable strawberry taste. Of course, you can buy perfectly splendid strawberry preserves. You no longer live the life of a subsistence farmer who puts up preserves to save the fruit she can't eat when it is ripe and abundant.

But you should make strawberry preserves all the same, out of an ambition to create beauty (the jars are little sculptures glinting in the larder) and this particular recipe illustrates sugar chemistry scientifically (see page 40) and, in steps 3 and 4, demonstrates a time-honored prescientific method still practiced in French homes.

Without probably knowing it, French cooks have an inherited right to strawberries, because strawberries are, historically, a French invention. I am not talking about the entire strawberry genus (*Fragaria*), which is a divine invention, in both senses of the word divine. But the strawberry of commerce is a deliberately cultivated hybrid that combines the virtues of two wild types of this aggregate fruit (the little seeds on the surface are the actual "fruits," aggregated on the fleshy and delicious "receptacle" you have up till now thought of as the fruit), one type originating on each of the American coasts.

From earliest antiquity, Europeans had loved the plant we now call wild strawberry or *fraise des bois,* but they had never been able to coax it to grow large and sweet. After the discovery of the Americas, plant explorers brought back *F. virginiensis* from Virginia and *F. chiloensis* from the Pacific coast of Chile. By a happy accident (and some exemplary international cooperation from the Royal Garden at Kew), both species ended up within pollination distance of each other in a greenhouse at what is now the Jardin des Plantes in Paris, where a green thumb named Jussieu (after whom a nearby street and Metro stop are named) noticed that they had given rise to a volunteer plant whose fruit combined the size of the insipid Chilean plant and the delicious flavor of the Virginian. From this happy accident spread the billions of tons of what we now think of as natural strawberries, the kind God made, except that he didn't. So the strawberry is one of the undoubted benefits to all people of the Columbus landfall and the European occupation of the New Hemisphere.

. . . in a greenhouse at . . . the Jardin des Plantes in Paris, where . . . they had given rise to a volunteer plant whose fruit combined the size of the insipid Chilean plant and the delicious flavor of the Virginian. From this happy accident spread the billions of tons of what we now think of as natural strawberries, the kind God made, except that he didn't.

1 cup sugar

About ⅓ cup water

1 pound strawberries, trimmed and washed

2 6-ounce (¾ cup) jam jars, boiled for 20 minutes

1. Dissolve the sugar in a small amount of water, say a third of a cup, preferably in an untinned copper pot. Bring to a boil, skim away impurities with a slotted spoon or skimmer, and continue boiling until the temperature of the sugar reaches 238 degrees on a candy thermometer. This is the soft-ball stage, when a small amount of the sugar dropped in cold water will form a malleable ball.

2. Lower the heat and slide in the strawberries. Cook for 7 to 8 minutes, until the strawberry liquid has dissolved into the sugar and combined with it to make a syrup.

3. Remove the strawberries and drain.

4. Meanwhile, continue boiling the syrup over medium-high heat, until you notice the rate of boiling accelerates. This signifies that evaporation is complete. Return the strawberries to the syrup.

5. From this point on, test the consistency of the syrup with the skimmer frequently. At first, the syrup will drip off the skimmer in a rapid stream. After a few minutes, it will visibly thicken on the skimmer and drip off slowly in large, well-spaced droplets. This is the *nappe,* the moment you have been waiting for, when the syrup "coats" the spoon (*nappe* in everyday French means tablecloth, something that covers something else—a *nappe de petrole* is an oil slick). Remove from the heat immediately and let cool for 10 minutes. Then fill the jam jars a little at a time, to warm the glass and also prevent the strawberries from floating to the top, which happens if you pour in the whole amount quickly.

About 1 pound strawberry preserves

Suckling Pig

A crisp, glistening suckling pig fresh from the oven with an apple in its mouth defines festive. This is not a dish for a romantic evening for two by the fire with flutes of champagne and soft music. Suckling pig is for raucous assemblies of revelers, for folks who like the idea of roasting a whole, greasy, tender animal taken from its mother's teat before it has had a chance to forage on its own, eat solid food, and turn into a nasty hog or sow. If this kind of thing makes you quiver with discomfort, no one is trying to shame you into wrestling with a snouted piglet in a hot oven. But someone has to do it if the feast is to take place. And here is a straightforward method.

There are many ways to roast a baby swine. At one of the annual press lunches that the Christian Brothers Winery used to host at Lutèce in New York, André Soltner, the gifted chef, stuffed the cavity of a *cochon de lait* with a subtle and aromatic super-sausage.* In the Philippines, suckling pig is almost the national dish. In her classic *Recipes of the Philippines* (1973),[†] Enriqueta David-Perez stuffs a small pig with tamarind leaves and thrusts a bamboo pole through it as a spit to turn it over a charcoal fire. For a sauce, she grinds the pig's liver, stirs in a cup of water, strains it and then cooks the purified chopped liver in a hash with $\frac{1}{4}$ tablespoon sautéed onion, $\frac{1}{4}$ cup bread crumbs, $\frac{1}{4}$ cup vinegar, $\frac{1}{4}$ cup sugar, salt, and a whole head of garlic, peeled, minced, and browned in $\frac{1}{4}$ cup lard. After seasoning with salt and pepper, she cooks until thick.

Viviana Carballo, a Cuban refugee from Castro who earned a prestigious *grand diplôme* at the Cordon Bleu in Paris and tested recipes in the *New York Times* food department for a time in the early seventies, developed this recipe for American kitchens and served it with a Cuban garlic sauce, *mojo de ajo:* Peel a small head of garlic and process with 1 teaspoon salt and $\frac{1}{2}$ teaspoon each of pepper, ground oregano, and ground cumin. Stir in the juice of two limes or two naranja agrias (see page 70) and 1/4 cups hot pork fat.

---

* During the cocktail period before the meal, I found myself talking to a man in a monk's habit. Assuming he was an actor hired for the occasion, I said: "I get it. You're a Christian Brother."

"Indeed, I am," he replied with beatific calm. "I'm Brother Timothy, the cellar master at the winery. What's your name?"

† I have been unable to establish the original date of publication. My copy is the nineteenth printing, 1973.

One 10- to 12-pound suckling pig, trussed   Vegetable oil

Salt   1 small apple

1. Preheat the oven to 450 degrees.

2. Rub plenty of salt into the skin of the pig. Cover the ears and tail with aluminum foil. Press some aluminum foil into a tightly compacted ball. Insert in the pig's mouth.

3. Oil the bottom of a roasting pan big enough to hold the pig. Set the pig in the pan on its side. And put in the oven with the pig's head facing out.

4. After 25 minutes or if the pig begins to smoke, reduce the heat to 375 degrees. Continue cooking for another 1¼ hours. Then turn the pig on its other side, baste liberally with additional oil, and put back in the oven headfirst.

5. After another 40 minutes, turn the pig on its belly, remove the foil from ears and tail, baste and return to the oven for another half hour or until a meat thermometer registers 180 degrees, the skin is crisp and dark, and the thighs move easily in their sockets. Remove from oven, present the whole pig to your guests, and then, out of their view, sever the head from the body. This allows residual steam to escape, instead of letting it soften the skin.[*] Reassemble the pig.

6. Remove the foil from the mouth and replace with the apple. Begin the carving process by cutting away the trotters. Then cut the skin into serving pieces. Carve the meat from the ribs.

Serves 8 to 10

---

[*] Hervé This proved this in an experiment conducted with Jeffrey Steingarten in 1993. He was testing Grimod de la Reynière's grotesque but correct assertion published in *L'Almanach des Gourmands* (1802–9).

Szechwan Dry-Fried Beef

In the sixties, the U.S. government did away with the so-called oriental exclusion act, and Chinese from Taiwan began arriving on American shores in great numbers. One of them, David Keh, got a student visa and worked part time in the kitchen of a restaurant on Maiden Lane near Wall Street called the Four Seas, nominally a Beijing- or Mandarin-style place owned by the Brazilian-Chinese shipping magnate C. Y. Tung. Because Tung liked the spicy food of Szechwan Province, Keh slipped a few Szechwan dishes into the menu without identifying them as such. Cognoscenti discovered them, and their reputation spread among tastemakers who'd never eaten Chinese food anything like it. So when the Four Seas burned down, Keh opened the Szechuan on upper Broadway, far from the madding crowds of Cantonese Chinatown. His gamble paid off in crowds and money that led to a series of other restaurants. Ellen and John Schrecker introduced me to this world, and their book, *Mrs. Chiang's Szechwan Cookbook* (1976) is still the best guide in English to this cuisine. This recipe and the one for anise ham (page 80) are adaptations of theirs.

To American restaurant culture, the Szechwan meant much more. It opened a window of opportunity on China that made President Nixon's visit to Beijing seem like a minor event. There is no single signature dish in Szechwan cooking, but dried beef is a standout and it contains the two key ingredients that mark the style. They are both nominally "peppers," although neither is related to the true pepper, the black pepper or *piper nigrum.* The original Szechwan pepper is the dull brown dried berry of the *huajiao* or *Pimpinella anisum,* a prickly ash tree native to Szechwan and belonging to the botanical family Umbellifera (named for the characteristic umbrella shape of its members' inflorescences). Other umbellifers include many of the world's major spice plants (anise, fennel). These are the "peppercorns" sold as Szechwan peppercorns.

Equally important to modern Szechwan cooking are chilies, *Capsicum* "peppers," which came to China after 1492. The chilies provide the spicy heat (in Chinese, *la*), and the Szechwan peppers bring their complex flavor and a mild tongue-numbing quality (*ma*).

The dry-frying technique for this dish must be carried out rigorously, yielding a brittle texture that is a sign the dish has been made properly. When a restaurant does not achieve this (unforgivable, since it can be done in advance), this is a clear sign that an ignoble rot has infected the kitchen. This tendency to decline has also, unfortunately, been a typical pattern in U.S. Szechwan restaurants.

1 teaspoon Szechwan peppercorns

2 scallions, trimmed and cut in 1-inch lengths, plus 2 scallions, trimmed and julienned

One 1-inch piece fresh ginger, peeled and julienned

⅓ cup soy sauce

4 teaspoons sesame oil

1 tablespoon sugar

2 tablespoons Chinese rice wine

2 pounds beef, top or bottom round, julienned

6 small or 2 large carrots, scraped and julienned

1 tablespoon salt

6 stalks celery, trimmed and julienned

6 tablespoons peanut or corn oil

8 dried red chilies, trimmed, seeded, and julienned

1. Spread the peppercorns out on a skillet and toast them over low heat, shaking the pan, until they have darkened. Let cool and pulverize in a clean electric coffee mill or a mortar. Place them in a bowl with the 1-inch scallion pieces, julienned ginger, soy sauce, 2 teaspoons sesame oil, sugar, rice wine, and the beef shreds. Toss and let marinate for an hour.

2. Toss the carrot shreds together with 2 teaspoons salt in a bowl and let stand for a half hour, to draw out the water. Drain and pat dry. Set aside.

3. Toss the julienned celery with the remaining 1 teaspoon salt in another bowl; let sit for a half hour. Drain and pat dry. Set aside.

4. Heat 3 tablespoons peanut or corn oil in a wok or skillet over high heat until it begins to smoke. Reduce the heat to medium and add the julienned carrots. Stir-fry for a minute. Then add the julienned celery and continue stirring for another 5 minutes, or until the shreds have stiffened. Remove with a slotted spoon and reserve.

5. Wipe out the wok with paper towel. Add 3 fresh tablespoons oil and heat as before. Pick out and discard the scallions from the beef. Then put the julienned beef shreds and chili strips in the oil and stir-fry for a few minutes while the marinade boils away. Add the carrot and celery slivers. Stir-fry briefly; then reduce the heat as low as possible. Add the scallion shreds and continue cooking, while the beef dries and darkens, for an hour, stirring occasionally. Remove from the heat and let stand until ready to serve.

6. Just before serving, stir the remaining 2 teaspoons sesame oil into the beef mixture. Return to high heat and stir-fry briefly.

Serves 8

Tamales con Rajas
(Mexican Steamed Cornmeal with Chili Strips)

Consider the strangeness of the Mexican diet before the Cortés landfall in 1519. Meals were almost exclusively vegetarian. There were none of the domestic animals usual in Old World agriculture: no cattle, no horses, no sheep, no goats. As a consequence, Mexicans cooked without animal fat or dairy products. The cheese so omnipresent in Mexican food of today was unknown. No wonder the Aztecs ate worms and grasshoppers and pond slime. The wonder is that they evolved the dishes that became the basis of one of the world's most diverse and opulent cuisines.

The tamal is one of those dishes. More even than polenta, it is the fullest and finest exploitation of corn in cookery. From the simplest possible means, alkali-extracted cornmeal and dried corn husks, arose a vast lexicon of dishes, varied in size and flavor and, of course, in ingredients added to the cornmeal from pork to beef to refried beans. But you know all that and so does everyone else, because the tamal has made the leap from an exotic survival to a staple of American fast food available on Web sites and from little booths in parking lots in Greenville, Mississippi.

Is this progress? I think so. Tamales are a tonic for the jaded palate. Steaming brings out the complicated, lightly musty aroma of corn. There is the texture to think about as well, a kindred problem to the assessment of mashed potatoes, but here granularity is a plus, or at least an essential factor.

Since 1519, the expanded variety of ingredients in Mexico and Mexicans' access to cheese and lard have obviously transformed and broadened the scope of tamal cuisine. Modern, Europeanized life has also narrowed the field in one other respect. No one any more eats tamales of the type mentioned in Nahuatl codices: tamales containing pieces of human flesh. It has been argued that Aztec cannibalism was an outgrowth of protein deficit in a society without animal husbandry. This theory runs up against the afta nutritional fact that the combination of corn and beans abundantly available in pre-Hispanic Mexico furnishes the complete protein profile other societies (and now Mexico) get from meat.*

---

* The codices quash another theory—that cannibalism never existed at all. Since cannibalism in Aztec life was always part of ritual murder, it is a small logical step to see it as little different from the consumption of other mammal meats in the religious sacrifices of Homeric and biblical tradition. No one can say why the Aztecs did not recoil from eating one another, but one reason must be that they liked it. By all accounts human flesh is tasty, and if you wonder what that taste is, take the Polynesian phrase "long pig" as a guide.

The recipe here should pose no problems for the squeamish. It is meatless, though not vegetarian. It is also authentic for the Mexico of today.

1 pound cornmeal of the type labeled for tamales (*masa harina*), about 2 cups

½ cup heavy cream

1½ teaspoons baking soda

Salt

½ cup lard, at room temperature

½ cup milk, approximately

One 10-ounce can Italian tomatoes, drained, seeded, and chopped

2 tablespoons butter, softened

5 chilies poblanos, roasted over an open flame, skinned, seeded, and cut in thin strips (*rajas*)

1 medium onion, peeled and sliced

One 8-ounce package of dried corn husks, soaked until pliable and drained

10 ounces of Mexican or Puerto Rican white cheese (*queso asadero* or *queso del país*), cut in 24 slices

1. In a mixing bowl, beat together the cornmeal, cream, baking soda, and salt.
2. Beat the lard or whisk it until it is smooth and light in texture. Then beat it into the cornmeal mixture.
3. Beat the milk into the cornmeal mixture gradually, until you have a smooth dough. Test this by dropping a small ball of dough into cold water. It is ready if it floats.
4. Stir together the tomatoes, butter, chili strips, and onion.
5. Take a corn husk and spread with the cornmeal mixture. In the center, put a spoonful of the chili mixture and a slice of cheese. Fold the sides of the leaf over each other, then fold over the ends to make a package. Pull a thin strip off a corn leaf and use it to tie up the package. Continue until you have used up all the ingredients. This recipe should make about 24 tamales.
6. Put water in a steamer. Set the rack in the water. Line the rack with corn leaves. Put in the tamales, standing up with the tied ends on top. Cover with more corn leaves. Then cover the steamer with a dish towel and then the steamer lid. Bring to a boil, lower the heat to a simmer, and steam for 1 hour. Make sure the water does not run out. You will probably have to add more boiling water several times. The tamales are done when the filling pulls away easily from the leaf.

Serves 12 as an informal hors d'oeuvre or snack

Consider the strangeness of the Mexican diet before the Cortés landfall in 1519. Meals were almost exclusively vegetarian. There were none of the domestic animals usual in Old World agriculture: no cattle, no horses, no sheep, no goats. . . . The cheese so omnipresent in Mexican food of today was unknown. No wonder the Aztecs ate worms and grasshoppers and pond slime.

Tempura

Deep-frying was not a feature of traditional Japanese cuisine. When two Portuguese traders in a Chinese junk were blown by a typhoon onto the shore of a minor island called Tegashima near Kyushu in 1543, they were the first Europeans to set foot in Japan. A contemporary chronicle reports that they sold a musket to a Tegashiman notable, the first firearm acquired and shot by a Japanese. Soon after, other Portuguese brought with them a highly developed vocabulary of fritters. The Japanese latched on to the method and adapted it to the restrained spirit of their elegant foodways. The word *tempura* itself is a vestige of this adaptation, since it derives from the Portuguese word for seasoning, *tempero*.*

Tempura is best done in an austere batter of flour and water. Many Japanese add egg, however, to produce a golden, crisper surface. I say, what is the point of making a Japanese classic if you are going to turn it into the Asian equivalent of beer-battered shrimp?

2 dozen jumbo shrimp, with tails left on
1 cup flour, approximately (the low-gluten flour called *tempura ko* if possible)
1 cup ice water
1 cup cold water
2 inches dried kelp (*dashi konbu*)
One half 5-gram package of dried bonito flakes (*katsuo bushi*)

3 tablespoons light soy sauce
1 tablespoon rice wine (mirin)
1 tablespoon sugar
Oil for deep-frying
½ cup grated Japanese white radish (daikon)
1 tablespoon grated ginger

1. Run a knife point along the underbelly of the shrimp so that they will stay flat when cooked.
2. Mix the flour with a cup of ice water in a bowl. Stir briefly to blend.
3. To make *dashi* stock for a dipping sauce: In a large saucepan, pour a cup of cold water over the dried kelp. Bring to a boil. Remove the kelp and then remove the saucepan from

* There are said to be four hundred Portuguese loan words in Japanese. The most famous case is *arigato* (thank you in Japanese), which supposedly began as *obrigado* (thank you in Portuguese). This is a false etymology. *Arigato,* or rather an archaic form of it, is recorded as early as the eighth century in Japanese.

the heat. Add the bonito flakes without stirring and let steep for a minute or two. Strain through a dish towel. Squeeze out as much liquid as you can.

4. To complete the dipping sauce: Stir 3 tablespoons light soy sauce, 1 tablespoon rice wine (mirin), and 1 tablespoon sugar into the *dashi*.

5. Heat the oil for deep-frying to 360 degrees.

6. Put a small amount of additional flour in a bowl. Hold the shrimp by their tails and dredge in the flour, then dip in the batter.

7. Deep-fry three at a time until golden brown, This should take only a couple of minutes.

8. Drain on a paper towel.

9. Meanwhile, heat the dipping sauce but do not boil.

10. When all the shrimp are done, place them on a cloth in a basket. Serve with the dipping sauce. Pass the grated daikon and ginger separately as condiments for the dipping sauce.

Serves 4

Terrine of Foie Gras

Well into the seventies, you could not buy fresh (raw) foie gras in the United States. Importation was (and is) illegal, and there was no domestic industry. Now we have a dependable supply of fabulous homegrown livers. They are all duck livers; geese need to graze and aren't adapted to the intensive production methods that now prevail. The basic principle is the same as it has been since the Romans, who discovered that geese would eat more than they needed and that this hyperdiet would cause their livers to swell to great size, sometimes over 5 pounds, and to develop remarkable tenderness and delicacy of flavor.

You do not have to be a connoisseur to see why people will pay large sums for foie gras (which simply means fat liver in French). Like most superb things—truffles, the red wines of Burgundy's Domaine de la Romanée-Conti, the voice of Luciano Pavarotti in his prime, Lee Miller's breasts as photographed by Man Ray, a Goya portrait—foie gras is just obviously wonderful.

In the summer before my senior year in college, I was taken to La Pyramide in Vienne, south of Lyon. Three cold hors d'oeuvres materialized from the kitchen where one of France's great chefs of the immediate postwar period, Fernand Point, had presided until his death in 1955.* It was seven years later and his widow Mado had kept his ship scudding ahead under full sail.

I'd been sent out to the street to retrieve the wallet my father had forgotten in the car; so I'd missed the ordering phase and didn't know what I was eating. On one plate was a rectangular slice whose outer edge was bread and inside it was a disk of rich, meaty dull pink. I tasted it and wanted more. What was it? *Foie gras frais en brioche,* lightly poached foie gras encased in eggy brioche.

This was fancy food, no doubt about it, but also dramatically simple food. Plain, unadulterated liver, barely cooked, and some (very good) bread.

---

* Once, at the end of lunch, Point heard two men arguing loudly with each other over the check. As they kept grabbing it from each other, Point went over to quiet them. Somehow they had to decide who would get to pay. One of the men suggested a footrace, from the restaurant's doorway to the eponymous stone pyramid up the street. The winner would cover the bill.

   Point found a starting pistol somewhere and out they went. A small crowd gathered. The pistol went off, the men ran toward the Pyramid, neck and neck. And when they reached the monument, they just kept on running.

I had eaten foie gras before, the canned variety, so diluted with filler that it hadn't impressed me much. But the thing itself was a stunner.

But what about the ducks? I once visited a barn in Sullivan County, New York, in the heart of the old borscht belt, and talked to an Israeli who'd learned his trade at home from Hungarian refugees. When he walked by the cages of his precious, waddling moulards, they rushed toward him, eager to have more grain pushed down their throats through a tube. If a duck can be called happy, they were happy. They felt no pain that I could see. Their livers regularly increase the sum of human happiness.

Salt

White pepper, freshly crushed

1 whole raw foie gras of duck, about 1½ pounds

1. Bring a large pot of lightly salted water to a boil.
2. Preheat the oven to 200 degrees F.
3. Cut the two lobes of the liver apart. Trim away any membrane or green bile spots. Then, probing with your fingers, locate the vein system in each lobe and pull it out.
4. Blanch the lobes in the boiling water for 2 minutes. Remove with a slotted spoon, pat dry, and season liberally with salt and pepper.
5. Line a 5-cup terrine mold or 5-cup square metal cake mold with plastic wrap, leaving a 5-inch overhang on all sides. Set the lobes in the mold and fold the wrap over the foie gras, completely covering it.
6. Cut a piece of lightweight cardboard so that it will make a cover for the mold.
7. Take an ovenproof pan just a bit larger than the mold. Cover its bottom with 6 layers of paper towel. Set the mold on the paper towel.
8. Set the pan in the oven and cook for about 40 minutes or until a meat thermometer registers 115 degrees F.
9. Set the mold in a pan of ice water. Weight the cardboard with several heavy cans. This forces out the fat from the liver. When fat completely covers the liver, remove the cardboard, cover the mold with plastic wrap, and refrigerate for 72 hours (or as long as 3 weeks). To serve, remove the fat from the surface, unmold onto a serving platter, and cut into serving slices.

8 servings

Tortilla Española
(Spanish Cold Omelet)

This is *not* the Mexican flat bread made from cornmeal. It *is* a thick potato omelet, often served cold, which is the most typical of all dishes eaten in Spain. The word tortilla means a little torta or pie. Clearly, the term itself is pre-Columbian, although the omelet could not have been made before the conquest of Peru and the subsequent export of the potato, a native of the Andean highlands and a staple of life for the Incan civilization, to Spain through Seville.

Conversely, when Cortés and his band of soldiers conquered Aztec Mexico in 1519, they encountered "tortillas" at every turn and on every table in their new colony. Although these circular unleavened breads already had an indigenous name (actually many names: *tlaxcalli* in Nahuatl, *dzita* in Mixtec, *totopo* in Zapotec, and so on), the conquistadores baptized them with the word they had grown up applying to circular starchy "pielets."

The Spanish potato tortilla is likely to be a successor to some pre-Columbian starchy, egg-bound pie. Various Old World vegetable surrogates for the potato come to mind, and there is indeed, in Spain today, in the gastronomically primordial region of Catalonia, a tortilla (*truita* in Catalan) based on *samfaina,* the ubiquitous local "ratatouille" of eggplant, zucchini, red bell peppers, and tomato seethed in olive oil. Leave out the New World émigré peppers and tomatoes and you have the makings of a tortilla before 1492.

However it began, the tortilla of today is a dish whose identity is fought over by purists. To add onions or not, that is the question. I think it is fine either way. Perhaps most Spanish cooks vote for onions. But those defenders of the *fé* Lourdes March and Alicia Ríos eschew *la cebolla* altogether in the recipe they published in *The Heritage of Spanish Cooking* (1992), as did Colman Andrews's source Angela Paba in the directions she gave him for his *Catalan Cuisine* (1999).

All Spanish tortillas are flipped—some cooks do it more than once—to promote even cooking of the thick, six-egg batter. And this maneuver, universal to the experience of any Spaniard who has ever made or witnessed the creation of the dish he knows better than any other, has entered the language as an idiom. *La tortilla se ha dado la vuelta* (literally, the tortilla has turned over) means something like the shoe is on the other foot or it's a different story now.

Whatever you do, don't brown the potatoes.

Various Old World vegetable surrogates for the potato come to mind, and there is indeed, in Spain today, a tortilla (*truita* in Catalan) based on *samfaina*, the ubiquitous local "ratatouille" of eggplant, zucchini, red bell peppers, and tomato seethed in olive oil. Leave out the New World émigré peppers and tomatoes and you have the makings of a tortilla before 1492.

1⅓ cups olive oil

1½ pounds potatoes, peeled and thinly sliced

Salt

1 large onion, peeled and thinly sliced, optional

6 eggs, lightly beaten

1. Heat the olive oil in a deep, 8-inch nonstick skillet over medium heat.
2. Pat dry the potato slices, sprinkle with salt, and slide them into the oil. Cover and cook for 5 minutes. Stir to keep the potatoes from browning or sticking together. (Add the onion now, if you are adding onion). Cook another 15 minutes, covered, or until the potato slices have softened. Drain the potatoes in a colander. Reserve the oil for future frying. Clean the pan and coat it generously with some of the reserved oil, bottom and sides.
3. Stir the eggs and potatoes together. Taste and add salt if necessary. Heat the skillet. Then pour in the egg-potato mixture. Lower the heat immediately to low-medium. Cook for 2 minutes or until just set, shaking the pan to keep the omelet from sticking. The timing matters. Don't worry about a small amount of unset egg on top. Invert a dinner plate (or, better still, a special earthenware tortilla plate) over the skillet.
4. Turn the omelet over onto the plate. Then, right away, slide the inverted omelet back into the skillet. Cook for another minute or two. Then transfer to a serving plate. Serve while hot or at room temperature.

Serves 6

Tripes à la Mode de Caen

Tripe is the generic term for the stomachs of ruminants, i.e., cud-chewing animals (cows, sheep, camels, llamas). I say stomachs because all ruminants have several, a chain of digestive chambers with different specialized roles to play in the processing of grass and other cellulose rich pasturage. The cow has four stomachs, in order of use: the rumen, the reticulum, the omasum, and the abomasum. After the cow chews the grass with her thirty-two teeth and reduces it to a mass or cud, she swallows it and sends it to the rumen, a large sac that collaborates with the honeycombed reticulum in chemically attacking the cud. Eventually, the cow regurgitates the cud and chews it some more. It then goes to the leafy omasum (aka "the book"), which subjects the cud to hydrochloric acid and sends it on to the abomasum, a true stomach in the human sense and with much the same function.

I mention all this because in its traditional form, tripe in the style of Caen (the Norman cathedral town) contains pieces of all four stomachs. Unless you have cattle of your own and intend to slaughter them for the sake of this remarkable and legendary dish, you will not be able to make it authentically. The truth is that few ordinary people, even ordinary Caennois, ever did this themselves. They bought their tripe from a *tripier,* a vanishing specialty within the butcher profession. *Tripiers* do the unpleasant, arduous, and smelly task of cleaning and parcooking tripe.

In the United States, you will easily find only one of the four stomachs,* the reticulum or honeycomb tripe, named, if you have never seen it, because it is made up of white cells the size of a quarter. One thing they do is catch indigestible solid matter such as nails and prevent them from rupturing the cow's digestive system. Some farmers feed cows little magnets that lodge in the reticulum and make sure that metal objects stay there and do not descend further into the animal.

Supermarket tripe is totally pure and white and clean, but it is slippery and gelatinous. It will not taste "funny" when you are done with it. It will be rich and so ready to gel in its cooking liquid that warm plates are essential for serving it. This is a cheap and easy dish to make. It cooks while you sleep.

---

* I have seen at least three, in the meat section of the Grand Central Market in downtown Los Angeles, but I have only tasted or cooked honeycomb tripe.

2 pounds honeycomb tripe

3 medium carrots, scraped and cut in
    rounds

½ pound salt pork, sliced as thin as possible

1 sprig parsley

1 bay leaf

1 sprig thyme or ¼ teaspoon ground

6 cloves garlic, peeled

3 whole cloves

1 cup chicken stock, approximately

1 cup dry white wine

Salt

Pepper

1. If you are using frozen, ready-to-cook tripe, simply defrost and rinse. Fresh tripe should be soaked for several hours.

2. Preheat the oven to 250 degrees.

3. Cut the tripe into 2-inch squares.

4. In a heavy casserole, place one third of the tripe in an even layer on the bottom. Cover with a layer each of half the carrots and then half the pork. Cover that with the parsley, bay leaf, thyme, 3 garlic cloves, and 2 of the whole cloves.

5. Add another layer of tripe (half of what remains). Top it with layers of the remaining carrots and salt pork. Add the remaining garlic and the clove. Add a final layer of all the remaining tripe. Pour in the chicken stock and white wine. Add additional stock, if necessary, to bring the liquid level even with the top of the solid ingredients. Season lightly with salt and pepper.

6. Cover the pot with a double thickness of aluminum foil. Press the lid on to make a hermetic seal. Bring to a boil on the stove; then place in the oven and cook for 12 hours.

7. Remove the casserole from the oven. Adjust the seasoning of the broth. Spoon away the excess fat, discard the bay leaf, and serve. Or for a more elegant effect, remove the tripe pieces with a slotted spoon. Discard all other solid ingredients. After the liquid reaches room temperature, cool in the refrigerator so that the fat rises to the surface and solidifies. Skim off the fat, reheat the sauce, return the tripe to it, heat to a simmer, and serve on warm plates.

4 servings

Truite au Bleu

In the compleat angler's creel, you will find a small wooden club called a billy (smaller than the policeman's billy club or nightstick and not coated with dark varnish), used to stun fish when landing them. If you are going to make *truite au bleu* authentically, you will need a billy or its equivalent. Here is Escoffier's recipe from *Ma Cuisine* (1934):

> *Start with live trout in a tank. Keep a shallow pot of salted and vinegared boiling water ready. Ten minutes before you want to serve them, take the trout out of the tank and stun them by hitting them on the head. Gut and clean them rapidly. Put them down on a plate and sprinkle them with vinegar. Then slip them into the boiling water, where they will immediately curl up [recroquevillent] and their flesh will flake [se brisent]. It takes only a few minutes to complete the cooking.*

Before you call PETA, reflect that stunning a fish before gutting it is undoubtedly more humane than letting it choke to death in a creel or boil to death by being plunged while still alive into the pot. This latter method is mentioned as an alternative to stunning in *Larousse Gastronomique* (1938). The goal of Escoffier's method is freshness, of course, but it goes beyond that. The reflexive shudder when the trout hits the boiling water makes him flex, curving head toward tail. And he solidifies in that position, reaching the table in the classic pose of blue trout, an image of perfect freshness, as if (or actually) caught in the moment of death (or if you prefer, the last moment of life). As far as I know, the role of the vinegar was originally to provide an attractive flavor, just as lemon might. But someone discovered that it gave the fish's flesh a gentle azure hue, whence *truite au bleu*.

The classic sauce is melted butter, served separately. And boiled potatoes. Perhaps you will be tempted to make the dish in the classic way. (Despite the savage sound of the method, it isn't much different from what happens to any trout pulled from a tank or kept alive on the way back from the stream in a Ziploc bag filled with water.) But if not, be assured that the same result, except for the curled shape, is available to people who start with fresh dead trout from a fish market.

The court bouillon can be frozen and used another day.

2 quarts cold water

1 cup white wine vinegar, approximately

1 large carrot, scraped and chopped

1 large onion, peeled and chopped

1 tablespoon chopped parsley

1 sprig thyme

1 bay leaf

1 tablespoon salt

1 teaspoon pepper

6 trout

Sprigs parsley for garnish

½ cup melted butter or mayonnaise with
capers added

1. In 2 quarts of cold water, add vinegar, carrot, onion, parsley, thyme, bay leaf, salt, and pepper, to make a court bouillon. Bring to a boil and cook until the carrot pieces are tender.

2. Reduce the heat so that the court bouillon just trembles. Moisten the fish with vinegar, slide into the court bouillon, and cook for 8 minutes. Drain. Decorate with sprigs of parsley.

3. These trout can be served hot or cold. If hot, serve with melted butter. If cold, use mayonnaise into which some capers have been stirred.

Serves 6

Vinaigrette

Since Roman times (and no doubt from still earlier periods), people have eaten vegetables so customarily in an oil or fat medium that they felt no need to talk about it. Then, as now, greens were cooked in oil or animal fat. What made something a salad was the addition of vinegar. Whence vinaigrette.

Somewhere buried in the dawn of human cuisine, the addition of vinegar to vegetables must have had to do with preservation and the culinary effect of vinegar on food. In ancient days, in Mediterranean cultures abundantly supplied with old wine but not awash in citrus juice, vinegar would have been a crucial source of acid taste and a major ingredient in food preservation. We see this today in a hundred different marinades and barbecue sauces, which are really salad dressings disguised with spices or ketchup and used to tenderize and flavor meat and fish. (The primordial connection between salads—now thought of as the epitome of fresh food—and preservation is also strongly suggested by the word *salad*, so obviously connected with salt, the prime active ingredient in that other great pickling medium, brine.)

It seems logical to assume that people had oil and butter and animal fat before they had vinegar. But once vinegar was available to them, they would have cast about for something to dilute its strength. They might have used water, but they didn't. Instead they proceeded to invent vinaigrette, an improvisation of genius when viewed with hindsight. And the discovery is most easily explained if we imagine that cooks already accustomed to mixing greens with oil, decided to add a little vinegar to it, hoping thereby to liven up the oil and to dilute the acridity of the vinegar. Or the process may have worked in reverse. Early cooks may have tried preserving food in vinegar and then added oil, already a common medium for vegetables, in order to dilute the vinegar and make the food more palatable. Once they had tasted the mixture, they would have realized, as has everyone in the ensuing centuries, that it was a delicious combination. From there it would have been a simple step to advance from preserving vegetables in vinaigrette to eating them fresh and raw with the same sauce.

The basic formula is a culinary universal: four ingredients in geometrically decreasing order of importance. 3 parts oil to 1 part vinegar (of medium strength), and salt, pepper (as well as mustard, wine, and chopped herbs), according to taste. In other words, there is no recipe, just a general notion of proportion between oil and vinegar and a very general idea of seasoning.

What oil, then? Cold-pressed virgin olive oil? Peanut oil? If you are olive-averse, peanut or corn oil is for you. Gustatorially cautious souls will not only shun olive oil but vinegar too, taking refuge in lemon juice for the acid balance to the oil. I vote here for an assertive vinaigrette worthy of the name, and sharpened, as well as emulsified (oil and vinegar by themselves don't blend for long) by a splash of mustard, and further empowered with garlic.

³⁄₄ cup cold-pressed extra virgin olive oil

¹⁄₄ cup red wine vinegar

¹⁄₄ teaspoon salt

4 turns of a pepper mill

1 teaspoon mustard

1 clove garlic, peeled and minced

Combine all the ingredients in the salad bowl. Whisk together just before adding the salad.

Enough dressing for salad for 8

Vitello Tonnato
(Tuna-ed Veal)

Vitello Tonnato & the Roaring Zucchinis is a young Bavarian rock group specializing in music of the forties through sixties of Ray Charles and Louis Jordan, and especially in the repertoire of Louis Prima, the king of Las Vegas night clubs of the sixties. It is unclear from their publicity whether they actually cook or consume the cold roast veal smeared with tuna mayonnaise known to gastronomes as *vitello tonnato*. But the group's name is an unlikely yet convincing proof of the universality of the dish. There are many people—my wife is one—who will assert that *vitello tonnato* is the best of all summer meat dishes. She had support in her enthusiasm from our dog Ilka (*RIP*), who gobbled half a platter of *vitello tonnato* intended to serve 8, in the 1980s, while we were briefly absent from the kitchen. Given adequate security, this is definitely a fine thing to make in advance. The emulsified fish combines improbably well wlth the veal. The assembled dish looks beautiful.

One 2½-pound veal roast	1 bottle dry white wine
12 ounces tuna, canned in oil	1 recipe Mayonnaise (page 121)
1 medium onion, peeled and sliced thinly	Capers
6 anchovy fillets, roughly chopped	6 lemon wedges
Salt and pepper	

1. In a heavy pot just large enough to hold the veal, combine the veal, tuna, onion, chopped anchovies, salt, and pepper. Pour the white wine over the meat.
2. Bring the liquid to a boil, lower the heat, cover, and simmer for an hour. Uncover and cook for another half hour.
3. Put the meat in a clean container. Let cool.
4. The remaining cooking liquid should be palpable but thick. If it is thin, return to the boil and reduce until you get the desired consistency. Pour into a processor and process with the steel blade until you have a smooth paste, the smoother the better.
5. Cut the meat into thin slices.
6. Whisk the capers into the mayonnaise and then gradually whisk the mayonnaise into the tuna puree. Spread the sauce over the veal slices as you arrange them in an overlapping

line on a serving platter. Cover with plastic wrap and refrigerate overnight. An hour before you want to serve it, remove from the refrigerator and let it return to room temperature. With a rubber spatula, pick up any excess sauce and smear it over the veal. Decorate with the lemon wedges.

Serves 6

Waterzooi
(Belgian Chicken Stew)

Waterzooi is the most famous Belgian dish. If this seems like faint praise, you haven't spent much time eating in Belgium. Anyway, waterzooi is a fine thing. I heard about it first in a guide to European restaurants privately printed in Detroit by Lester Gruber, proprietor of the London Chop House, Detroit's best restaurant (yes, I know, this is like calling waterzooi the most famous Belgian dish) when I was growing up there. Not that I ever ate there. My parents, out of puritanism, not penury, usually avoided the most expensive restaurant wherever they went, except in France. One night, they had Les and Cleo Gruber to dinner, and all I heard about it the morning after at breakfast was how much the Grubers drank.

Les Gruber was an authentic gastronome and a bosom pal of James Beard. His little guide was judicious and, in my experience, infallible. Somewhere in it, he called waterzooi one of the world's ten greatest dishes.

Waterzooi is indeed a fine, rich, and improbably light masterpiece of ordinary, rich ingredients blended with a modest mastery, a very Belgian achievement. Actually, waterzooi is Flemish, and I am told that in Flemish it means literally a water stew, combining water with a form of the verb *ziedem,* to seethe.

There are three kinds of waterzooi, with fish, with rabbit, and with chicken. All of them are, as Nika Hazelton explains in *The Belgian Cookbook* (1970), midway between soup and stew— and served in soup bowls. Ghent is the home of the chicken waterzooi, Nika's and my favorite.

1 large (6- to 7-pound) roasting chicken or capon	4 sprigs parsley
5 tablespoons butter	3 sprigs thyme
5 stalks celery, trimmed and sliced	1 bay leaf, crumbled
thin(?)	¾ cup heavy cream
5 leeks, trimmed, degreened, and sliced crosswise	4 egg yolks, lightly beaten with the cream
1 large onion, peeled and chopped	Juice of 1 lemon
2 cloves	Salt
	White pepper

1. Cut the chicken into large pieces. In particular, split the carcass into breast and back and then split both of them. This will allow packing the chicken more efficiently into the pot and thereby permit using less cooking liquid.
2. Melt the butter in a large, heavy pot just big enough to contain the chicken pieces in a single layer. Add the celery, leeks, onion, cloves, parsley, thyme, and bay leaf. Sauté over medium heat until the vegetables have just begun to soften. Do not brown.
3. Put the chicken on the vegetables. Pour in enough water to cover the chicken.
4. Bring to a boil, cover, lower the heat, and simmer until the chicken is tender. This could occur in as little as 30 minutes.
5. Take the chicken pieces out of the broth and put in a bowl to cool sufficiently so they can be handled. As soon as you can, pull off the skin and discard. Then cut the flesh from the bones in as large pieces as possible. Put the chicken in a bowl, cover, and keep warm in a low oven.
6. Strain the cooking liquid into a saucepan and reduce to about 4 cups or a little more, over high heat.
7. In a serving dish large enough to hold the chicken and the sauce, pour in the egg yolk/cream mixture. Gradually whisk in the sauce and the lemon juice. Season with salt and white pepper. Then put in the chicken pieces. Bathe in sauce and serve immediately with buttered bread and rice.

Serves 4 to 6

Wiener Schnitzel
(Viennese Breaded Veal Cutlets)

Anna Maria Schwarzenberg sent us to Figlmüller in the Wollzeile near the Stephansdom, Vienna's cathedral, for the best schnitzel in town. She ought to know, we thought, since her mother, the princess, was Austria's most famous *feinschmecker*. Figlmüller is a tourist attraction but not a tourist trap. In a pleasantly boisterous atmosphere, it serves enormous breaded veal cutlets, pounded thin so that they are larger than their plate. With salad and a glass of wine (no beer at Figlmüller) you can feel as happy as it is possible to be in Vienna.

Behind this *gemütlich* vision lurks disagreement and pettiness. Should this dish be made only with veal, as tradition dictates, or can a serious person choose to make it with pork, as many Austrians do? Princess Schwarzenberg has not answered my e-mail seeking a firm decision. Perhaps she found that her ruling on a similar question concerning the authenticity of Sacher torte led to even more disputation than before she entered the fray. There are other questions perhaps more important than the veal-pork dilemma. There is, for instance, the issue of lard versus vegetable oil (don't even think about olive oil; butter maybe, but never olive oil). And you might want to consider if a half hour of marination in lemon juice is obligatory for an ideal cutlet. And wouldn't veal scallopine from a butcher be just as good, if not better, than meat you sliced and pounded yourself?

I feel uncharacteristically rigid about these matters, like some cranky dispossessed Austrian nobleman with a dueling scar.* Tradition leads to a superior schnitzel.

Veal is a more distinguished meat than pork, especially when pounded mercilessly. If you slice your own schnitzels, you will get larger pieces than your butcher is likely to be selling for scallopine. The lemon marination tenderizes the veal and infuses it with an appealing tangy perfume. Lard also adds character, while vegetable oil is neutral.

---

* After they signed the Yalta treaty dividing up the spoils of World War II, Churchill, Roosevelt, and Stalin celebrated with brandy and cigars. Churchill pulled a silver lighter from his vest and lit the first round of cigars, holding the lighter so that the others could see its inscription: "To the defender of Europe from the people of Europe."

   For the second round, Roosevelt produced a gold lighter dedicated "To the Savior of the World from the People of the World."

   Finally, it was Stalin's turn. His lighter was encrusted with large jewels of many colors. On it was a platinum plaque engraved in large Gothic letters that said: "To Count Esterhazy from the Vienna Jockey Club."

Wiener schnitzel is a simple tavern dish raised to a high level of clarity and spirit by meticulous attention to the choice of materials, the finesse of their treatment, and their presentation. So what might be dismissed as pedantic fidelity to tradition turns out to be, in this case, crucial to the quality of a dish so simple and exposed that nothing can hide even small mistakes or slightly rounded corners.

2½ pounds top round of veal or boned pork loin

3 eggs

6 tablespoons milk

1½ cups flour

1½ cups bread crumbs

Lard or vegetable oil for deep-frying

4 lemon wedges

1. Cut the veal or pork loin into four equal segments.
2. Take a segment and slice halfway through it at the middle of the segment. Without removing the knife from the meat, rotate the blade 90 degrees and cut straight through to within ½ inch of the right side. Then reverse the blade and cut through almost to the edge of the left side. Open the segment out by grasping the two flaps at the original center cut. Prepare the other four segments in this manner.
3. Pound the segments between two oiled pieces of plastic wrap until they are ¼ inch thick.
4. Beat the eggs with the milk. On the left side of the egg-milk bowl, spread the flour on a dinner plate. Do the same thing with the bread crumbs on the right side of the bowl. Dip each meat segment in the flour, then in the egg-milk mixture, and, finally, in the bread crumbs. Let rest between sheets of wax paper until ready to fry. This resting period is a necessary step; it lets the breading solidify and adhere to the meat.
5. Heat the lard or oil to 360 degrees or until it just begins to smoke. Slip a schnitzel gently into the oil. Fry for a minute on each side, or until golden. Remove with a skimmer and drain on paper toweling. Continue this way with the remaining three schnitzels.
6. Let the oil cool to around 325 degrees. Refry each schnitzel for a minute on either side. Drain and serve immediately with a lemon wedge on each schnitzel. The schnitzels should overlap the plate on at least one side.

Serves 4

Zabaglione
(Egg-Yolk Foam)

Here is what to do when you have a lot of yolks left over from making an angel food cake or meringues with the whites that came with them. Or you could start out intending to make this golden foam and freeze the whites for another day.

That much is certain about zabaglione. There also seems to be general agreement that it is an Italian dish, with an alternate spelling—*zabaione*—that some authorities prefer, for reasons they do not choose to disclose. I'm fine with either, since they are phonological equivalents. I am also prepared to believe a French authority (*Larousse Gastronomique* [2001]) that the word derives from a Neapolitan dialect verb, *zapillare,* to foam. And I am very pleased to note, in the same tome, that *sabayon* is conceded to be a gallicization of the same word and thing, with extended uses evolved in the French kitchen.

In the classic, operatic presentation, a singing waiter finishes belting "O Sole Mio" and picks up a sun-bright, round-bottomed copper pan (the easier to whisk yolks in) and pours in the premixed ingredients, whisks them together over moderate heat, and continues his attack, while grinning at you from the exposed kitchen and making well-rehearsed small talk until he spoons the thickened spume into wineglasses and passes them around your table with a flourish, as if he were distributing the elixir of love. The *echt* Roman variation, served at that center of Anglo-Italian elegance, Caffè Greco, is flavored with dry Marsala in which some ground cinnamon and vanilla have been infiltrated.

You may prefer a more restful option in your home, chilled zabaglione with strawberries. Or you could play the French card and use sabayon as a sauce on almost any dessert.

6 egg yolks	1 cup fortified wine such as Marsala,
1 cup sugar	sherry, madeira, tawny port, or dry
	white wine
	3 tablespoons dark rum (if using white wine)

1. Beat the egg yolks and sugar together with a whisk or an electric mixer until the mixture turns smooth and lemon yellow. This can be done before the meal begins if you cover the mixture.

2. Stir in the wine and then transfer the mixture to a heavy, nonaluminum pan. Specialty

shops sell purpose-built zabaglione pans, attractive round-bottomed copper affairs that give better results than flat-bottomed pans your whisk can't cover completely. You could also use a round-bottomed copper egg-white-beating pan, if you already have one.

3. With a large balloon whisk, whisk vigorously and without pause over low-medium heat until the mixture turns thick and foamy. Obviously, you want to be careful not to overcook and scramble the yolks.

4. If you are using white wine, whisk in the rum off heat. Serve immediately in wineglasses. Or let cool, chill, and serve at room temperature with sliced strawberries or other fruit mixed in.

Serves 4

Selected Bibliography

ACHAYA, K. T., *Indian Food: A Historical Companion*. Delhi: Oxford, 1994.

ALEJANDRO, REYNALDO. *The Philippine Cookbook*. New York: Coward-McCann, 1982.

American Heritage Cookbook. New York: Scribner's, 1980.

ANDREWS, COLMAN. *Catalan Cuisine: Europe's Last Great Culinary Secret*. New York: Macmillan, 1992.

BEACH, S. A., ET AL. *The Apples of New York*. Albany, N.Y.: State of New York Department of Agriculture, 1905.

BHUMITCHITR, VATCHARIN. *The Taste of Thailand*. New York: Atheneum, 1988.

CHILD, JULIA, ET AL. *Mastering the Art of French Cooking*. Vol. 1. New York: Knopf, 1961.

———. Vol. 2. New York: Knopf, 1970.

CRÈVECOEUR, J. HECTOR ST. JOHN DE. *Letters from an American Farmer* [1782]. New York: Signet, 1963.

CROZE, AUSTIN DE. *Les plats régionaux de France* [1928]. Luzarches, France: Daniel Morcrette, 1977.

DAVID-PEREZ, ENRIQUETA. *Recipes of the Philippines*. Manila: National Book Store, 1973.

DAVIDSON, ALAN. *The Oxford Companion to Food*. New York: Oxford University Press, 1999.

DOMÈNECH, IGNASI. *La Teca, La Veritable Cuina Casolana de Catalunya*. Barcelona: Març 80, 1994.

FERNANDEZ, DOREEN G., AND EDILBERTO N. ALEGRE. *Sarap, Essays on Philippine Food*. Manila: Mr. and Ms. Publishing, 1988.

FINAMORE, ROY. *One Potato, Two Potato*. Boston: Houghton Mifflin, 2001.

GEORGIEVSKY ET AL. *Ukrainian Cuisine*. Kiev: Technika, 1975.

GLASSE, HANNAH. *The Art of Cookery Made Plain and Easy* [1747]. London: Prospect, 1983.

GRIMOD DE LA REYNIÈRE, ALEXANDRE BALTHAZAR LAURENT. *Manual des Amphitryons* [1808]. Paris: Métailié, 1983.

GRINGOIRE, T., AND L. SAULNIER. *Le Répertoire de la cuisine*. Paris: Dupont et Malgat, 1914.

HAZELTON, NIKA. *The Belgian Cookbook*. New York: Atheneum, 1970.

HELOU, ANISSA. *Lebanese Cuisine*. New York: St. Martin's, 1998.

Jaffrey, Madhur. *An Invitation to Indian Cooking*. New York: Knopf, 1973.

L' Antiartusi. Milan: Pan, 1973.

Larousse Gastronomique. New York: Clarkson Potter, 2001.

McGee, Harold. *On Food and Cooking, the Science and Lore of the Kitchen*. New York: Scribner's, 1984.

March, Lourdes. *Hecho en Casa, Conservas, Mermeladas, Licores*. Madrid: Alianza, 1986.

Montagné, Prosper. *Larousse Gastronomique*. Paris: Larousse, 1938.

Novo, Salvador. *Cocina Mexicana o Historia Gastronomica*. Mexico City: Porrua, 1967.

Owen, Sri. *The Classic Asian Cookbook*. New York: DK Publishing, 1998.

——. *Indonesian and Thai Cookery*. London: Piatkus, 1988.

Page, David, and Barbara Shinn. *Recipes from Home*. New York: Artisan, 2001.

Piccinardi, Antonio. *Dizionario di Gastronomia*. Milan: Rizzoli, 1993.

Ríos, Alicia, and Lourdes March. *The Heritage of Spanish Cooking*. New York: Random House, 1992.

Rojas-Lombardi, Felipe. *The Art of South American Cooking*. New York: HarperCollins, 1991.

Saint-Ange, Madame. *La Cuisine de Madame Saint-Ange*. Paris: Larousse, 1925.

Schrecker, Ellen, with John Schrecker. *Mrs. Chiang's Szechwan Cookbook*. New York: Harper & Row, 1976.

Seranne, Anne. *The Home Canning and Preserving Book*. New York: Barnes & Noble, 1955.

Simeti, Mary Taylor. *Pomp and Sustenance, Twenty-Five Centuries of Sicilian Food*. New York: Knopf, 1989.

Vatanapan, Pojanee. *Thai Cookbook*. New York: Harmony, 1986.

Vitali, Benedetta. *Soffritto, Tradition and Innovation in Tuscan Cooking*. Berkeley, Calif.: Ten Speed Press, 2001.

Volokh, Anne. *The Art of Russian Cuisine*. New York: Macmillan, 1983.

Wilson, C. Anne. *Food and Drink in Britain, from the Stone Age to the 19th Century*. London: Constable, 1973.

Wolfert, Paula. *Couscous and Other Good Food from Morocco*. New York: Harper & Row, 1973.

Index

Abdalla, Michael, 104–5

adobo, chicken (Filipino chicken stew), 33–34

ajo blanco con uvas (white garlic soup with grapes), 86–87

ajwain, in poori (Indian bread puff), 161

Alaska, baked, 4–5

Alciatore, Jules, 137

almond extract, in soufflé, 193–94

almonds:

    in *ajo blanco con uvas* (white garlic soup with grapes), 86–87

    in *bstilla* (Moroccan pigeon pie), 24–26

    in *chiles poblanos en nogada* (Puebla chilies stuffed with pork in walnut sauce), 37–39

    in macaroons, 113–14

    in Paris-Brest (cream-puff cake), 142–44

Alsatian sauerkraut and pork stew (choucroute), 45–46

American dishes:

    apple pie, 1–3

    baked Alaska, 4–5

    chocolate fudge, 40–41

    chocolate pudding, 43–44

    clam chowder, 47–49

    doughnuts, 73–75

    macaroni and cheese, 111–12

    oysters Rockefeller, 137–38

    pizza, 157–58

    shrimp, crab, and okra gumbo, 189–90

    Southern fried chicken, 195–96

American Heritage Cookbook, 40

American processed cheese, in macaroni and cheese, 111–12

anchovy fillets:

    in pizza, 157–58

    in *vitello tonnato* (tuna-ed veal), 225–26

Andrews, Colman, 216

anise:

    in *pho bo* (Vietnamese beef soup), 153–54

    star, fresh ham with (tipan), 81

Antiartusi, L', 111

apple:

    pie, 1–3

    in suckling pig, 205–6

Apples of New York, The (Beach et al.), 1

apricot preserves:

    in bread pudding, 21–23

    in genoise à l'orange, 89–90

    in *savarin valaisanne* (yeast-risen ring cake soaked with Swiss pear brandy from the Valais Region), 185–87

apricots, in plum pudding, 159–60

artichokes, in *escabeche* of vegetables (cold braised vegetables in vinegar sauce), 78–80

Art of Cookery, Made Plain and Easy, by a Lady, The (Glasse), 198

Art of Russian Cooking, The (Volokh), 6, 65

Art of South American Cooking, The (Rojas-Lombardi), 31

bacon:

    in chicken soup, 35–36

    in choucroute (Alsatian sauerkraut and pork stew), 45–46

    in *daube de boeuf à la provençale* (Provençal beef stew), 69–71

    in oysters Rockefeller, 137–38

    unsmoked, spaghetti with eggs and (*spaghetti alla carbonara*), 197

baked Alaska, 4–5

baking soda, in *tamales con rajas* (Mexican steamed cornmeal with chili strips), 209–10

Barthe, Louis, 10

broccoli, in *escabeche* of vegetables (cold braised vegetables in vinegar sauce), 78–80

bstilla (Moroccan pigeon pie), 24–26

bulghur, Lebanese raw lamb with (kibbeh nayeh), 104–6

butter:
  clarified, in lamb biryani (Indian lamb and rice ragout), 107–8
  rum (hard sauce), 160
  sauce, white (*beurre blanc*), 8–9

cabbage, black (*cavolo nero*), in *ribollita* (Tuscan "reboiled" bean and greens soup), 173–74

cakes:
  cream-puff (Paris-Brest), 142–44
  genoise à l'orange, 89–90
  yeast-risen, soaked with Swiss pear brandy from the Valais region (*savarin valaisanne*), 185–87

candied citrus peel, in plum pudding, 159–60

cannellini beans, in *ribollita* (Tuscan "reboiled" bean and greens soup), 173–74

cannelloni (spinach-and-ricotta-stuffed pasta roll-ups), 27–30

capers:
  mayonnaise with, in *truite au bleu*, 221
  in *vitello tonnato* (tuna-ed veal), 225–26

caramel, crème (caramelized pudding), 60–63

Carême, Antonin, 53, 122, 185

carom, in poori (Indian bread puff), 161

casseroles:
  Cuban beef (*ropa vieja*), 181
  Valencian rice (*paella valenciana*), 139–41

Catalan Cuisine (Andrews), 216

catfish, in *cioppino* (Russian fish pie), 53–55

caviar, in crepes, 64–66

cavolo nero (black cabbage), in *ribollita* (Tuscan "reboiled" bean and greens soup), 173–74

ceviche de lenguado (citrus-cured flounder), 31–32

chapati, in poori (Indian bread puff), 161

Cheddar cheese:
  in macaroni and cheese, 111–12
  in moussaka (eggplant baked with ground lamb), 128–29

cheese:
  macaroni and, 111–12
  white, in *tamales con rajas* (Mexican steamed cornmeal with chili strips), 209–10
  see also specific cheeses

chicken:
  Burgundian, stewed in wine (coq au vin), 50–52
  in *croquetas* (Spanish croquettes), 67–68
  in fried rice, 82–83
  in *paella valenciana* (Valencian rice casserole), 139–41
  Southern fried, 195–96
  Thai red-curry (*gaeng pet gai*), 84–85

chicken soup, 35–36

chicken stews:
  Belgian (waterzooi), 227–28
  Filipino (chicken adobo), 33–34
  Moroccan, with wheat pellets (couscous chick chick), 56–57

chicken stock:
  in crayfish bisque, 58–59
  in jambon persillé (parsleyed ham), 101–3
  in onion soup, 133
  in *tripes à la mode de Caen*, 219–20

chickpea(s):
  in couscous chick chick (Moroccan chicken stew with wheat pellets), 56–57
  Lebanese puree of, with sesame cream (hummus bi tahini), 98–100

Child, Julia, 11, 170, 71

chiles poblanos en nogada (Puebla chilies stuffed with pork in walnut sauce), 37–39

chilies, green:
  in lamb biryani (Indian lamb and rice ragout), 107–8
  in *pho bo* (Vietnamese beef soup), 153–54

crepes, 64–66

Crèvecoeur, J. Hector St. John de, 1

croquetas (Spanish croquettes), 67–68

Croze, Austin de, 50, 51, 170

Cuban beef casserole (*ropa vieja*), 181

cucumber:
    in Peking duck, 150–52
    in tomato gazpacho, 86–87

Cuisine de Madame Saint-Ange, La (Saint-Ange),
    60–61, 170–71

culantro, in *pho bo* (Vietnamese beef soup),
    153–54

Curnonsky (Maurice Edmond Sailland), 51

currants, in plum pudding, 159–60

curry, Thai red-:
    chicken (*gaeng pet gai*), 84–85
    sauce (*gaeng pet*), 85

custard pie, savory, from Eastern France (quiche
    Lorraine), 170–72

daikon (Japanese white radish), in tempura,
    212–13

dashi konbu (dried kelp), in tempura,
    212–13

daube de boeuf à la provençale (Provençal beef
    stew), 69–71

David, Elizabeth, 121

David-Perez, Enriqueta, 205

Davidson, Alan, 12, 116, 124

Dell'Osso, Anna Maria, 111

dill-mustard sauce, 92
    in gravlax, 91–92

ditalini, in *pasta e fagioli alla pordenonense*
    noodles and beans in the style of
    Pordenone), 195–96

Dizionario di Gastronomia (Piccinardi), 113

Domènech, Ignasi, 27

dopiaza, 107

dough, pie-crust (pâte brisée), 147–48
    in quiche Lorraine (savory custard pie from
    Eastern France), 170–72

doughnuts, 73–75

duck:
    fat, in mashed potatoes, 118–20
    à l'orange (duckling with orange sauce), 76–77
    Peking, 150–52
    in terrine of foie gras, 214–15

Dumaine, Alexandre, 59

dumplings, Lyonnais pike, with crayfish sauce
    (*quenelles de brochet, sauce nantua*),
    167–69

Dutch dishes:
    doughnuts, 73–75
    hollandaise sauce, 93–94

eggplant, baked with ground lamb (moussaka),
    128–29

eggs, spaghetti with unsmoked bacon and
    (*spaghetti alla carbonara*), 197

egg-yolk foam (zabaglione), 231–32

English dishes:
    bread pudding, 21–23
    plum pudding, 159–60
    rum butter (hard sauce), 160
    standing rib roast with Yorkshire pudding,
    198–99

escabeche of vegetables (cold braised vegetables
    in vinegar sauce), 78–80

Escoffier, Auguste, xvii, 191, 200, 221

Esposito, Raffaele, 157

Farmer, Fannie, 4

Fernandez, Doreen, 33–34

Festive Baking (Iaia), 74

Filipino chicken stew (chicken adobo), 33–34

Finamore, Roy, 120

fish:
    caviar, in crepes, 64–66
    pie, Russian (coulibiac), 53–55
    pike dumplings, Lyonnais, with crayfish sauce
    (*quenelles de brochet, sauce nantua*), 167–69
    salt cod puree (*brandade de morue*), 16–17
    sole miller-style (*sole meunière*), 191–92
    trout, in *truite au bleu*, 221–22

ginger:
  in fresh ham with star anise (tipan), 81
  in lamb biryani (Indian lamb and rice ragout),
      107–8
  in Moroccan pigeon pie (*bstilla*), 24–26
  in *pho bo* (Vietnamese beef soup), 153–54
  in pork vindaloo (spicy Indian pork stew from
      Goa), 162–63
  in Szechwan dry-fried beef, 207–8
  in tempura, 212–13
gingersnaps, in sauerbraten (German marinated
      pot roast), 183–84
Glasse, Hannah, 198
Goa, spicy Indian pork stew from (pork vindaloo),
      162–63
goose fat, in mashed potatoes, 118–20
Grand Marnier:
  in genoise à l'orange, 89–90
  in soufflé, 193–94
grapes, white garlic soup with (*ajo blanco con
      uvas*), 86–87
gravlax, 91–92
Greek dishes:
  moussaka (eggplant baked with ground lamb),
      128–29
  navarin de mouton printanier (lamb stew with
      spring vegetables), 130–31
green beans, in *paella valenciana* (Valencian rice
      casserole), 139–41
greens and bean soup, Tuscan "reboiled"
      (*ribollita*), 173–74
gremolata, in osso buco alla milanese (Milanese
      veal shanks), 134–35
Gringoire, T., xvii, 76
groats, kasha, in coulibiac (Russian fish pie),
      53–55
Gruber, Lester, 227
Gruyère cheese:
  in moussaka (eggplant baked with ground
      lamb), 128–29
  in onion soup, 133
Guérard, Michel, 7

Guide Culinaire, Le (Escoffier), xvii, 191, 200
gumbo, shrimp, crab, and okra, 189–90

Haeberlin, Paul, 118
halibut:
  in *ceviche de lenguado* (citrus-cured flounder),
      31–32
  in *quenelles de brochet, sauce nantua*
      (Lyonnais pike dumplings with crayfish
      sauce), 167–69
ham:
  in choucroute (Alsatian sauerkraut and pork
      stew), 45–46
  fresh, with star anise (tipan), 81
  parsleyed (jambon persillé), 101–3
  and veal, Roman breaded (*saltimbocca alla
      romana*), 182
  see also prosciutto
hambone, in *pasta e fagioli alla pordenonense*
      (noodles and beans in the style of
      Pordenone), 145–46
hard sauce, 160
  in plum pudding, 159–60
Hazelton, Nika, 227
Helou, Anissa, 98, 104
Heritage of Spanish Cooking, The (March and
      Ríos), 216
Hess, Karen, 73–74
hollandaise sauce (Dutch sauce), 93–94
Home Comfort Cook Book, The, 111–12
honey, in Peking duck, 150–52
honeycomb tripe, in *tripes à la mode de Caen,*
      219–20
Hong Kong salt shrimp, 97
hummus bi tahini (Lebanese chickpea puree with
      sesame cream), 98–100

Iaia, Sarah Kelly, 74
ice cream:
  in baked Alaska, 4–5
  vanilla, small cream puffs with chocolate sauce
      and (profiteroles au chocolat), 164–66

mussel(s):
  soup (Billi Bi), 10–11
  steamed in wine (*moules marinière*), 126–27
mustard:
  in mayonnaise, 121–23
  in steak au poivre (steak with pepper sauce),
    200–201
  in vinaigrette, 223–24
mustard-dill sauce, 92
  in gravlax, 91–92

navarin de mouton printanier (lamb stew with
    spring vegetables), 130–31
New Orleans dishes:
  oysters Rockefeller, 137–38
  shrimp, crab, and okra gumbo, 189–90
New York Times Cookbook (Claiborne), 170
ngo gai, in *pho bo* (Vietnamese beef soup),
    153–54
noodles, *see* pasta
Novo, Salvador, 37
nuoc mam (Vietnamese fish sauce), in *pho bo*
    (Vietnamese beef soup), 153–54

okra:
  in fried rice, 82–83
  shrimp, and crab gumbo, 189–90
olives:
  in *ceviche de lenguado* (citrus-cured flounder),
    31–32
  in *chiles poblanos en nogada* (Puebla chilies
    stuffed with pork in walnut sauce),
    37–39
  in *daube de boeuf à la provençale* (Provençal
    beef stew), 69–71
omelet, 132
  Spanish cold (*tortilla española*), 216–18
*On Food and Cooking, the Science and Lore of the
    Kitchen* (McGee), 40, 65
onion soup, 133
orange(s):
  duck à l' (duckling with orange sauce), 76–77

  genoise à l', 89–90
  in marmalade, 116–17
orzata, in soufflé, 193–94
osso buco alla milanese (Milanese veal shanks),
    134–35
Owen, Sri, 82
Oxford Companion to Food, The (Davidson), 12,
    116, 124
oxtail, in *pho bo* (Vietnamese beef soup), 153–54
oysters Rockefeller, 137–38

paella valenciana (Valencian rice casserole),
    139–41
Page, David, 43
pancetta:
  in *daube de boeuf à la provençale* (Provençal
    beef stew), 69–71
  in *spaghetti alla carbonara* (spaghetti with
    unsmoked bacon and eggs), 197
Paris-Brest (cream-puff cake), 142–44
Parloa, Maria, 40
Parmesan cheese:
  in cannelloni (spinach-and-ricotta-stuffed pasta
    roll-ups), 27–30
  in *lasagne al forno* (Bolognese baked wide flat
    noodles), 109–10
  in omelet, 132
  in oysters Rockefeller, 137–38
  in *risotto alla milanese* (Milanese boiled rice),
    178–80
  in *spaghetti alla carbonara* (spaghetti with
    unsmoked bacon and eggs), 197
parsleyed ham (jambon persillé), 101–3
pasta:
  cannelloni (spinach-and-ricotta-stuffed pasta
    roll-ups), 27–30
  Chinese rice vermicelli, in *pho bo* (Vietnamese
    beef soup), 153–54
  couscous chick chick (Moroccan chicken stew
    with wheat pellets), 56–57
  lasagne al forno (wide flat noodles, Bolognese
    baked), 109–10

pork *(cont.)*:
    rind, in *daube de boeuf à la provençale* (Provençal beef stew), 69–71
    roast, in milk (*maiale in latte*), 115
    spareribs, in *pasta e fagioli alla pordenonense* (noodles and beans in the style of Pordenone), 145–46
    vindaloo (spicy Indian pork stew from Goa), 162–63
    see also bacon; ham; pancetta; prosciutto
pork, salt:
    in clam chowder, 47–49
    in coq au vin (Burgundian chicken stewed in wine), 50–52
    in crayfish bisque, 58–59
    in *tripes à la mode de Caen,* 219–20
port, tawny, in zabaglione (egg-yolk foam), 231–32
potato(es):
    in chicken soup, 35–36
    in clam chowder, 47–49
    in *navarin de mouton printanier* (lamb stew with spring vegetables), 130–31
    in *pasta e fagioli alla pordenonense* (noodles and beans in the style of Pordenone), 145–46
    in *ribollita* (Tuscan "reboiled" bean and greens soup), 173–74
    shoestring, Bolivian-style sautéed chopped meat with (*picadillo boliviano*), 155–56
    in *tortilla española* (Spanish cold omelet), 216–18
potatoes, mashed, 118–20
    in shepherd's pie, 188
pot roast, German marinated (sauerbraten), 183–84
preserves:
    raspberry, in crepes, 64–66
    strawberry, 202–4
preserves, apricot:
    in bread pudding, 21–23
    in genoise à l'orange, 89–90

in *savarin valaisanne* (yeast-risen ring cake soaked with Swiss pear brandy from the Valais region), 185–87
profiteroles au chocolat (small cream puffs with chocolate sauce and vanilla ice cream), 164–66
prosciutto:
    in *croquetas* (Spanish croquettes), 67–68
    in *saltimbocca alla romana* (Roman breaded veal and ham), 182
Provençal beef stew (*daube de boeuf à la provençale*), 69–71
puddings:
    bread, 21–23
    caramelized (crème caramel), 60–63
    chocolate, 43–44
    plum, 159–60
    rice, 175–77
    Yorkshire, standing rib roast with, 198–99
Puebla chilies, *see* chilies, poblanos

quenelles de brochet, sauce nantua (Lyonnais pike dumplings with crayfish sauce), 167–69
quiche Lorraine (savory custard pie from Eastern France), 170–72

rabbit, in *paella valenciana* (Valencian rice casserole), 139–41
radish, Japanese white (daikon), in tempura, 212–13
ragout, Indian lamb and rice (lamb biryani), 107–8
raspberry preserves, in crepes, 64–66
Recipes from Home (Page and Shinn), 43
Recipes of the Philippines (David-Perez), 205
Répertoire de la cuisine (Gringoire and Saulnier), xvii, 76
Reynière, Grimod de la, 164, 166, 185
ribollita (Tuscan "reboiled" bean and greens soup), 173–74
rib roast, standing, with Yorkshire pudding, 198–99

rice:

   Chinese vermicelli, in *pho bo* (Vietnamese beef soup), 153–54

   in crayfish bisque, 58–59

   fried, 82–83

   in lamb biryani (Indian lamb and rice ragout), 107–8

   Milanese boiled (*risotto alla milanese*), 178–80

   pudding, 175–77

   in shrimp, crab, and okra gumbo, 189–90

   Valencian casserole (*paella valenciana*), 139–41

   wine, *see* wine, rice

ricotta cheese:

   -and-spinach-stuffed pasta roll-ups (cannelloni), 27–30

   in *lasagne al forno* (Bolognese baked wide flat noodles), 109–10

Ríos, Alicia, 140, 216

risotto alla milanese (Milanese boiled rice), 178–80

roast, *see* beef

Roden, Claudia, 128

Rojas-Lombardi, Felipe, 31

Roman breaded veal and ham (*saltimbocca alla romana*), 182

ropa vieja (Cuban beef casserole), 181

Rose, Peter G., 73

rum:

   dark, in zabaglione (egg-yoke foam), 231–32

   in hard sauce, 160

Rumford, Count (Benjamin Thompson), 4

Russian dishes:

   beet borscht, 6–7

   coulibiac (fish pie), 53–55

Saint-Ange, Eugénie, 60–63, 170–71

Saint-Gelais, Mellin de, 58

salmon:

   in coulibiac (Russian fish pie), 53–55

   in fried rice, 82–83

   in gravlax, 91–92

salt cod puree (*brandade de morue*), 16–17

saltimbocca alla romana (Roman breaded veal and ham), 182

Santich, Barbara, 78

sauces:

   beurre blanc (white butter), 8–9

   chocolate, small cream puffs with vanilla ice cream and (profiteroles au chocolat), 164–66

   crayfish, Lyonnais pike dumplings with (*quenelles de brochet, sauce nantua*), 167–69

   dill-mustard, 92

   hard, 160

   hollandaise (Dutch sauce), 93–94

   orange, duckling with (duck à l'orange), 76–77

   pepper, steak with (steak au poivre), 200–201

   Thai red-curry (*gaeng pet*), 84–85

   Vietnamese fish (*nuoc mam*), in *pho bo* (Vietnamese beef soup), 153–54

   vinegar, cold braised vegetables in (*escabeche* of vegetables), 78–80

   walnut, Puebla chilies stuffed with pork in (*chiles poblanos en nogada*), 37–39

sauerbraten (German marinated pot roast), 183–84

sauerkraut, Alsatian, and pork stew (choucroute), 45–46

Saulnier, L., xvii, 76

sausages, hot Italian, in meat loaf, 124–25

   see also kielbasa

savarin valaisanne (yeast-risen ring cake soaked with Swiss pear brandy from the Valais region), 185–87

schnitzel, wiener (Viennese breaded veal cutlets), 229–30

Schrecker, Ellen and John, 107

Schwarzenberg, Anna Maria, 229

serrano peppers, in *ceviche de lenguado* (citrus cured flounder), 31–32

sesame cream, Lebanese chickpea puree with (hummus bi tahini), 98–100

shallots:

   in *beurre blanc* (white butter sauce), 8–9

Moroccan, with wheat pellets (couscous chick chick), 56–57
stews, pork:
  Alsatian sauerkraut and (choucroute), 45–46
  vindaloo (spicy Indian pork stew from Goa), 162–63
stout, in plum pudding, 159–60
strawberry preserves, 202–4
sturgeon, in coulibiac (Russian fish pie), 53–55
suckling pig, 205–6
suet, in plum pudding, 159–60
sultanas, in bread pudding, 21–23
Swedish gravlax, 91–92
sweet potato, in *ceviche de lenguado* (citrus-cured flounder), 31–32
Swiss pear brandy from the Valais region, yeast-risen cake soaked with (*savarin valaisanne*), 185–87
Szechwan dry-fried beef, 207–8
Szechwan peppercorns:
  in fresh ham with star anise (tipan), 81
  in Hong Kong salt shrimp, 97
  in Szechwan dry-fried beef, 207–8

tagliatelle, in *pasta e fagioli alla pordenonense* (noodles and beans in the style of Pordenone), 145–46
tahini, hummus bi (Lebanese chickpea puree with sesame cream), 98–100
tamales con rajas (Mexican steamed cornmeal with chili strips), 209–10
Teca, La Veritable Cuina Casolana de Catalunya, La (Domènech), 27
tempura, 212–13
terrine of foie gras, 214–15
Thai dishes:
  gaeng pet (red-curry sauce), 85
  gaeng pet gai (red-curry chicken), 84–85
Thompson, Benjamin, Count Rumford, 4
Thorne, John, 111–12
tipan (fresh ham with star anise), 81

tomato(es):
  in *chiles poblanos en nogada* (Puebla chilies stuffed with pork in walnut sauce), 37–39
  in couscous chick chick (Moroccan chicken stew with wheat pellets), 56–57
  in *daube de boeuf à la provençale* (Provençal beef stew), 69–71
  gazpacho, 86–87
  in *homard à l' américaine* (American lobster), 95–96
  in *paella valenciana* (Valencian rice casserole), 139–41
  in pork vindaloo (spicy Indian pork stew from Goa), 162–63
  in shrimp, crab, and okra gumbo, 189–90
  in *tamales con rajas* (Mexican steamed cornmeal with chili strips), 209–10
tomato paste:
  in *lasagne al forno* (Bolognese baked wide flat noodles), 109–10
  in osso buco alla milanese (Milanese veal shanks), 134–35
  in *ropa vieja* (Cuban beef casserole), 181
tomato puree:
  in *lasagne al forno* (Bolognese baked wide flat noodles), 109–10
  in moussaka (eggplant baked with ground lamb), 128–29
tortilla española (Spanish cold omelet), 216–18
tripe, honeycomb, in *tripes à la mode de Caen*, 219–20
trout, in *truite au bleu*, 221–22
truite au bleu, 221–22
tuna, in *vitello tonnato* (tuna-ed veal), 225–26
turbot, in *ceviche de lenguado* (citrus-cured flounder), 31–32
turnip, white, in *navarin de mouton printanier* (lamb stew with spring vegetables), 130–31
Tuscan "reboiled" bean and greens soup (*ribollita*), 173–74

wine, rice:

    Chinese, in fresh ham with star anise (tipan), 81

    Chinese, in Szechwan dry-fried beef, 207–8

    mirin, in tempura, 212–13

wine, white:

    in Billi Bi, 10–11

    in choucroute (Alsatian sauerkraut and pork stew), 45–46

    in coq au vin (Burgundian chicken stewed in wine), 50–52

    in crayfish bisque, 58–59

    in *daube de boeuf à la provençale* (Provençal beef stew), 69–71

    in *escabeche* of vegetables (cold braised vegetables in vinegar sauce), 78–80

    in *homard à l' américaine* (American lobster), 95–96

    in jambon persillé (parleyed ham), 101–3

    in *moules marinière* (mussels steamed in wine), 126–27

    in osso buco alla milanese (Milanese veal shanks), 134–35

    in *saltimbocca alla romana* (Roman breaded veal and ham), 182

    in *tripes à la mode de Caen,* 219–20

    vinegar, *see* vinegar, white wine

    in *vitello tonnato* (tuna-ed veal), 225–26

    in zabaglione (egg-yoke foam), 231–32

Wolfert, Paula, 24, 56

Wright, Clifford A., 109

yeast-risen cake soaked with Swiss pear brandy from the Valais region (*savarin valaisanne*), 185–87

yogurt:

    in lamb biryani (Indian lamb and rice ragout), 107–8

    in moussaka (eggplant baked with ground lamb), 128–29

Yorkshire pudding, standing rib roast with, 198–99

zabaglione (egg-yolk foam), 231–32

zucchini, in *ribollita* (Tuscan "reboiled" bean and greens soup), 173–74